This book is a must read for anyone who has an interest or appreciation of Augusta's colorful history. Basically the book is intended to portray the history of Lake Olmstead but it is much more than that. In some respects it is the history of the City of Augusta but always with ties to Lake Olmstead-from the development of the Augusta National Golf Club, the Masters Golf Tournament, the Augusta Canal, local politics and Augusta as a winter resort to name of few.

In the early 1980s, as a part of the plans to develop the Riverwalk along the Savannah River, the City of Augusta undertook a major initiative to establish itself as a major water sports venue. Little did we realize at the time that we were merely re-establishing a long standing tradition that started a century earlier in Lake Olmstead as documented by the author.

In recent years we often hear from visitors about the hospitality they experienced while visiting Augusta. I have often wondered where this tradition started or was it just an example of "Southern hospitality". After reading this engaging book you will understand that it is merely a part of our heritage dating back a century ago!

The name of book may be a little confusing. Most people might recognize the "green jacket" reference but the "twelve monkeys" may leave you scratching your head. Rather than spoil the surprise I encourage you to read the book for this and many other reasons.

Dayton L. Sherrouse, AICP
Augusta Canal National Heritage Area

12 MONKEYS &
A GREEN JACKET

❖

I hope you enjoy the read!
Best wishes!

R

Robert A. Mullins

Library of Congress Control Number:		2014905795
ISBN:	Hardcover	978-1-4931-8970-0
	Softcover	978-1-4931-8971-7
	eBook	978-1-4931-8969-4

This book was printed in the United States of America.

Rev. date: 05/12/2014

To order additional copies of this book, contact:
Xlibris LLC
1-888-795-4274
www.Xlibris.com
Orders@Xlibris.com
544025

CONTENTS

ACKNOWLEDGEMENTS

I would like to thank all the people responsible for preserving our history from the *Augusta Chronicle* to Reese Library at Georgia Regents University. In particular, I thank Carol Waggoner-Angleton and Jessica Huey for their assistance in locating historical photographs from the Special Collections at Reese Library. Joe Casella and Travis Bateman were extremely helpful in documenting the history of motor boat racing at Lake Olmstead. Marlene Spears and Jamie Spears were equally as helpful with documenting water skiing. Tom Lee provided relentless enthusiasm and encouragement eagerly reading numerous manuscript drafts. I would also like to thank Dayton Sherrouse, Rebecca Rogers and Julie Boone at the Augusta Canal Authority, the Augusta Genealogical Society, as well as the Superior Court Clerk's Office. Special thanks are deserved by my assistants Savanna Fisher and Bethany Davis. They both dove into this project with incredible enthusiasm and determination.

FOREWORD

The view of Lake Olmstead from my front porch transports the viewer into an enchanting trip through history. Spanish moss droops with profusion from the old oak trees around the lake. There is nothing more beautiful than the moon reflecting on the water, except possibly the brilliantly colorful summer time fireworks detonated from Lake Olmstead Stadium. Then there are the owls and the "laughing" ducks or mallards. Instead of the gaily decorated boats performing in brilliant regattas, ducks and other waterfowl skim across the lake providing a relaxing wildlife regatta.

Nine years ago, I purchased property on Lake Olmstead. The property was deteriorating and overgrown, but glimpses of the past emanated throughout the urban jungle. There were remnants of two gold fish ponds connected by a stream bed and system of waterfalls made from native sandstone. Old light fixtures were mounted high into the trees from the house to the waters' edge. Down by the edge of the lake through the thick underbrush was an old fire pit and the last boat house on a lake once lined with boat houses. On the second floor of the boat house was an apartment or party room of sorts with large windows overlooking the lake. Electrical lines were still connected and old musical equipment filled the room. Visions of the raucous soirées that had taken place in this envious "room with a view" filled my head.

My first desire was to preserve the boat house. I called and made appointments with several local engineers involved with historical preservation projects, but they provided little hope. Regrettably, the boat house had deteriorated beyond the point of repair. There were no preservation funds available and costs were monumental. Signs of recent adventurous activity by uninvited guests in the party room raised the specter of potential liability risks. In the end, the decision was made to tear down the boat house and erect a floating dock. Fortunately, I was able to save an old fire pit adjacent to the boat house.

Several years later, I came to learn that a water skier used to call the boat house home. Unbeknownst to me, his name was intricately linked with Lake Olmstead as Augusta's Water Ski King, Jimmy Spears. In researching the history of water skiing on Lake Olmstead I had the pleasure of meeting Jimmy's widow, Marlene Spears and his son, Jamie Spears. Both were tremendously helpful, especially with their contribution of photos and an understanding of the history of skiing at Lake Olmstead.

Also raising my awareness of the rich history of the canal and Lake Olmstead was my office at the Enterprise Mill located on the Augusta Canal in downtown Augusta. Perched on the top floor of the original granite flour mill structure built in 1848, my office overlooks the Augusta Canal Discovery Center boat dock from which the Petersburg boat replicas depart.

One might ask how I derived the title of "Twelve Monkeys and a Green Jacket." The reference to the "twelve monkeys" is symbolic of the efforts Augustans made to secure exciting fun-loving amusements and family entertainment. The "Green Jacket" is a continuing symbol of Augusta's former status as a "winter colony" for the wealthy and efforts to promote tourism.

This book explores Southern history, and more importantly the history of Augusta, through one of the Southeast's most historically renowned lakes, Lake Olmstead. Created as a byproduct of the Augusta Canal's enlargement of 1873, the beautiful 100-acre lake was once known for its placid sheets of water and the social venues built upon its shores. Lake Olmstead and its surrounding banks have been a part of Augusta's history for over 140 years. Until the creation of Clarks Hill Lake, Lake Olmstead was Augusta's primary water front venue. From motorboat racing to water skiing, it provided numerous recreational opportunities.

Although the glorious lake side clubs and recreational facilities have long since vanished, the allure and rich history of the lake holds fast. Today, its waters are polluted and filled with trash. Swimming has not been allowed for over 60 years. Private residences, including my own, now border the north side of the lake, while a city park encompasses its south side. Next to the park, stand Lake Olmstead Stadium (where Augusta's minor league baseball team currently plays), the old city stockade (which now hosts the local humane society), a National Guard armory, and subsidized public housing. The ski ramp that saw so many exhilarating jumps and records established was removed years ago.

The book originally was intended to be limited to the history of Lake Olmstead, but it soon became obvious that surrounding events played a significant role in the lake's development, as well as its demise. Therefore, the book would be incomplete without its coverage of Augusta's role as a "winter colony" for wealthy northerners. What happened to one of the greatest luxury resort of the south—the Bon Air Hotel? Why is the Partridge Inn the only remaining grand hotel in operation today? What happened to the Forrest Ricker Hotel and the Hampton Terrace Hotel?

The other question that often eludes a knowledgeable response is how did Augusta come to be known for one of the greatest golf tournament in the world, the Masters? Included in the book is a chapter on the foundation of the Augusta National, a club which may or may not have ever been established without the social prosperity brought forth to Augusta by the many events hosted on or near

Lake Olmstead. Wealthy philanthropists flocked to Augusta in the well-tempered winter season to take advantage of the lavish resorts which boasted golf, horses, and boating to the visiting masses.

Respect and pride for Augusta's "forgotten gem" has eluded the community, due in part to the lack of awareness as to its history and significance. This book affords a clearly painted picture of how Lake Olmstead went from being one of the most heralded places in Augusta, to being merely a "forgotten gem" of its once beloved community. It is intended to raise awareness on both the currently wasted potential of the lake, as well as the amount of respect her rich history warrants.

The research process has been long, but fascinating discoveries virtually appeared around every corner. I hope that the social history and scenes described in these pages will transport the reader through time and capture their imagination.

I

Introduction

In 1872, engineer Charles A. Olmstead convinced the Augusta City Council to utilize the flawed aqueduct through which the Augusta Canal was routed over Rae's Creek as a dam, creating what would become a lake of unsurpassed scenic beauty and most popular entertainment, recreational, and social venues. Named Lake Olmstead after its creator, the one-hundred-acre man-made lake would woo the souls of those who were fortunate enough to experience both its serene sheets of water and the social accord generated by the many future events to be held on its shores. Lake Olmstead and its majestic shoreline has been a prolific part of local history for over 140 years.

Founded originally as a water diversion tactic, the lake soon became known by Augustans for the matchless social opportunities it afforded. Couples crammed into the three-thousand-seat theater (casino) at Lake View Park to see the renowned theatrical performances. After the show, they danced the night away to the sweet music of the orchestra or took a romantic stroll down Lovers Walk, a discreet tree-lined path paralleling the lakeshore. Families spent the day at the lake soaking up all the eagerly anticipated amusements. Children merrily chatted as they ventured through the zoo petting the deer and laughing at the monkeys while taking heed of the porcupines. Girls and boys tested their speed at the skating rink and clambered onto their favorite horse at the merry-go-round. Older children enjoyed the bowling alleys and dru-chute coaster. During the summer months, families and children played in the water and made sand castles at the beach.

Figure 1. Lovers Walk, Lake View Park, Augusta, Georgia *(1906)*

The exclusive Lakeside Club hosted regal nighttime regattas, with whimsically decorated boats following in tow behind a steam launch of musicians. Members meticulously decorated their craft in hope of taking home one of the many prizes awarded. Society's elite danced in the pavilions overlooking the lake's clear waters. Thunderous rumbles followed by dazzling colors and bright lights lit up the night sky from the recurrent fireworks shows.

One is immediately drawn in by the allure and romanticism created by the lake's rich history. Although its current state raises eyebrows to the question of its once-pristine aesthetics, Lake Olmstead, with its hilly banks covered in imposing virgin oak trees, was at one point in time the most beautiful spot imaginable. During the spring, great masses of white dogwood blossoms graced its shores, while purple wisteria drooped from the old trees in enchanting profusion. The fragrance from the plum bushes was intoxicating, and the hillsides were covered in green grass speckled with white and purple violets. Wild strawberries grew in abundance on the banks of the majestic tree-lined shores.[1] An early nineteenth-century writer observed, "[T]he time is coming when art will join nature to bring out its full possibilities. When that is done Lake Olmstead will come into its own and its fame will spread throughout the country."[2]

Lake Olmstead's stately tree-lined shore and the allure of its serene waters stirred the soul of many a man. It was a place of "moss-burdened trees and wild honeysuckle [grew] in profusion, moving up to the rolling hills of Lakemont, where added romance was to be found as the shadow of the mellow moon dance on the waves of historic Lake Olmstead."[3] Romanticism sprung from its placid waters. In the late nineteenth century, one would take a trolley car, a horse and buggy, a bicycle, or simply walk to Lake Olmstead. Gentlemen could take their ladies to a vaudeville show overlooking the lake or dance the night away at one of the two pavilions. Couples strolled along the enchanting wooded shoreline or rowed out to the middle of the lake to gaze at the stars shining brilliantly in the night sky. Newsman John F. Battle described the romantic enticement of the lake.

> Yes, it was the dance pavilion, the Casino and the canoe where *girls* held sway and sort of *made monkeys of men.* There was some powerful courting in those days at old Lake View. Many a lad and lass marched to the altar following those sparkling days at the park.[4]

The courting at Lake Olmstead was simply unrivaled, often making monkeys of enamored young men.

Lovers Walk was quite a special spot. In 1933, Jesse Watkins, a veteran deputy of the sheriff's office, was often tasked with breaking up some of the petting parties at Lake Olmstead. "Recently, during our rounds of the Lakemont region, we 'flushed' a couple. 'Move on, and hurry up about it,' remarked one of the officers. And forthwith the cuddling flapper invited us to go to a place where they have high temperatures the year round due to the fact that a sinister man holds the upper hand."[5]

Today, Lake Olmstead is merely "a forgotten relic" of Augusta, a remnant of the glorious past, when it was the jewel of not only Augusta but of the entire South. The early social clubs and recreational facilities have long since vanished. Private residences now border the north side of the lake, the Augusta Canal creates the eastern border, and a city park encompasses its south side. The lake's waters have become polluted, and swimming has not been permitted for over sixty years. Lost in the abyss of local history, this "diamond in the rough" no longer receives the love and attention she was once provided by the city of Augusta and its residents. Hope for this stunning remnant of Augusta's fruitful history hinges on both the appreciation of her past and the acknowledgment of the immense need to preserve her future.

Figure 2. Geological map of Georgia

Distinguishing Geography

Local geography and early history laid the framework for the creation of Lake Olmstead. Augusta is located in mideastern Georgia, across the Savannah River from both North Augusta and Aiken, South Carolina. Sited at the head of the navigable section of the Savannah River, Augusta is just below the granite shoals created by the Fall Line at the junction of the Piedmont Plateau and the Coastal Plain, the Fall Line on which Augusta stands lies 140 miles from the Atlantic Ocean and 150 miles from the Blue Ridge Mountains, and once formed the ancient coastline of the Atlantic Ocean. The geological boundary of the Fall Line generally runs in a parallel line to the current Atlantic Coast and is characterized by Piedmont crystalline rocks to the north and Coastal Plain sedimentary rocks to the south. Waterfalls or rapids slowly formed over time, as streams and rivers flowed from the more erosion-resistant rock of the Piedmont area to the more easily eroded strata of the Coastal Plain.

Because of the falls and rocky shoals, river navigation naturally terminated at the Fall Line, consequently resulting in numerous settlements and cities, such as Macon, Georgia; Augusta, Georgia; Columbia, South Carolina; Raleigh, North Carolina; Richmond, Virginia; Baltimore, Maryland; Lowell, Massachusetts; and Trenton, New Jersey. The waterfalls and elevation change along the fall line also made it a significant source of water power and a prime location for grist mills, textile mills, and other water-powered industries.

Princess Augusta

The Fall Line made the area a natural location for an Indian trading post for the surrounding tribes of Creek, Yuchi, and Shawnee Indians. As the new American colonists expanded their exploration up the Savannah River from the coast, they quickly recognized its importance as a trade center. In 1735, the trustees of the newly chartered colony of Georgia directed that a fort be built on the Savannah River, just below the shoals, at the terminus of river navigation.[6] Within the next year, the King's Fort was finished and garrisoned with men and cannons.

Several years later, in 1739, Augusta was officially founded by British general and trustee James Edward Oglethorpe (1696-1785). During his visit to the fort in 1739, Oglethorpe resolved to name the fort in honor of his good friend, Prince Frederick Louis of Wales. Prince Frederick had recently married his new bride, Augusta, daughter of Fredrick Drake of Saxe-Gotha, and welcomed a daughter into the world, whom they also decided to name Augusta. In the honor of the birth of the prince's daughter, Oglethorpe respectively christened the fort Augusta.

Augusta soon became the second town in the colony of Georgia, the thirteenth British colony. Augusta subsequently served as the capital city of Georgia several times in the seventeen hundreds, but most significantly during 1786-1796, shortly after the Revolutionary War (1775-1783). Currently, Augusta is the second largest city in Georgia and the largest city in the Central Savannah River Area.[7]

II

The Augusta Canal

Lake Olmstead's creation is a fortuitous consequence of the incredible growth of cotton as Georgia's number one crop and Augusta's transition from one of the largest inland cotton markets in the United States to a manufacturing center. In the middle seventeen hundreds, tobacco farming was a major industry in Georgia. However, a young man named Eli Whitney (1765-1825) from Westborough, Massachusetts, would soon change that. After graduating from Yale University, Whitney was hired to tutor children in South Carolina. On his journey south, he met Catharine Greene, widow of infamous revolutionary war general Nathaniel Greene (1742-1786). She invited him to read law at her Mulberry Grove plantation near Savannah, Georgia. It was here that he perfected his cotton gin, automating the process of separating the seed from the raw cotton. After Eli Whitney's invention of the cotton gin in 1793, local farmers shifted their emphasis from tobacco to growing cotton. In Georgia, annual cotton production rose from one thousand bales in 1790 to twenty thousand bales in 1801. Twenty years later, annual cotton production was as high as ninety thousand bales and would soon reach over five hundred thousand bales.[1]

After harvesting the cotton fields, traders would either ship the cotton to Charleston, South Carolina, via rail or Savannah, Georgia, via boat. At the time, the Charleston-Hamburg Railroad was the longest railroad in the world with 136 miles of track.[2] It was also the first railroad in the United States to be powered entirely by steam and provide regularly scheduled passenger service. Alternatively, traders would ship the cotton down the river to Savannah, Georgia.

The thriving economy of Augusta, however, stagnated during the economic depression of the early 1840s. Although Augusta was still a substantial trade center, Henry Harford Cumming (1799-1866) believed Augusta could replicate the success of other cities in the United States that had recently made the transition from inland cotton markets to manufacturing centers. According to Cumming, the key to transforming Augusta into a manufacturing giant would be found through the construction of a canal system, which would provide manufacturing power and enable more efficient transportation of goods and products.

Figure 3. Henry H. Cumming (*Courtesy of David Connolly*)

Henry was the sixth of nine children and came from a powerful and prominent family. His father, Thomas Cumming (1765-1834), was a merchant by trade but was driven by civic service. He was Augusta's first mayor and president of one of Georgia's strongest banks, the Bank of Augusta. Henry's younger brother, Alfred (1802-1873), a former general in the Mexican War, also served as Augusta's mayor prior to his appointment by President James Buchanan as the first territorial governor of Utah in 1857. When Henry was twenty years old, his neighbor, John Forsyth, United States minister to Spain, appointed Henry as his attaché. As a result, Henry traveled extensively in Europe. When he returned to Augusta, he practiced law and soon became a director of the Georgia Railroad and Banking Company (a powerful railroad and banking company at that time).[3]

Cumming chose to focus plans for his canal on those of the city of Lowell, Massachusetts, in order to gain the conceptualization needed for this ambitious project. The inception of Lowell's integrated canal system in the 1820s helped Lowell develop into a center of textile production, marking the beginning of America's industrial transformation.[4] Its six-mile canal system powered ten major textile mill complexes, employing over ten thousand workers by the mid eighteen hundreds.[5]

John Edgar Thomson (1808-1874), an esteemed transportation expert of his time, was hired to survey and design the original canal construction.[6] Thomson had initially come to Augusta in 1834 to serve as the chief engineer of the newly chartered Georgia Railroad Company. A second-generation civil engineer,

Thomson followed in his father's footsteps. His father, John Thomson, had supervised construction of previous canals in the northeast, the first railroad in Pennsylvania, and numerous highways.[7] By 1845, Thomson had completed the railroad from Augusta to Marthasville (present day Atlanta, Georgia), the longest railroad track in the world at the time, slightly longer than the Charleston-Hamburg Railroad. Using his conservative but technologically innovative managerial skills, Thomson went on to become president of the Pennsylvania Railroad, quickly making it the largest business enterprise in the world.

Thomson's innovations included using coal for fuel instead of wood and substituting steel rails for iron. He reduced the cost per mile of track from 1.9¢ to 0.98¢ and increased the railway system from 250 miles of track to six thousand miles of track.[8] Thomson's innovations would be instrumental in Augusta's transition into a major manufacturing center. In fact, the city of Thomson, Georgia, situated approximately thirty miles west of Augusta on the Augusta-Atlanta railway, owes its name to him.[9] Thomson would die childless in 1874 at age 66, leaving much of his fortune to help orphans of workers killed while working on the railway. The J. Edgar Thomson Foundation is still in operation today.

Figure 4. William Phillips and his daughter Belle (*Historic American Engineering Record*)

A young local engineer, William Phillips, Esq. (1804-1877), would also help Cumming convince skeptics within the city of Augusta that a canal would bring rapid growth and prosperity to Augusta. In the fall of 1844, Thomson and Phillips began trudging through the thickets and briars upstream of Augusta with their compasses and transits to survey the canal's path. Phillips provided the following accounting.

> In September, 1844, at the request of Col. Henry H. Cumming, an examination of the falls in the neighborhood of Augusta was commenced, with a view of ascertaining the practicability of rendering them available for manufacturing and other purposes.[10]

The next year work began on the Augusta Canal with expectations that it would function as a source of power, water, and transportation, almost literally fueling Augusta's transformation. Work on the first level of the canal, approximately seven miles in length, was finished two years later in 1847. Locks were installed seven miles above Augusta, diverting river water through the canal. The canal was approximately forty feet wide at the channel's crest, twenty feet wide at the base, and five feet deep.

Figure 5. Rae's Creek Falls from the Port Royal & Western Carolina RY
(*Historic American Engineering Record*)

In constructing the canal, one of the numerous obstacles faced by canal engineers was Rae's Creek. Named after John Rae, an Irish Indian trader who came to the Augusta area in 1734,[11] the creek intersected the canal's path to downtown Augusta. Flowing some twenty-five feet below the bottom of the canal, the creek was the only major hitch in Thompson's plans.[12] Ultimately, the decision was made to route the canal over the creek, thereby eliminating convergence of the two waterways. An intricate wooden aqueduct (basically a wooden bridge) was constructed, routing the canal over Rae's Creek. Inevitably, the wooden aqueduct began to decay, much more rapidly than Thomson would have hoped. In the 1850s, Italian masons were hired to rebuild the aqueduct. This beautifully constructed stone structure can still be viewed today from many vantage points along the creek.

By 1847, there was a saw and grist mill as well as a cotton mill, known as the Augusta Factory, constructed along the banks. Led by Jacobez Smith, who arrived from Petersburg, Virginia, the Augusta Factory truly exemplified the positive impact of the canal's establishment for Augusta. When operating at capacity, the Augusta Factory operated 5,280 spindles and two hundred looms with an annual production of two million yards of cloth. By 1890, the mill operated thirty thousand spindles and 807 looms, with an annual production of fourteen million yards of cloth. According to its president, Stewart Phinizy (1851-1918), at the height of its production, the mill employed almost six hundred employees and was valued at $1 million.[13]

Figure 6. Petersburg Boat on the Augusta Canal (*Historic American Engineering Record*)

The canal was an instrumental transportation artery. Receiving their name from a now-defunct town in Wilkes County, cigar-shaped boats known as Petersburg boats shipped cotton and cargo from farms upstream of Augusta on the Savannah River and Augusta Canal. The boats or barges, usually piloted by a six-man crew, were some seventy feet long, five to six feet wide, and could carry as many as sixty cotton bales. After the cotton was harvested, the fall trip to Augusta was highly anticipated.

> During every autumn of the years that followed, heavily loaded flatboats floated down the Broad and Little Rivers into the Savannah River, while wagons drawn by four or six horses traveled the post roads to Augusta, the nearest cotton market. Planters on horseback accompanied these caravans and returned later with household purchases for the winter. The trip to Augusta was the greatest pleasure of the year, for the men stopped at wayside inns to meet old friends and exchange the news.[14]

Guided by poles, the boats would travel down the canal to Thirteenth Street, where cotton was loaded onto wagons then transported to Augusta's riverfront. Petersburg, once the third largest town in Georgia, however, suffered irreversible desolation when an epidemic of yellow fever swept through the town.

Confederate Powder Works

As the American Civil War began in 1861, Augusta seceded from the Union, and Confederate soldiers took charge of the US Arsenal in Augusta, originally established to protect the city from Indian attacks. Gunpowder for the troops was in short supply, and Confederate president Jefferson Davis (1808-1889) knew his troops did not have a chance without it. Therefore, Davis appointed Confederate colonel George Washington Rains (1817-1898), a veteran of the Mexican War, to locate a manufacturing site for the necessary gunpowder. Due largely to the Augusta Canal and the power generated by its coursing waters, coupled with the railroad facilities and river transportation, Colonel Rains selected Augusta as the location for the Confederate States Powder Works facilities.[15]

Figure 7. Colonel George Washington Rains (*Historic American Engineering Record*)

Colonel Rains's older brother, General Gabriel J. Rains (1803-1881), had previously devised the first modern mechanically fused high explosive antipersonnel land mine, known as Rains Mines. Because of their fiery reputation, Colonel Rains and his brother, Gabriel, were often referred to by the Confederacy as the Bomb Brothers.

> George Rains and his brother Gabriel created explosive solutions to the Confederacy's problems during the war. George created the gunpowder, and Gabriel used it to create landmines lethal to Federal soldiers.[16]

The Rains brothers were truly an explosive pair.

Building of the massive powder works plant began in September 1861, with Major C. Shaler Smith, Raines's architect of choice for the project, guiding the way. Twelve rolling mills were soon constructed, each with ten-foot-thick walls. Granite for their foundations was mined from Stone Mountain in nearby Atlanta, Georgia. Brick was manufactured locally.[17] Each building was spaced one thousand feet apart from the other to minimize fire hazard potential between them. Thirty-gallon water tanks were also placed above the boilers of each building and were rigged to drench the powder if a fire were to ignite.

The Powder Works structures, costing approximately $385,000, were scattered along the banks of both the river and canal and stretched over two miles. Interestingly, the Powder Works were the only buildings ever constructed solely by the Confederate States. It was soon apparent that President Davis undoubtedly chose the right man for the job in Colonel Raines. Thanks to Rains, the first gunpowder was produced and ready for Confederate troops by April 13, 1862. While most of the men were engaged in the fighting, local women gathered daily at the Powder Works to pack ammunition, pausing at noontime each day to pray for their men in battle. By the end of the Civil War, the Confederate Powder Works had produced over 2.75 million pounds of high-grade gunpowder and still had over seventy thousand pounds remaining.

Figure 8. Sibley Mill with Confederate Powder Works Chimney (c. 1903)

Fortunately for future generations, Colonel Rains began a campaign soon after the war ended, seeking to preserve the Confederate Powder Works chimney as a monument to the fallen Confederate soldiers. On November 5, 1872, he presented a petition to the city council for the preservation of the tall chimney.

In the projection of the centre portion of the first building, or the one nearest the city, with its chimney, I conceived the design of making it not only subserve [sic] its necessary purposes in connection with the general plan, but also to give it the appearance of a grand monumental structure, as is well seen from the front view. For this purpose the chimney was placed centrally, and its necessary dimensions considerably enlarged.

This noble structure has the design of a magnificent obelisk monument of nineteen feet base, and about one hundred and sixty feet in altitude, constructed of the best materials and chaste ornamental workmanship. The whole developed with the elegant taste and true proportions which characterized the genius of my young architect, C. Shaler Smith.

Should this portion of the buildings cease to be valuable for any use to which they may be applied, would it be asking too much from the city of Augusta that the designated parts, or at least the noble obelisk, be allowed to remain forever as a fitting monument to the dead heroes, who sleep on the unnumbered battlefields of the South?[18]

The tall Confederate Powder Works chimney still stands today, as the last tangible remnant of Rains's legacy.

Rains remained in Augusta after the Civil War, albeit largely as a winter resident. Regardless of his residency status, he was an active Augusta resident. He accepted a chair at the local Academy of Richmond as a professor of chemistry and natural science. He also served on Augusta's Board of Health for several years and as the dean of faculty for the medical department of the University of Georgia.[19]

Enlargement

Within twenty years after its construction, the canal proved to be an inadequate source of water power to support the surrounding businesses. The city of Augusta was threatened with numerous lawsuits from some of these businesses, quickly spawning a movement to enlarge the canal.[20] The movement to enlarge the Augusta Canal began in 1870, with the encouragement of Augusta's young mayor, Joseph Vicessimus Henry Allen (1830-1883). Major Allen had served in the Civil War under General W. H. T. Walker and Ambrose R. Wright.[21] Allen, an insurance agent by trade, was a staunch public servant and responsible for first organizing the city police.[22]

Businessmen and industrialists predicted that if the canal was enlarged, at least thirty additional textile mills were prepared to locate to Augusta.

Alternatively, city engineer and canal chief engineer William Phillips endorsed the enlargement as a means of controlling floods, which had remained a recurring problem throughout Augusta's history.

In March of 1872, after Augusta's citizens voted by referendum in favor of enlarging the canal, the enlargement began under the direct supervision of then mayor Charles Estes. Estes, a lawyer by profession, was no stranger to canal work. Having worked himself on the Erie Canal, Mayor Estes had made many professional connections, which he promised to employ in order to benefit Augusta's plans for further economic expansion. He soon hired Charles A. Olmstead, who had worked with Estes as the chief engineer on the 350-mile Erie Canal linking Buffalo, New York, and Lake Erie to the Hudson River.

Hundreds of laborers were employed during the project. Although most of the workers were African Americans, a group of two hundred Chinese laborers were also brought in by an Indianapolis construction company. Some historians claim that this resulted in one of the oldest Chinese communities in the United States. However, according to the Chinese Consolidated Benevolent Association (CCBA) of Augusta, Georgia, after the enlargement of the canal in 1875, most of the Chinese men drifted off to work elsewhere. According to the 1880 Census, only ten Chinese men were reported as living in Augusta along with eight Chinese grocery stores.[23]

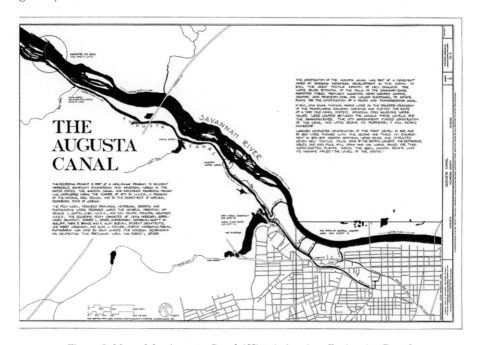

Figure 9. Map of the Augusta Canal (*Historic American Engineering Record*)

During the enlargement project, Mr. Hosch, the superintendent of the canal work, established a settlement on the banks of the canal near the aqueduct and Lake Olmstead. Hosch's "headquarters" incorporated the Hotel (a very comfortable frame building built of rough boards), a storehouse, a blacksmith and wheelwright shop, an office, a post office, and a store.[24] Mr. Hosch was a hospitable gentleman notorious for welcoming guests to his dinner table with both an ample kitchen and great culinary skills. The Hoschville settlement, however, dwindled away soon after the canal enlargement was completed.

As a progressive enticement to encourage Augusta's continuing development, Mayor Charles Estes directed Augusta officials to offer anyone responsible for bringing in outside capital for development along the canal a commission of 3 percent. To be eligible for the commission, the investment had to be in real estate, buildings, and/or machinery to be used solely for the manufacturing of cotton, wool, iron, or other goods on or near the Augusta Canal below Rae's Creek using the canal's water power for its machinery.[25]

In 1876, the expansion of the Augusta Canal was finally completed. The enlarged canal was 150 feet wide and eleven feet deep. Although Charles Olmstead estimated that the enlargement would cost $371,610.56, before the project was said and done, he was proven to be off by at least $600,000, as the final cost of the enlargement project totaled $972,883.00.[26]

Figure 10. Lake Olmstead, showing one of the islands (*Historic American Engineering Record*)

III

Lake Olmstead Is Born

When the canal was originally built, it was routed over Rae's Creek via a wooden aqueduct. Within years, the wooden aqueduct started to fail and leak. To remedy the problem, Henry Cumming asked for the assistance of Frederick A. Barton from Springfield, Massachusetts. Barton came to Augusta and directed the construction of an ornate stone aqueduct.[1] Rae's Creek would subsequently flow through two huge arched culverts. However, as the canal enlargement project began, Charles Olmstead resolved to dam Rae's Creek for cost-saving measures. Olmstead hired Italian stonemasons to plug the granite aqueduct through which the canal was routed over Rae's Creek.[2] After, stone was ferried down the canal from local quarries, and the aqueduct plugged water from the canal, and Rae's Creek flooded Lake Olmstead's basin in early 1873.[3]

Engineers predicted that the lake's reservoir could cover more than 132 acres and contain one or two islands within its banks.[4] Although there are no islands in the lake today, there was at least one island in the lake when it was formed. In fact, in 1881, W. A. Walker submitted a petition to the city council to purchase one of the islands so that he could build a pleasure house.[5]

The dam was completed in 1873, resulting in a 113-acre lake surrounded by a wooded basin. A stunning portrayal of the event was preserved by a local news correspondent.

> What this broad sheet of water covers was eight months ago a beautiful valley, finely wooded with oak and bay, and through the bottom the merriest of laughing brooks danced down toward the river; but the improvements suggesting themselves, caused the valley to be cleared and an immense dam thirty feet high to be made across the lower end. The brook flowed on against the dam, and water backing upon water changed fairy-like into a lake.[6]

The new lake was located on the northwestern edge of the city, commencing at a point near Washington Road and extending to the aqueduct. It was envisioned that the drive from Augusta to the lake would be one of the most delightful little excursions in the world.

Colonel George W. Rains described the placid waters of Lake Olmstead as "beautifully clear and very pure."[7] The lake was befittingly named after its creator, Charles Olmstead. "Olmstead plugged up the old aqueduct, where the canal once went over Rae's Creek," said Tom Robertson, a local civil engineer and former chairman of the Augusta Canal Authority. "The canal bank then became a dam, and the dam formed the lake they called Lake Olmstead."[8]

The Rae's Creek Basin, in which Lake Olmstead was formed, was one of uncommon beauty. The basin was largely wilderness and contained one of the last old-growth forests in the Augusta area. The forest began in Summerville and continued down to Watkins's store at Lake Olmstead. One former Augustan recalled, "If you have never explored this forest, it is well worth your while . . . . If a ramble through the woods does not bring you bodily and mental rest and refreshment, you had better see your doctor at once."[9]

Much of the land on which Lake Olmstead occupied was formerly owned by Judge Eberneazer Starnes, who had purchased it from Isaac Henry. Other land submerged by the lake is believed to have included property owned by former governor John Milledge, whose estate, Overton, was located only a few blocks from the lake.

An 1873 sales advertisement for a 105-acre farm located next to Rae's Creek at the head of Lake Olmstead presented a glimpse into the neighboring property. This farm consisted of forty acres of bottom land, with the remaining sixty-five acres being located on the hill above the lake. Improvements on the farm included a three-room farmhouse, a double house for servants, a good ginhouse, a "finely arranged" barn, a Griswold cotton gin, and several vineyards.

This place offers extra inducement to parties wishing to purchase, as it borders on the new Lake just made by enlarging the canal, and only a short distance from the city, and is bound to be enhanced in value as soon as factories are built in the neighborhood of it.[10]

Just north of the lake was the Woodlawn area. With its beautifully kept villas, mansions, and thick pine groves, the ambience of majesty and distinction blanketed the area.

Figure 11. Beech Springs, Lake View Park

IV

Pure Water and the Great Flood of 1888

The area around the head of the lake was heralded for its prolific springwater. Residents would visit the area regularly to drink the pure inestimably blue springwater.[1] Other springs in the area included Coleman's spring, which feeds into the Augusta Canal north of Lake Olmstead. From the 1770s to 1817, the spring once furnished water to the Coleman household, Bedford Plantation, and the town of Bedford, which then existed south of National Hills shopping center.

Lake Olmstead, although never utilized for such, was often seen as a possible drinking water source. Augusta's original water source, Turknett Springs, became inadequate by the early 1880s due to the rapid increase in Augusta's population. By 1860, Augusta had a population of 12,493, more than double its population of just five thousand in 1830.[2] It was at that time the second-largest city in Georgia and one of only 102 US cities to have a population over ten thousand. Colonel Rains, the former director of the Powder Works and member of Augusta's Board of Health, recommended utilization of water from Lake Olmstead.

Lake Olmstead's water could be utilized and eventually take the place
of the Turknett Springs water . . . . When the city finances will permit, I
should propose to make use of the beautifully clear and very pure water
from the middle or upper part of Lake Olmstead, by means of a conduit
leading to the reservoirs, and thus dispense with the canal water for city
purposes.[3]

Jones S. Davis, Esq., superintendent of the Sibley Mills and architect for the Sibley
and Enterprise Mills, concurred. "Augusta would eventually see the necessity
of taking her water from Rae's Creek which now flows into Lake Olmstead. This
creek never muddies and the water is as clear, pure and fresh as a living spring."[4]

In 1882, some local businessmen proposed the construction of a new
waterworks to draw water from Lake Olmstead to ensure that Augusta's drinking
water would be free from impurities.

We propose the following as a basis of negotiation for giving the city of
Augusta a full supply of pure water from Lake Olmstead . . . . The water
is to be conveyed from the Lake by steam or water power, or both, to
some eligible position on the Hill, into one or more reservoirs . . . . Our
works to be of sufficient capacity to supply at least ten million gallons
water per day.[5]

It was projected that if the water from Lake Olmstead could be connected with the
city's water mains, it would supply an enormous amount of water for fire purposes
yet still maintain the lake level for recreation and enjoyment.

Figure 12. The Great Flood of 1888 (*Historic American Engineering Record*)

Although plans to draw drinking water from Lake Olmstead were never formally implemented, the lake did serve as a temporary source of water for Augusta in 1888. In the early morning hours of September 11, 1888, Augusta suffered a horrendous flood, when an engorged Savannah River rose almost two feet within two hours. It was the first time since 1840 that Augusta was entirely submerged. Buildings were inundated up to their second-floor windows. Serious damage was caused to the canal and railroads, with Hawks Gully on the canal taking the brunt of the damage. "The bridge across Broad, at Hawk's Gully, was loose early in the day, and floated off into the fields. A cow had taken refuge on it, and there she remained at nightfall, never abandoning her bark."[6]

Another Erie Canal engineer credited with designing the headgates and locks during the canal's enlargement, Byron Holley, was telegraphed to come to Augusta and assist the city council with the necessary repairs to the canal. Water supply was also an issue. On September 15, to address the problem of a water supply, approximately 250 workmen began construction of a dam at the wasteweir at Lake Olmstead. The temporary dam was located across the canal just above the mouth of Lake Olmstead.

Although bridges and streets suffered washouts and several houses were destroyed and cellars filled with water, Augustans' spirits remained high.

These casualties are far from wrecking a sturdy city like Augusta, and the stranger who walks along her solid business blocks, looks on her mammoth mills and cotton warehouses, sees the busy sir and listens to the confident language of her people, finds it hard to realize that two days ago the whole town was submerged by angry waters . . . . Augusta, the bravest and most beautiful city in Georgia will ere long be again the brightest and busiest as well.[7]

Augusta rebounded well from the flood of 1888.

Even though Lake Olmstead would not serve as more than a temporary source of drinking water, the canal would. In the late 1890s, Augusta replaced its former water pump station with a new pump station on the first level of the canal. The Greek-revival brick structure still stands today and demonstrates the use of hydro mechanical power to power its pumps.

V

Boating Aficionados

As predicted before its creation, Lake Olmstead immediately became a social gathering place, especially for the early boating aficionados. Within a year of its birth, sailboats and rowboats would become virtually an everyday scene on the lake. The boating fever, however, would have to wait until the outcome of the grand lottery and the mad rush to become the first commodore to launch his vessel on the newborn lake.

The Grand Lottery and the Platt Mutiny

As water filled Lake Olmstead's basin, the boating men of Augusta struggled with anticipation and excitement as to which privileged commodore would be the first to launch his vessel on the serene virgin waters of the lake. Social structure at the time ordained that the honors be determined in a manner befitting of Southern gentlemen. Having enthusiastically discussed the matter for several months, the boating aficionados decided that the honor and privilege of placing the first boat on Lake Olmstead would be bestowed upon the winner of a lottery. What they didn't know was that a plot was being hatched to undermine the "grand" lottery.

The "grand" lottery even aroused the interest of persons as far away as New York. Perhaps the best accounting of the lottery and its spoliation was preserved by a correspondent from the *New York Clipper* newspaper. The following belated portrayal appeared in the *New York Clipper* on July 12, 1873, and was subsequently reprinted locally in the *Daily Chronicle & Sentinel* on July 13, 1873.

> A correspondent in Augusta, Ga., sends us the following concerning a newly made lake two miles from that place. A quiet drive west from Augusta through the village of Harrisburg over the two canals, brought us to the beautiful shore of Lake Olmstead, on whose mirrowed [*sic*] bosom rested one tiny craft, the *Home Made*, so small looked she, as the

sunset danced over the water about her, that one could never think of her as being a pioneer—an honor not easily won in the very grasp of the boating men of America—yet the waters of Lake Olmstead had never known the dip of an oar or even the ripple of a bow until this little craft came upon them, and the story as my companion told it was this . . .

Now began the boating men to look about and ballot for a crew to whom might be given the honor of pulling the first boat upon these untouched waters; but ere they could decide, this little nutshell of a boat was secretly taken overland to the lake, and one twilight, with her crew of three men aboard, shot out from a hidden inlet and skimmed rapidly along, proclaiming themselves, with a hearty cheer, pioneers of the water. Long faces were worn next day by the crew who watched anxiously for the issue of the election, and the committee decided to ballot no more.[1]

Before the lottery could take place, the handsome young Platt brothers, Henry C. and W. Edward Platt, secretly carried their "little nutshell of a boat" overland to the lake and, at twilight on May 6, 1873, shot out onto the lake from a hidden inlet boastfully proclaiming themselves as the pioneers of the water. Defiantly, the Platt brothers stole the honor of placing the first boat on Lake Olmstead, when they skimmed across the lake's vast waters in their self-built boat, the *Home Made*.[2]

Soon after, Henry Platt also purchased and placed what was known as a traveling canoe rigged with a mainsail, jib, and dandy on the lake. The *Louie*, as it was named, was fourteen feet, six inches in length, thirty inches wide, and constructed principally of oak, with mahogany decks. All its brass work was nickel plated. The traveling canoe was made to carry a single person and designed in such a way that its rigging could be stowed within its body, which also served as a sleeping compartment for its captain. Proudly displayed on the *Louie*'s mast was a colorful silk flag, a present to Mr. Platt from his young lady friend in Madison, Wisconsin.[3]

The rebellious Platt brothers and their family would make a lasting imprint on Augusta's history, not only by placing the first boat on Lake Olmstead, but also through their advancement of the funeral business and community service. Henry and Edward's father, Charles Platt (1814-1873) had moved to Augusta from New York after studying modern embalming in 1837. Although Charles initially opened a fine furniture store known as Platt's Emporium on Broad Street, he was most notorious for introducing the process of embalming to the South and assisting in the burial of such people as Major General David E. Twiggs, General W. H. T. Walker, Governor Charles A. Jenkins, and General Leonidas Polk. Charles also helped organize the Clinch Rifles in 1861 during the Civil War.[4]

When Charles Platt died in 1873, his son, Edward, a.k.a. "Boss" Platt (1853-1929), closed his father's furniture store to focus on the funeral business.

Edward, educated in Stuttgart and the University of Heidelberg, organized the Georgia Funeral Directors' Association and was elected as its first president in 1877. He was also issued the first embalming license in the state of Georgia. After serving as chief of Augusta's first volunteer fire department, Edward successfully campaigned for a paid fire department.[5] Not as much is known about Edward's brother Henry. Although Henry was born in Augusta, he eventually moved to Nantucket where he worked as a photographer.[6]

Figure 13. Early Boathouse at Lake Olmstead (*Historic American Engineering Record*)

Kenny's Sailboat and the Tiger

While the Platts launched the first boat on Lake Olmstead, Captain P. J. Kenny, one of the canal's workers, holds the honor for launching the first sailboat on the lake during the humid morning of June 7, 1873.[7] Another sailboat, the *Sallie*, was also soon anchored on the waters of the lake by Mr. John S. Costello, of the McCabe & Costello Firm, once a leading dry-goods house.[8]

Captain Kenny had won much admiration a couple of months earlier when he tracked and captured a tiger in the "jungles" adjacent to the canal. For several weeks, a dreadful tiger had afflicted Columbia County slaughtering cows, sheep, and goats, "to say nothing of the unknown human bodies which the ferocious animal has borne away and hid in the dark, or its own rapacious entrails."[9] No one knows for sure where the ferocious animal came from, but it was conjectured that it had escaped from a traveling animal show.

When Kenny received news of the tiger's movement into the thick vegetation near the canal where he was quartered, he gathered together a posse of tiger hunters. With burning torches lighting the way, Kenny and his fellow warriors set off in the darkness of night in search of the ferocious beast. After several long hours of tracking the beast, the men came upon the tiger and lassoed him. As if he had escaped from a traveling menagerie show, the tiger became quite passive.

The tiger was restrained in a notably secure cage and loaded onto a mule-drawn wagon toward the city in hopes of obtaining a handsome reward. The tiger, however, had other plans. As the armed party of men grew close to the city, a furiously blinding rainstorm burst open upon the group. The men and their horses sought immediate shelter. Unbeknownst to the captors, the excited tiger made a "desperate and successful effort to break the small bars which had hitherto restricted his liberty."[10] Once free, the deadly beast made his way down Hawk's Gully to the Savannah River. With his captors' guns aimed and firing, the tiger, jumping the rocky shoals, made his way to the other side of the river. Although a disappointment to Kenny and his posse, the escape was not a total loss. "We regret that our citizens were deprived of the sight of the captured tiger, but are gratified to know that our Carolina friends will now have to look after him."[11] With the dangerous tiger in South Carolina, at least it was no longer a menace to Augusta.

Inaugural Sailing Regatta

Soon after Rae's Creek filled Lake Olmstead's reservoir, Augustans began talking of inaugurating a sailing regatta. Members of the zealous Augusta Boat Club began practicing daily on the lake and canal. It maintained a clubhouse on the canal after consolidating with the Rebel Boat Club.[12] Promoted by club president William J. Cranston, Esq. (1848-1893), a local cotton broker, the first recorded sailboat race at Lake Olmstead took place between two crews on Friday afternoon, July 16, 1875.[13] So avid was the Boat Club they even requested inclusion of a regatta at the next State Fair in Macon, Georgia. "We feel assured that nothing at the State Fair would please visitors better than a few exciting boat races."[14]

Daily practice and zealous enthusiasm did not, however, ensure continuous victories. With the robust shipping and railroad ties between Augusta and Charleston, South Carolina, the two cities became sporting rivals. The Palmetto Boat Club of Charleston issued an interstate boating challenge to the Augusta Boat Club and even bequeathed Augusta with home-course advantage. Augusta fervently accepted, and the sailing regatta was rapidly scheduled to take place on

July 23, 1879, at Lake Olmstead. The *Charleston News* reported that the "Palmetto Crew is training hard for the Augusta Regatta on the twenty-third on Lake Olmstead."[15]

As race day finally arrived, droves of spectators seeking to witness the event packed the canal steamers hauling people from downtown Augusta to Lake Olmstead. The Augusta Boat Club gave its best effort, but ultimately, the Palmetto Crew's training paid off as it emerged victorious. Although disappointed, Augustans were proud to hear Charleston's president applaud the length and beauty of Lake Olmstead.[16]

Armstrong's Steamers

Although many credit the team of Robert Livingston and Robert Fulton for inventing and operating the first commercial steamboat in 1807, William Longstreet had already successfully built and navigated his steamer on the Savannah River a year earlier.[17] By the 1870s, steamboats or steamers, as they were often called, were making daily trips between Augusta and Savannah, Georgia. Over seventy different steamboats navigated the Savannah River during the early to late eighteenth century.[18] The vessels were mainly used for shipping purposes and transportation. That changed with the introduction of pleasure steamers on Lake Olmstead. In the spring of 1877, Mr. N. W. Armstrong, superintendent of the Canal Steamboat Company, introduced his new pleasure boat, the *Wade Hampton*.[19] Similar to other canal boats of the period, the *Wade Hampton* was pulled by a horse or mule along the canal's towpath. Mr. Armstrong, however, was convinced that small steamboats could be run on the canal and Lake Olmstead, just as they were on the Erie Canal.

Armstrong, who also worked as a realtor and clerk for the Enterprise Mill, purchased and mounted a propeller on his newest boat, the *Augusta*. However, the one-horsepower engine proved to be undersized for propelling the boat. Armstrong then transferred it to his yawl boat, a two-masted sailboat similar to a sloop or cutter. "With this it works finely, propels it easily at the speed of about six miles per hour, and without any washing of the banks."[20] Mr. Armstrong paraded guests, including Mayor John Meyer, on his trips back and forth to the canal locks and dam and around Lake Olmstead. In the meantime, he sent north for a four-horsepower engine to propel a larger boat.

Figure 14. The Steamboat *Toccoa* (c. 1912)

The mode of transportation on the canal and Lake Olmstead was soon revolutionized. Steam was rapidly superseding horse, mule, and pole power. By 1883, the steamer *Julia* had found a home in Augusta and was transporting parties of patrons back and forth on the canal and Lake Olmstead. The longest of the trips was the trip to the canal headgates and back, which took four hours. Several years later, in 1887, a young gentlemen's club known as the AGCH Club, launched a lightweight steamboat onto the lake.[21] Within the next several years, another steamer, the big launch, *Anita S.*, would also ride the waves on Lake Olmstead, making the lake seem more like a harbor than a lake.

Boating fever was firmly entrenched at Lake Olmstead. As reported in the *Augusta Chronicle*, boating fever had caught on in Augusta and was approaching epidemic form. "The bank of the canal, along the rock pile at the basin, is becoming lined with boathouses, and any afternoon rowing parties may be encountered anywhere between Lake View Park and the canal basin."[22] Even the local YMCA was not immune from boating fever. The YMCA had a boathouse on Lake Olmstead, which provided members access to rowboats and canoes at reduced rates.[23] Boating parties and picnics at the lake had become regular afternoon and evening affairs.[24]

Cries for Help

With the escalation of boating came numerous and often quite humorous accounts of boaters in need of rescue. One such occurrence took place on a warm spring day in 1899. Two army lieutenants with hundreds of spectators looking on endured an impromptu bath in Lake Olmstead. The two fell into the lake while attempting to change places in their rowboat.[25] One lieutenant, holding his pistol out of the water, ploddingly swam to shore. His companion, unable to swim, was blowing and gurgling water before he was reached by a nearby boat.

Another instance occurred on a cold November night in 1902. Cries for help, mixed with exclamations of "murder" and "police" and the rapid gunfire of pistols, generated sensational excitement around the lake.[26] On the return trip to the city after spending the afternoon at the Canal Locks, a party of six couples, hosted by William E. Moore, was stranded when their steam launch became stuck on a mudbank near the mouth of the lake. In response to the cries for help, a gang of four men started out to rescue the stranded party. Only two of the men, however, made it to the stranded revelers, as the other two men became frightened at the darkness and had to be taken back to shore. The stranded launch was eventually pulled off the mudbank and the party brought to shore.

P. W. Norman, a night watchman at the lake, was frequently called on for help from stranded boaters. One of Norman's impressive rescues occurred on the night of July 14, 1903. A group of fifty moonlight excursionists had set out on their large pleasure boat for a trip to the Canal Locks and back. They were having a splendid time with seven kegs of beer, a dozen boiled hams, and fifty loaves of bread on board. Around midnight, the towrope used to traverse the canal broke, and the boat ran aground in the mouth of the lake. After he and his assistant heard several gunshots, followed by the screams of frightened women, Norman sent out a rowboat out to rescue the stranded party. Ungratefully, the drunken pleasure-seekers hurled insults at Norman after being rescued. Norman was about to summon the police in hopes of halting the unruly ruckus, but fortunately, the party continued on its journey to the Locks.

Norman came to the rescue again on the night of May 5, 1904, when a young man and lady overturned in the lake.[27] However, it was P. W. Norman who had to be rescued in 1907. Norman challenged Ed Simms to a swimming contest, betting Simms that he could swim across the Savannah River and back before he could. At 10:00 p.m. on May 2, 1907, with numerous spectators watching, the two men jumped into the river and swam to the South Carolina side. About halfway back across, Norman tired and began calling for help. Simms, who was in the lead, swam back to Norman and, holding the weary Norman out of the water, swam back to the bank on the Georgia side of the river.[28]

As the popularity of Lake Olmstead grew, one of the underlying problems with its subsequent development came to light. Lake Olmstead was located on the line between the city limits of Augusta and Richmond County. As early as 1883, a case came before the city's recorder court regarding the necessity to have a city license to sell liquor at the Park. Although it was argued that Lake View Park was not within the city limits, the recorder promptly decided that under the act, approved in December 1882, the city limits included the waterline of Lake Olmstead and the Park was in this limit. The parties arraigned were fined $50 each.[29] Unfortunately, the location of Lake Olmstead meant that neither the city nor county had uniform jurisdiction over the lake. As time went on, this would cause significant problems.

VI

Augusta's Winter Colony

An essential attribute contributing to the allure of Lake Olmstead was its location. It was located on the west end of the city adjacent to the historic hilltop community of Summerville. Summerville, commonly referred to as the Hill, is situated on the sandhills overlooking Augusta and the Savannah River Valley. During the late eighteenth century and early nineteen hundreds, the Hill would see phenomenal growth as a winter colony and tourist center for wealthy northerners seeking to escape brutal northern winters. The yearly presence of northern visitors led to the development of an infrastructure featuring affluent sporting opportunities, such as golf and polo, as well as swanky resort hotels with ongoing social functions and entertainment. Augusta's newest recreational jewel, Lake Olmstead, would benefit greatly from its location, just over a mile from the center of Augusta's blossoming winter colony.

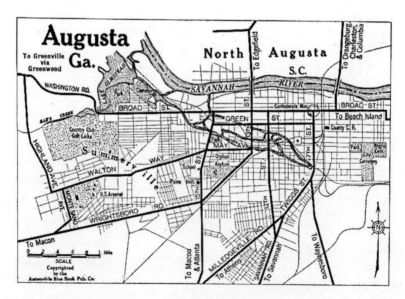

Figure 15. Map of Augusta during the early 1900s

The Hill

What made the Hill so desirable was its climate. Summerville is perched along a crest of sandhills rising above the coastal plain and stretching along the Fall Line from Chester, South Carolina, to Augusta. Formed over twenty-five million years ago, the sandhills were once beach dunes of the ancient Atlantic Ocean coastline. By comparison, the Hill is approximately three hundred feet higher in elevation than Augusta.[1]

Due to its elevation and highly permeable soil, Summerville is cooler and less humid than the city. It also did not have many of the health troubles associated with the low-lying area of the Savannah River, such as yellow fever and malaria, both mosquito-borne infectious diseases. Although the fever was a perilous threat to downtown Augusta in the early eighteen hundreds, Summerville was largely unscathed.

The advantageous climate of the Hill persuaded the US government to relocate its arsenal from its location near the Savannah River to the Hill. Established to protect Augusta from the surrounding Cherokee and Creek Indians, the US Arsenal housed troops that saw action during the Indian Wars, including the Seminole War of 1835. Additionally, the arsenal served as a major supply and manufacturing center for the US Corps. In 1844, Major General William Tecumseh Sherman (1820-1891), then a lieutenant, was assigned to the arsenal for six months.[2] Of course, Sherman would go on to become one of the most well-known union generals during the Civil War, due largely to his famous March to the Sea. Although Sherman torched Atlanta, he bypassed Augusta, leading many to speculate his reasons.

In 1820, swamp fever was so ravishing in Augusta it nearly obliterated the entire garrison stationed at the US Arsenal. Only seven of the thirty enlisted men survived.[3] The following is an excerpt from an October 1, 1825, letter from Major Matthew M. Payne, the commanding officer at the arsenal.

> I regret to state that circumstances have compelled me to remove the garrison from the arsenal. About the 17th of September a fever of the most alarming character made its appearance at this post. Assistant surgeon, Dr. T. P. Hall, was attacked on the 17th and died on the morning of the 21st of yellow fever. A private of the company, who was attacked on the 21st, died on the morning of the 24th, and not well enough men of the garrison to bear the corpse to the grave. Under such circumstances a removal became absolutely necessary. I therefore directed the quartermaster to rent a house on Sand Hills for the reception of the sick, retaining at the post only three well men of the command.

General Gaines, who is here, urged in the strongest terms an immediate removal. So unfavorably is the general impressed with the locality of the post, that he says it would be better to abandon it altogether than to keep them here during the summer and fall months.

Respectfully, &c.,

M. M. PAYNE, *Major United States Army.*[4]

Several years later, in 1826, the US government fled its location by the river and relocated the arsenal to the Hill, purchasing approximately seventy-two acres of Freeman Walker's Bellevue plantation.[5] Freeman Walker (1780-1827) and his younger brother, Valentine, had come to Augusta from Virginia in 1797 to join their older brothers, George and Robert, in studying law. Walker would proceed to have a noteworthy impact on Augusta through his lengthy and remarkable political career. He was a member of the State House of Representatives from 1807-1811, served as a Democratic Republican to the United States Senate from 1819-1821, and served as mayor of Augusta from 1818 to 1819 and 1823.

The arsenal would play a significant role in the wars that followed, but in 1955, the arsenal was permanently closed. The former arsenal site is now the location of Georgia Regents University, formerly Augusta State University.

As the climate of the Hill continued to draw people from the city, a separate village known as Summerville was established and incorporated in 1861. Many of Augusta's prominent and wealthy families moved to the Hill. As such, it was historically home to many of Augusta's most influential people, including George Walton (1749-1804), a signer of the Declaration of Independence; John Milledge (1757-1818), a former Georgia governor and founder of Athens, Georgia, and the University of Georgia; and Thomas Cumming (1765-1834), Augusta's first mayor and president of the powerful Bank of Augusta.

By the 1890s, Summerville had become a prominent winter resort. The village transformed itself from a small summer resort for local residents into a winter playground for wealthy northern bankers, industrialists, and politicians. Summerville soon became home to two of Augusta's most prominent tourist hotels and Augusta's first golf courses.[6] In recognition of its historic value, Summerville was added to the National Register of Historic Places in 1980.

Figure 16. Streetcar on Broad Street (ca. 1903)

The Bon Air Hotel and Partridge Inn, both located about a mile from Lake Olmstead, were the foremost of Augusta's early grand hotels. Both were built on the Hill overlooking Augusta and coincided in part with the 1866 development of a horse-drawn trolley line running from Fifth and Broad Streets up the hill through Summerville to the Augusta Arsenal. Another early hotel on a hill, albeit on the other side of the Savannah River, was the Hampton Terrace Hotel in North Augusta, South Carolina. At the time, it was deemed the largest wooden structure in the world. Finally, in 1928, a year before the Great Depression, the last of Augusta's grand hotels was opened, the Forrest Hills-Ricker Hotel.

Bon Air Hotel

The Bon Air Hotel, built on the Hill overlooking Augusta, was the largest of the grand hotels in Augusta. The Bon Air began as a dream of Dr. William H. Tutt (1823-1898), a community leader in Augusta, who had made his fortune selling patented medicines such as Tutt's Liver Pills and Tutt's Golden Eagle Bitters. These medicines were extremely popular, and advertisements for these mail-ordered concoctions filled newspapers around the nation. A nineteen hundred advertisement from an Oregon newspaper espouses not only the benefits of Tutt's Liver Pills but exemplifies the vast region in which they were sold.

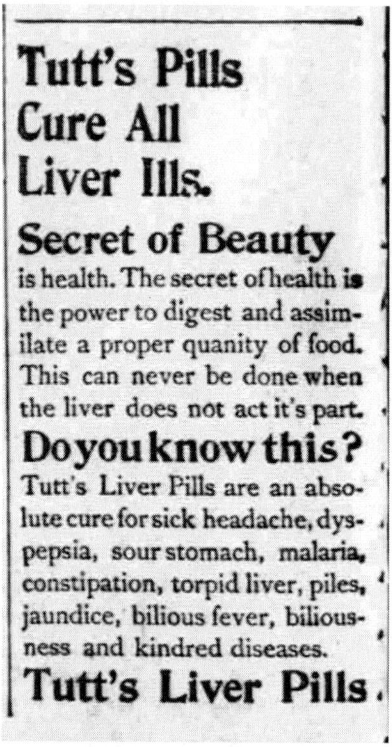

> **Tutt's Pills Cure All Liver Ills.**
>
> **Secret of Beauty** is health. The secret of health is the power to digest and assimilate a proper quanity of food. This can never be done when the liver does not act it's part. **Do you know this?** Tutt's Liver Pills are an absolute cure for sick headache, dyspepsia, sour stomach, malaria, constipation, torpid liver, piles, jaundice, bilious fever, biliousness and kindred diseases. **Tutt's Liver Pills.**

Figure 17. Advertisement for Tutt's Liver Pills from the July 9, 1900 *Morning Oregonian*

Tutt had also been instrumental with the development of the Augusta Canal, serving on several important committees. An unrelenting proponent of Augusta, Tutt also successfully campaigned for Augusta to host the Cotton States Mechanics and Agricultural Fair, bringing throngs of people to Augusta.[7]

Dr. Tutt, with his wealth and financial means, correctly believed that a resort hotel on the Hill would attract wealthy tourists from the North. On May 28, 1888, Tutt purchased the four-acre Hillsides estate of Mrs. Anna McKinne Winter for $12,500 as the site for his hotel. Opened to the public on December 2, 1889, the Bon Air was majestically constructed with 105 guest rooms. The expansive four-storied Victorian building with towers and turrets, staircases, and verandas was ready to receive "the Yankee elite."[8] In recognition of the "soothing, cooling breezes that wafted through and around Summerville," Dr. Tutt named the hotel Bon Air.[9]

Figure 18. The original Bon Air Hotel (c. 1900)

The Bon Air was one of the finest hotels in the South, renowned for its gourmet food, golf, tennis, and horseback riding. The hotel featured wooden stairs, door facings, wainscoting, and floors made from curled Georgia pine. A broad veranda extended around the entire front and south side of the hotel. A large octagon-shaped solarium enclosed by glass windows on all sides crowned the top of the hotel, offering a spectacular view of the Savannah River Valley. The grounds were embellished with the finest of luxuries, including beautiful landscaping, bowling alleys, and lawn tennis courts. The Bon Air was so popular that within several years, an additional 145 rooms were added. A full-service livery stable operated by George H. Kernaghan was located at the bottom of the hill, providing guests fine saddle and driving horses.[10] Kernaghan had made his fame and fortune racing horses on the "turf" circuit and operated his livery stable for over thirty years. He was also a renowned breeder, selling two of his mares, Lizzie and Jennie, for $6,000 each.[11]

Golf would prove to be the Bon Air's legacy. Anne Osborne, an Augusta historian, noted "at the turn of the century, a new game was introduced among the elite."[12] In 1897, the hotel and a group of prominent Augustans organized the Bon Air Golf Club. The Club originally leased ninety acres of land on the east end of Milledge Road from Alfred S. Bourne to construct a nine-hole golf course but subsequently acquired additional land to expand its course on the west side of Milledge Road. Within the next couple of years a 6,174-yard, eighteen-hole course, known as the Hill course, was established with the help of both David Ogilvie, a Scotland native, and Dr. William Henry Harison Jr., the founding president of the Augusta Country Club.[13] The Hill course had sand greens until 1927, when renowned golf architect Donald Ross installed grass greens.[14]

The Bon Air hosted a full schedule of golf events for men and ladies during the winter months (January through March), including the Governor's Cup and the Bon Air Cup. Golf in Augusta soon began to prosper. The Bon Air developed another eighteen-hole golf course on a 185-acre adjoining tract, known as the Lake course. The 5,833-yard Lake course overlooked Lake Olmstead and extended along the lakefront and border of Rae's Creek. It had the first grass greens in Augusta.[15]

Figure 19. View of Lake Olmstead from the Lake course

The Bon-Air Golf Club would eventually become part of the Augusta Country Club, organized in 1899 and chartered in 1900. Together, they would contribute significantly to Augusta's growth as a tourist destination. After many years of usage by the Country Club, utilization of the Lake course was gradually discontinued during the 1930s. In 1942, the Lake course was sold for approximately $25,000.[16] Shortly thereafter, a residential neighborhood, Country Club Hills, was developed on the property.

The prestigious Bon Air entertained some of America's most elite dignitaries, including American novelist and author of *The Great Gatsby*, F. Scott Fitzgerald (1896-1940); industrialist, philanthropist, and founder of the Standard Oil Company, John D. Rockefeller (1839-1937); US president and subsequent Supreme Court justice William H. Taft (1857-1930); US president Warren

G. Harding (1865-1923); and British prime minister Sir Winston Churchill (1874-1965).

The grand hotel was a source of alliance between Augustans and prominent politicians and businessmen. One such instance was the ensuing friendship of President William H. Taft and the Honorable Joseph R. Lamar. Lamar was born in Elbert County, Georgia, and attended the Academy of Richmond County in Augusta, Georgia. He lived down the street from Woodrow Wilson, another Augustan destined for prominence. After attending the University of Georgia, Lamar obtained his law degree from Washington and Lee University School of Law. Later, he would go on to serve in the Georgia House of Representatives and on the Georgia Supreme Court. In 1911, President Taft appointed Lamar to serve on the United States Supreme Court, a position he held until his death in 1916.

The Bon Air was also home to a group known as the Conversation Club. According to research by Tom Robertson, a local civil engineer, the Conversation Club gathered regularly at the Bon Air Hotel in the 1920s. The group composed largely of a wealthy group of Northerners vacationing in Augusta, and several local leaders would gather each morning before they set off to play golf to discuss life, politics, sports, and various current events. Among the members were Judge Kenesaw Mountain Landis, the first commissioner of Major League baseball; Canadian prime minister Robert Borden; Nobel Prize winner Nicholas Murray Butler; and Harvey Samuel Firestone, the founder of the Firestone Tire & Rubber Co. "It was a very diverse group but they all had two things in common: money and a love for golf," Mr. Robertson said.[17]

Regrettably, in the early morning of February 4, 1921, at the height of its success, disaster struck the Bon Air when it suffered a devastating fire and was utterly destroyed. News of the fire was a front-page story in virtually every American newspaper, as well as in numerous papers throughout Canada and Mexico.

Initially, it was announced that the Bon Air would not be rebuilt. However, financing paired with the leadership of Col. Sanford Cohen and former mayor, Thomas G. Barrett (1862-1929), ensured that it was rebuilt. Col. Sanford Cohen, a prominent promoter, aggressively sought financing and secured the support of the Chamber of Commerce's Committee of Fifty, a powerful group of local leaders. Led by young lawyer Joseph B. Cumming Jr. and banker Walter Lane, the committee passed a resolution endorsing both the rebuilding of the Bon Air Hotel and a pledge to raise $50,000 of the amount necessary to insure its success.[18] While Cohen was acquiring local support, Thomas Barrett was persuading Walton H. Marshall, manager of the Vanderbilt Hotel chain, to invest in the Augusta landmark. With significant funding from the Vanderbilt family, the hotel was rebuilt as the Bon Air-Vanderbilt Hotel at a cost of over $1,000,000.[19]

Figure 20. View of downtown Augusta and Walton Way from the Bon Air
(*Robert A. Mullins Collection*)

The Bon Air-Vanderbilt reopened with much fanfare on January 8, 1923.[20] The hotel was so successful during its first season that an additional one hundred rooms were added for the second season. The hotel's success, however, diminished over the years with the development of Florida as the new winter travel destination. The Bon Air was purchased by the Sheraton Corporation in 1945 but subsequently declared bankruptcy and closed its doors on September 27, 1960.[21] For a short time thereafter, the Bon Air was turned into a retirement community. Today, apartments at the Bon Air provide federally subsidized housing for seniors and disabled people.

Partridge Inn

Figure 21. Partridge Inn (*Courtesy of the Partridge Inn*)

Building off the early success of the Bon Air Hotel, Morris W. Partridge (1869-1947), a seasonal cashier/bookkeeper at the Bon Air Hotel, acquired property across the street for what would soon be another grand hotel, the Partridge Inn. The notorious landmark began as a two-story private residence of the Meigs family who moved to Augusta from Connecticut in the early eighteen hundreds.[22] After purchasing the property in 1892, Partridge began offering guest accommodations in the old Meigs house during the winter season. Morris Partridge quickly gained the reputation as a gracious and charismatic host.

Figure 22. View of the Partridge Inn from the Bon Air (*Robert A. Mullins Collection*)

Over the next thirty-seven years, numerous expansions and improvements were made, eventually resulting in a five-story building with 145 rooms and a quarter mile of galleried porches and balconies.[23] Although one of its wings was built of brick, the hotel was mostly wooden with a facade punctuated with verandas, balconies, and porches. A penthouse suite crowned the sixth floor, offering a panoramic view of Augusta and the Savannah River Valley. There were "delightful sun parlors and palm rooms enclosed in glass" as well as a roof garden.[24]

The Inn contained space on the bottom floor for local shops and businesses. The Summerville post office was located there, as were the Summerville Drug Store, Stark Cleaners, and the Van Dyck Linen Shop.[25] Even indoor putting greens were available. Mindful of its guests, the Inn also boasted quail hunting, excellent saddle horses, a riding master, and stables to house the polo horses of its numerous guests.

Figure 23. Indoor putting green at the Partridge Inn (*Courtesy of the Partridge Inn*)

In 1923, the Partridge Inn experienced the pinnacle of its first golden age when it hosted a gala banquet for President Warren G. Harding. The *Augusta Chronicle* acknowledged the banquet as the greatest banquet in Augusta's history.

> Augusta staged the greatest banquet in its history last night when President Warren G. Harding and other distinguished men in national affairs were guests of honor.[26]

Economics and Partridge's death eventually took its toll on the grand hotel. The Partridge Inn was converted into apartments during the 1960s and 1970s. By the 1980s, it was slated for demolition. Fortunately, however, the Partridge Inn was protected and revitalized after several years of extensive renovations. The Partridge Inn is the only remaining grand hotel of Augusta still operating today.

Hampton Terrace Hotel

Figure 24. The Hampton Terrace Hotel

On the beautiful bluffs of the Savannah River across from Augusta stood the Hampton Terrace Hotel, a magnificent hotel and one of the largest wooden structures ever built. The hotel was the creation of James Urquhart Jackson (1856-1925), a young railroad official who often dreamed of building a city on the bluffs.

Jackson was a very determined and ingenuous young man. After graduating from the University of Georgia, Jackson began his career selling stocks and bonds in Augusta, investing the money he made in building numerous regional railways, such as the Augusta and Knoxville, the Georgia Southern and Florida, the Augusta Southern, and the Marietta and North Georgia railroad systems.[27] Jackson, through his construction of the Marietta and North Georgia railway, enabled the initial development of Georgia's marble quarries. It was said that he used the first marble column taken from the mines in building his home in North Augusta.

Built in 1902 on the corner of Forest Avenue and Carolina Avenue, Jackson's home, now known as Rosemary Hall, had twenty-two rooms and boasted fifty-foot marble columns.[28] Jackson also organized and negotiated the sale of marble for several major buildings, including the New York Stock Exchange Building and the Minnesota State Capital Building.[29]

Figure 25. Number 6 Volunteer Fire Company baseball team): (1) C. W. Jackson, (2) M. Twiffs, (3) Charles Crawford, (4) Tom Alexander, (5) W. T. Craig, (6) Frank Dorr, (7) James Urquhart Jackson, (8) F. Von Kamp, (9) John Jackson, (10) P. Greene, (11) B. Wilson, (12) H. Preston, (13) ? Cain, (14) E. J. Miller Sr., (15) W. Rhett, (16) Francis Nixon, (17) William F. Law, Captain, (18) George Howard, (19) R. E. Stallings, (20) Harry C. Robert, (21) W. Verdery, (22) Lewis A. Robert (*Georgia Regents University, Reese Library Special Collection,* ca. 1880s)

His dream of building a city on the Savannah River bluffs overlooking Augusta began to take shape when he and his brother Walter purchased 5,600 acres of what is now North Augusta, South Carolina, from Mrs. Mattie Butler Mealing. Mealing had inherited her father's extensive plantation two years earlier. To increase access between Augusta and his new town, Jackson built the Thirteenth Street Bridge over the Savannah River. He also purchased Augusta's trolley system in 1897 and ran a line across his new bridge to North Augusta.

In April of 1902, Jackson began construction of the Hampton Terrace Hotel. The five-story hotel contained three hundred rooms and accommodations for five hundred guests. The wooden structure itself was longer than two football fields and contained enough glass to put windows into seventy standard residential homes.[30] The Hampton, located on the knoll across from Augusta, commanded a stunning view of Augusta and beyond. Amenities on the hotel's grounds included a golf course, tennis courts, riding stables, and a 1,500-acre game preserve. It was completed the next year at a cost of $536,000.[31] An early twentieth-century postcard image of the picturesque Hampton Terrace Hotel described it as "the most magnificent winter resort in the world." Many famous families and dignitaries, such as John D. Rockefeller, Marshall Fields, and Harvey Firestone, were frequent guests.[32] President Howard Taft regarded the golf course as "challenging as well as impressive."

Figure 26. The Hampton Terrace Hotel Golf Course (ca. 1905)

Catastrophe struck the Hampton Terrace Hotel on New Year's Eve in 1916, when the hotel's wiring short-circuited and it burned to the ground, leaving nothing but the brick chimney standing. Apparently, no one died in the fire, but the scene was dramatic.

One young woman was seen rolling a trunk down the terrace toward the
entrance gate. Others, scantily clad, carrying suitcases and their arms
full of wearing apparel, hurriedly placed themselves beyond reach of the
burning structure.[33]

The site was devastating. Regrettably, fire insurance was negligible, only
covering $200,000 of a loss estimated at over $750,000.[34] Although the Hampton
was never rebuilt, James U. Jackson is credited with building the town of North
Augusta. His dream of building a city became a reality in 1906, when the
community of North Augusta was incorporated.

The Fairgrounds

Along with the grand hotels, Augusta also had a central entertainment venue
adjacent to Lake Olmstead. The old fairgrounds were located on the downtown
side of Lake Olmstead at the intersection of Broad Street and Milledge Road,
comprising some eighty acres in between Wood Street and Lake Olmstead,
running all the way to the Augusta Canal. In addition to exhibit areas, the
fairgrounds had a large restaurant, an impressive music hall, a one-mile racetrack,
grandstands, stables, a poultry house, and numerous other outbuildings. The
fairgrounds were the scene of everything from horse racing, car and motorcycle
racing, to collegiate football games and horse shows. Close to Augusta's grand
hotels, it was a recreational and entertainment venue for local residents and
northern tourists.

Events held at Lake Olmstead would often spill over to the fairgrounds and
vice versa. Augusta's 1915 Labor Day celebration provides a typical illustration.
The day's events began with a parade from downtown Augusta to Lake View Park.[35]
Festivities were then formally opened with a day full of activities at both Lake View
Park and the fairgrounds, such as swimming races, foot races, freak races, a fat
man's race, and numerous other field sports. Local labor unions competed in
tug-of-war contests. After dinner, the crowd was treated to horse and motorcycle
racing and even a slow mule race. In proverbial Augusta tradition, the day-long
festivities concluded with dancing at the Lake View Pavilion.

Figure 27. Oxen plowing contest at the Fairgrounds
(*Georgia Regents University, Reese Library Special Collections*)

Numerous intercollegiate football games were hosted at the fairgrounds, including the University of Georgia Bulldogs' annual rivalry with Clemson University. In 1907, Georgia won the November 7 game by a score of 8-0.[36] Prior to construction of Sanford Stadium in Athens, Georgia would play Clemson at the fairgrounds five more times over the next six years, winning all but one game.

In 1908, lights were soon installed at the fairgrounds, which was in full swing for the special Night Society Horse Show held there on April 9, 1908. The facility was described as "one of the best horse show rings ever seen in the South."[37] There were over twelve different show classes, ranging from most beautiful model horse to best double carriage team. Big-band music provided entertainment to the crowd, with the last show class starting at 10:30 p.m.

Annually, the fairgrounds were used in connection with the Georgia-Carolina Fair, which emphasized that the fair was for people of both states. Typically, the directors of the fair association, speakers for the day, and band and other dignitaries in attendance gathered at the Confederate monument on Broad Street. In 1906, the Augusta Railway and Electric Company provided fourteen special cars for the procession from downtown to the fairgrounds. Music was performed by the Augusta Military Band, and a dedicatory poem was read by well-known Augusta poet, William H. Hayne (1856-1929).[38]

Another memorable occasion was the sixth annual Georgia-Carolina Fair held at the fairgrounds in November 1911. The opening of the fair was Monday, November 6.[39] James U. Jackson, president of the fair association from its inception, gave the opening address. To celebrate the opening day, a big airplane flew over the city. Thursday was Football Day featuring a gridiron challenge between Georgia and Clemson.

During Augusta's real estate boom in 1925, a group of Ohio businessmen led by A. A. Bratton and Luther L. Boger announced the purchase of six hundred acres west of Lake Olmstead and the fairgrounds.[40] The group intended to develop the fairground tract into a major tourist center to include the building of a new auditorium, a park, and tourist bungalows. Plans were to keep the racetrack in place for whippet racing and other events.[41] On the Broad Street side of the fairground tract, the group intended to construct a moving-picture theater and stores.

Contrary to the impressive proposition, with the onslaught of depression and hard economic times over the next couple of years, the fairgrounds began to deteriorate. In 1936, Augusta purchased about forty-five acres of the old fairgrounds for use as a borrow pit for a canal improvement project aimed at reinforcing the canal banks.[42] In 1941, Augusta's city council approved use of the property for construction of a one-hundred-unit public housing project.[43] Today, the old fairgrounds are the site of Olmsted Homes, a National Guard Armory, Lake Olmstead Stadium, and the local American Legion headquarters.

VII

Japanese Lanterns
Society Blossoms on Lake Olmstead

In its early years, Lake Olmstead was the scene of bountiful social and recreational affairs and one of the most popular social venues in Augusta. It was a time before moving pictures and automobiles, a time during which Augustans would take a trolley car on summer evenings to Lake Olmstead to watch vaudeville shows and paddle canoes "on the cool waters of the lake while fanned by a refreshing breeze."[1] By the turn of the century, two entertainment venues took up residence on the southeastern shores of Lake Olmstead, in a city known as one of the greatest club cities in the South.[2] Lake View Park, established in 1881, was the first social establishment on the lake. Nine years later, the exclusive Lakeside Club, located adjacent to Lake View Park, was organized. Unlike Lake View Park, the Lakeside Club was for members only.

Symbolic of this era were the use of Japanese lanterns casting rays of astonishing colors.[3] Traditionally, these paper lanterns, similar to luminaries, were used for cultural celebrations and festivals as symbols of hope and good wishes. During Lake Olmstead's early years, they were customary at lakeside soirees, adorning the clubhouses and grounds. Astonishing regattas and dances were both frequent and remarkable. Society was blossoming in Augusta on the shores of Lake Olmstead.

Lake View Park

Situated on a hill near the mouth of Lake Olmstead, Lake View Park afforded breathtaking views of the lake, the Carolina hills, and the Augusta Canal. Beginning on the north side of the terminus of Milledge Road and old Broad Street and stretching to the water's edge, the park occupied six acres. East of the park were the fairgrounds. Within the park itself, there were picturesque picnic grounds, cool springs, large wooden swings hanging from the towering trees, and a dance pavilion.

Never-ending fanfare greeted those attending the grand opening celebration of Lake View Park on Thursday evening, May 5, 1881.[4] Boats and streetcars ferried people from downtown Augusta to the new park. The *Steamer Julia*, piloted by Commodore Stoy, was busy bustling up and down the canal carrying patrons to the park. A popular community brass band, the Augusta Silver Cornet Band, played dance music as patrons and guests twirled the night away in the dance pavilion. A magnificent bombardment of fireworks over the lake capped off the evening's festivities.

The unrelenting party continued for weeks. On Monday night, May 16, 1881, another concert and dance featured the Augusta Brass Band, of whom W. Edward Platt was president.[5] Patrons flocked to Lake View Park, where, upon payment of a fifty-cent admission fee, they could join in the fun.[6] The caveat was that gentlemen were required to bring a lady guest to gain admittance. Trolley cars hauled people back and forth to the park in droves.

Within weeks of opening, Lake View Park became a popular picnic location for local groups. Some of the organizations staging picnics at the park included the Augusta Hose Company, Richmond Fire Company, St. John's M. C. Church Sunday School, and First Baptist Church Sunday School. The Deutscher Freundschaftsbund, a social and benevolent organization for the numerous local residents of German descent, hosted its social at the park. The German contingency in Augusta also organized a Deutscher Scheutzen Club devoted to marksmanship and good fellowship. Lake View Park was becoming an overwhelmingly popular venue for Augustans.

Figure 28. The Boat House, Lake View Park *(Credit: Augusta Canal Authority Collection)*

Over time, some historians have attributed development of the park to Frederick Law Olmsted (1822-1903), one of America's foremost landscape artists.[7] Although he was reportedly hired by the city of Augusta to design the park, there is no supporting evidence. Lake View Park was not owned by the city.

Before the creation of Lake View Park, the property was owned by Clarence Starnes. It was deeded to the newly formed Augusta Land Company in early 1874, shortly after the formation of Lake Olmstead. Incorporated a year earlier, the Augusta Land Company sought to obtain property with the objective of improving it and offering facilities and inducements for the growth of the city of Augusta and its suburbs.[8] Originally, the Augusta Land Company was led by Major James J. Gregg, son of William Gregg, founder of the Graniteville Mill. Gregg successfully obtained the financial backing of several British businessmen,[9] as well as mayor Charles Estes, who would lead the company after Gregg's death in 1876. Within a couple of years, the company acquired the Warren Place and much of the property between what would become the fairgrounds and National Hills, west of the city.[10]

In 1891, the Augusta Land Company sold Lake View Park to Joseph Oscar Mathewson (1836-1894), a director of the Charlotte, Columbia, and Augusta Railroad Company and general commission merchant, for $1,584.[11] Several months later, Mathewson sold the park to Major William T. Gary, an esteemed community leader and local railroad lawyer, for $2,640. Major Gary, a veteran of the Civil War, also served Augusta as a democratic state representative and Superior Court judge.[12]

Major Gary and July Walker

Major Gary was an avid and amusing storyteller. One of Major Gary's favorite stories to tell was from his days as US district attorney for the Southern District of Georgia. The story was set in Savannah, Georgia, when Gary appeared in the courtroom of United States judge Alexander "Aleck" Boarman of Western District of Louisiana.[13] Judge Boarman was on the bench presiding in place of the local judge, Judge Speer.

After proceeding through the first part of his criminal docket, Judge Boarman called the next defendant, July Walker. It seems that July Walker, a Negro man, had been charged with retailing spirituous liquors "without having first paid the special tax as required by law."[14] When July came for trial before the court, Judge Boarman asked him if he had a lawyer. July replied, "[N]o, boss." Judge Boarman then pointed to several lawyers who were present and told July to select one. Apparently, July looked around the courtroom and then back at the judge and said, "I believe I'd lak ter [sic] have you, boss."

Judge Boarman responded, "[W]ell, that's a little unusual, July, but if you say so I'll take the case and we'll see what we can do with it.[15] Call the first witness, Mr. District Attorney." So it was that Judge Boarman acted as defense counsel for a defendant upon whom he also had to pass sentence.

The prosecution presented evidence that July had obtained a cheap bottle of whisky and was selling it to others at ten cents a drink. It was reported that Judge Boarman "cross-examined the government's witnesses with the ardor of a young attorney trying his first case." However valiant his efforts, after the evidence was presented, Judge Boarman stated, "[T]hey've got you in a tight place."[16] Although Judge Boarman was not successful in his defense of July, July benefited from his representation. Instead of sentencing him, Judge Boarman simply told July to get back home and start hoeing.

In 1895, Major Gary sold the property to the Augusta Railway Company. Incorporated in 1889, the Augusta Railway Company, commonly referred to as the Street Railway, was led by its president, Colonel Daniel B. Dyer. Previously, the main transportation or streetcar company in Augusta was the Augusta & Summerville Railroad Company (A&S RR), incorporated in 1866. The A&S RR used horses and mules to pull its streetcars. After a legal battle with the A&S RR in early 1890, the Augusta Railway Company purchased the eight miles of track previously laid by the A&S RR and began construction of an electric railway system. Within a couple of years, the Augusta Railway Company constructed a power plant along the canal and converted virtually all the streetcars to electricity.

As part of the transfer of Lake View Park to the Augusta Railway, the Land Company required the Railway to enter into an agreement whereby the park would be deeded to the Railway in exchange for the Railway extending its trolley lines to Milledge Road (then referred to as High Street) and maintaining the new route on a regular thirty-minute schedule.[17] Additionally, the agreement required the Railway to convert Lake View Park into an amusement park maintained solely for "white" people. In accordance with the agreement, after the Railway built the trolley lines, the Augusta Land Company deeded Lake View Park to the Augusta Railway and Electric Company, the successor to the merger between the Augusta Railway Company and the Augusta Light Company.

Figure 29. Lake View Park, Augusta, Ga. (*Credit: Dayton Sherrouse Collection*)

Colonel Dyer Rides in from the Wild West

Lake View Park would continue to gradually develop over the years hosting picnics, midnight boat excursions, and dances. Sweet music from local brass bands often wafted across the serene water. Little did anyone know, but Lake View Park would soon flourish with the 1889 arrival of Colonel Daniel Burns Dyer (1841-1912) and his newly formed Augusta Railway Company. Leaving his good friend "Buffalo Bill" Cody behind, Dyer came to Augusta with his business associates, Samuel M. Jarvis, Col. R. M. Spivey, and Roland R. Conklin, to invest in electricity and streetcars. Having recently visited Augusta at the invitation of Walter C. Boykin (1852-1927), a local real estate agent, Dyer was enthralled by its scenic beauty and its investment opportunism. His wife, Ida Casey Dyer, reportedly had roots in the South as well.

Colonel Dyer was not your typical gentleman. Dyer was a soldier, pioneer, frontiersman, capitalist, journalist, politician, and a streetcar magnate. Black Beard, as he was known by the Indians, had served as the United States Indian agent in Kansas and worked with the Cheyenne and Arapahoe, as well as the Modoc Indians. After Oklahoma was opened up to white settlers, he was elected the first mayor of Guthrie, Oklahoma. Fondly, Colonel Dyer was often referred to as "the companion of the rich, the champion of the poor, and the sincere and helpful friend of everyone who knew him and asked his aid or advice."[18]

Dyer, the businessman, understood the implicit connection between community growth and the ability to increase his profitability from his investments in Augusta's infrastructure. Upon the arrival of Colonel Dyer and his associates, the local newspaper reported, "Augusta is ready to welcome such gentlemen with open arms, and they will meet with no obstacles in the way of anything which they propose that will benefit this goodly city."[19] His impact on Augusta would be monumental.

One of Dyer's first courses of business after arriving in Augusta was to charter the Augusta Railway Company and construct an electric streetcar system. He built electric trolley lines, expanding service from the Augusta Arsenal on the Hill all the way to downtown Augusta. Dyer invested in electrical utilities. The power plant he constructed on the Augusta Canal was the first electric system in the South operated by water power.[20] He too was responsible for providing the first significant lighting on Broad Street in 1892. He invested in the local newspaper and became an owner of the *Augusta Chronicle*. Dyer built Augusta's first modern office building on the corner of Broad Street and Eighth Street in 1891.[21] It was a five-story skyscraper complete with an electric elevator, which before that time had seldom been seen. Another of his ventures was the initiation of a horse show to increase the number of winter visitors to the city.

Colonel Dyer, the soldier, was steadfast in his support of local troops. During the Spanish-American War (April 25, 1898-August 12, 1898), Dyer provided land for what became known as Camp Dyer. Camp Dyer was home to the Tenth US Volunteer Infantry Regiment, an African American unit stationed in Augusta.[22] When Augusta troops requested use of the courthouse yard or the Richmond Academy grounds for a ten-day camp, Colonel Dyer offered Lake View Park and its two large pavilions in order to accommodate the troops. Colonel Dyer even arranged a visit by President McKinley to Camp Dyer, and "when that beloved man reviewed all the troops stationed here it was one of the great days in the history of this city."[23] Later, he would entertain President William Howard Taft when he vacationed in Augusta at his beautiful historic residence, Chateau Le Vert, former residence of George Walton.

Dyer, the transportation magnate, sought to connect transportation to sites of interest as a means of increasing tourism. He proposed a belt line between Lake Olmstead and the Locks on the Augusta Canal. The proposed line would provide multiple points of interest for passengers, such as Lake View Park, the Lake Golf Course, the Cross Country Club, the Jockey Club, Berckmans' Nurseries on Washington Road, and the headquarters of the Game Preserve.[24] The belt line, however, never came to fruition, as emphasis turned to automobile travel. Thus, in 1904, discussions turned toward constructing a boulevard that would circle the entire city of Augusta and Summerville.

Ever appreciative of Augusta's scenic beauty, Colonel Dyer sought to develop roads and a system of parks to take advantage of the area's natural beauty. "Parks," he said, "are the lungs of cities and the beneficial influence of healthy playgrounds for recreation can hardly be estimated."[25] The following excerpt is from an article written by Colonel Dyer appearing in the *Augusta Chronicle* in 1906.

> The object of this article is to consider a matter of the greatest importance to Augusta. It concerns the building of a system of parks and connecting them with a grand boulevard; encircling the city; making a series of parks and driveways broken by woods, water and open space that will give endless variety of view in ever-changing scenes.
>
> I recognize that there are many obstacles in the way of success; but I also recognize the great benefits present and future generations will derive from such an undertaking. Parks are said to be the lungs of cities and the beneficial influence of healthy playgrounds for recreation can hardly be estimated . . .
>
> If it is wished to waive all moral responsibility and obligations and rest in this matter on merely business expediency, then, I say, it will pay us to complete these parks and boulevards simply as an advertisement of our natural advantages as a winter resort. There is an actual commercial value in the artistic development of any city possessing the natural advantages we enjoy here and when this fact is realized the entire population will be behind every movement similar to the one aimed at here; for it will actually produce a dividend in dollars and cents to which we are all keenly awake and responsive if not devoted.[26]

Colonel Dyer perceived the economic value in highlighting the scenic beauty in the Augusta area.[27]

Although Dyer's grand boulevard with its series of parks was never constructed, Dyer would have a substantial impact on Lake View Park and the park and theater he built, known as Monte Santo Park. Soon after its development, the Monte Santo Park, located at the terminus of one of the railway's trolley lines, was subdivided and sold as residential lots. A highlight of the Monte Santo Theatre occurred in 1902 when Dyer transported nearly a hundred orphaned boys and girls from the orphan asylum to a special vaudeville show at the theater.[28]

Figure 30. The Lake, Lake View Park (*Credit: Dayton Sherrouse Collection*)

Colonel Dyer obtained an interest in Lake View Park in 1895, as president of the Augusta Railway Company. Needless to say, his interest was closely intertwined with his business pursuits. In order to enhance traffic to Lake View Park, Dyer developed a trolley line through the Harrisburg community to Lake Olmstead, at no expense to the city.

Colonel Dyer was not only interested in economic stimulation and infrastructure growth, but he was also an immense believer in innovative entertainment. Lake View Park and its patrons would benefit greatly from Dyer's introduction of high-tech entertainment. He introduced his newly acquired kinetoscope at Lake View Park in 1898. Invented by Thomas A. Edison and William Dickson in 1891, the kinetoscope utilized a strip of film, which passed rapidly between a lens and an electric lightbulb while a viewer peered through an external peephole.[29] Behind the peephole, a wheel spun with a narrow slit that acted as a shutter, providing a passing view of each of the forty-six frames, which passed by each second.

The next year, Dyer and his guests viewed motion pictures such as *Bathing at Milan* and *The Battle of San Juan* through Dyer's new vitascope.[30] The vitascope was a motion-picture projector patented by Thomas Armat in 1895.[31] One hot July night in 1899, however, instead of a vitascope exhibition, visitors were given a frightening electrical show.[32] That evening, Lake View Park was the center of a terrifying cyclonic storm. The furious storm with winds over fifty miles per hour came up abruptly from the north. The winds were so powerful that they blew the rain clean through the pavilion, in which seventy-five visitors had sought shelter. Women were crying. and children screamed. The long heavy benches in the pavilion could be seen through the lightning's flashing bursts, blowing around as if they were made of paper.

Colonel Dyer also added a quadruple-string organ to his entertaining innovations at Lake View Park.[33] Dyer's new organ made music automatically and had a force of sound that was four times greater than that of the ordinary pipe organ. It was powered by a quarter-horsepowered electric motor. Augustans cherished Dyer's efforts to amuse them, and he didn't stop with introducing Augusta to new innovative amusements any time soon. Dyer had large plans for Augusta.

Lake View Zoo—Twelve Monkeys

Soon after Colonel Dyer acquired his interest in Lake View Park, he presented his personal menagerie of both common and exotic animals to Augustans. Sparing no practical expenditure, Dyer sought to ensure the park had a collection of animals that were both interesting and educational. The zoo had monkeys, birds, alligators, deer, squirrels, and many other animals. Always seeking to add to his menagerie, in 1898, Dyer procured jack rabbits and prairie dogs from Kansas to add to his animal collection.[34] Colonel Dyer even secured a ferocious wildcat that was captured in Washington County, Georgia.[35]

Within the next couple of years, he added a tiger, as well as a herd of deer, a handsome pair of swans, several turkey rabbits, and a porcupine farm.[36] The porcupine farm served a dual purpose. Not only did it provide patrons a chance to see porcupines, the porcupines provided a lesson in deterrence to children keen on touching the animals.

> These affectionate little creatures are to be kept there to teach bad little children that it is not good form to rub the animals' fur, and in the winter the quills will be plucked and sold for toothpicks and things.[37]

A groundhog and a few tame turkeys were also acquired. Peafowl, although beautiful, were ostracized, because they made too much noise and would disturb performances at the casino.

The community, especially the children, enjoyed the zoo. Stories tracking the lives of the animals were commonplace in the local newspaper. For instance, in December 1898, the newspaper reported that the children of Augusta would be sorry to find out the deer in Lake View Park had either strayed or been stolen and had not been seen in four days.[38] Also, in August 1901, a large commotion occurred at the park when Tug Vason, a baby deer, escaped from his pen. Mr. Davis, the keeper of the deer, and a group of boys ran after the deer.[39] For almost an hour, little Tug led them on a cheery dance through the park. Tug was ironically captured when he tried to get back into his pen from the same hole through which he escaped.

Tug was not the only animal to emancipate himself from the zoo. An alligator, albeit unnamed, caused quite a stir on the third level of the canal when residents noticed him basking in the sun near the bridge at the corner of Kollock and Walker Streets. When frightened, the alligator slipped into the water but would shortly reappear and ramble lazily along the canal banks.[40] It was believed the alligator had made its escape several years earlier from Lake View Park.

Not all of Dyer's animals were fondly remembered. The prairie dog, brought into the zoo from Kansas, unfortunately had become quite a nuisance within several years of its arrival. The prairie dog is really not a dog at all but a charismatic, social, rabbit-size rodent. Prairie dogs live in underground burrows with extensive tunnels and chambers with defined nurseries, sleeping quarters, and even toilets. The perilous holes of the prairie dog pose significant danger to animals such as horses and cows. Their holes descend into the ground at a very steep angle for approximately fourteen or fifteen feet, then turn abruptly in a horizontal direction some nine or ten feet. Prairie dogs often live in large groups of several hundred animals in communities called colonies or towns. These towns are typically less than half a square mile. Some towns, however, are enormous. The largest recorded prairie dog town was located in Texas and covered a distance of some twenty-five thousand square miles and was reportedly home to approximately four hundred million prairie dogs.[41]

Soon after they arrived at Lake View Park in 1898, the prairie dog population escalated dramatically. Although park management attempted to control the growing population through rifle fire; at best, it was a slow and dubious method of extermination. Therefore, a war of extermination was declared. George H. Conklin, manager of Lake View Park, enlisted the assistance of N. L. Willet, a well-known columnist for the *Augusta Chronicle*, druggist and proprietor of N. L. Willet Seed Company, to command the war of extermination.[42] The two used a process known as the bisulfide of carbon method. About a tablespoonful of bisulfide would be poured on absorbent cotton or rags then dropped into the burrow and quickly covered with dirt. The volatile bisulfide was heavier than air and would seep downward to fill the burrow, thus poisoning the prairie dog. Within a week after the volatile drug was placed in the dogholes and the entrances covered up, all but a couple of the animals had been killed. A heavier dose of sulfide of carbon was dropped into the remaining holes, and the prairie dogs were no more.[43]

More than any other animals residing at Lake View Park, the monkeys were the highlight of the zoo. Keeping monkeys in captivity was not an easy task in those days, but the animal keepers at Lake View were zealously adept at it. Patrons enjoyed feeding the monkeys peanuts and popcorn, and the monkeys reciprocated by providing laughter and stories that have lasted through the years.

Not everyone had pleasant experiences with the Lake View monkeys. One particular instance involved a successful escape by a particularly intelligent and somewhat humorous monkey named Jumbo. It seems that during their trips to Lake View Park, the motorman and conductor of the Lake View trolley line discovered that Jumbo didn't like the sound of its ringing bells. Regrettably, they took great enjoyment in teasing poor Jumbo with the repetitive sounding of their trolley bells. Jumbo, however, knew his day of revenge would come.

Jumbo's opportunity for revenge finally came on Saturday morning, October 12, 1901.[44] On this particular morning, Jumbo successfully emancipated himself from his cage and headed for the nearest road. As he reached the road, Jumbo encountered the trolley driven by the dreadful motorman and conductor who had tormented him so callously. Astonishingly, Jumbo recognized them.

As the trolley car made its stop at Lake View Park, the motorman sounded the unbearable bell like he had done so many times in the past. Jumbo seized the opportunity and jumped onto the trolley, making a mad dash for the motorman, sinking his piercing teeth into his heartless hand. After the motorman finally shook Jumbo off, Jumbo proceeded to carry out his plan of vengeance on the conductor. Fortunately for the conductor, he also succeeded in escaping from Jumbo's clutches and withdrew to the end of the car, while Jumbo remained at the other end. Jumbo, however, became weary and, having wreaked havoc on the trolley, decided to continue his adventure elsewhere and see what was happening at nearby Devoe's store. When Jumbo entered the store, the startled customers and clerks ran, leaving Jumbo in full command of the store.

This was not the first instance of Jumbo's dazzling memory. Apparently, sometime before his tirade with the trolley motorman and conductor, a young man struck Jumbo while pretending to be congenial to him. When the young man came back two weeks later and once again put his hand into Jumbo's cage, Jumbo recognized him and ripped the skin from his fingers. Perhaps this young man should have learned a lesson from the porcupines.

Jumbo was not the only monkey at Lake View Park to make history. Another amusing animal character at Dyer's zoo was Pete the monkey, a resident of the zoo in the early nineteen hundreds. Pete's human visitors had introduced Pete to some dreadful habits, such as smoking too many cigarettes and taking small nips from bottles poked through the wire netting of his cage. Pete evidently had become "addicted to the use of the weed and spirituous drink early in life, much to the disgust of local school teachers and lady members of the Zoo."[45] Pete's rebellious character grew in reputation so much that when he died, a monument was erected in his honor, undoubtedly by those who led to his demise.

Management, encouraged by Pete's legacy, was determined to enlarge the park's assortment of monkeys. In honor of Pete, a new monkey house with space for twelve "chattering" monkeys was erected at Lake View Park in 1912. On the other hand, management resolved to carefully consider naming the monkeys in hopes of avoiding the pitfalls of the inevitable correlation between names such as Jumbo and Pete and the rebellious characters of the past.

Fire was the name given to the first monkey born at the new monkey house. According to proud park officials, Lake View Park was the only park in the South that had achieved success in raising monkeys. Fire was born on Friday, March 24, 1916, only two days after Augusta's devastating fire of 1916, and befittingly named after it.

Figure 31. Devastation from the Fire of 1916

The Great Fire of 1916 was the worst fire in Augusta history burning across twenty-five blocks of downtown Augusta, from Eighth Street to East Boundary, and destroying more than 740 buildings.[46] The fire apparently started from an unattended tailor's iron and, when fueled by strong March winds, soon became a devastating inferno. Although no casualties were attributed to the fire, Augusta suffered $10 million in damages. Among the losses were twenty thousand bales of cotton estimated at $1.2 million, an estimated three thousand people left homeless, and six hundred homes and commercial buildings destroyed.[47]

Casino and Other Amusements

Lake View Park continued to prosper into the twentieth century. James U. Jackson, founder of North Augusta, South Carolina, purchased the Augusta Railway and Electric Company from Dyer in 1902 and soon began to consolidate his railways, electric power, and land development businesses. Jackson had already added trolley lines between Augusta and North Augusta and begun the construction of the Augusta-Aiken interurban electric railway, as well as the Hampton Terrace Hotel.

The new Lake View Park management aggressively sought to add amusements for the whole family. In addition to the zoo, there were a skating rink, bowling alley, and an alligator pond, as well as rental boats and canoes. Its grounds were beautifully maintained. Under the direction of Mr. Foshee, a gardener of remarkable ability, the park's beauty continued to mature beneath the whispering pines. In the spring, the white blossoms of dogwood trees filled the air. Wisteria, with its sprays of purple and white, is drooped from its vines in bewildering profusion. The fragrance from the blooms on the plum bushes filled one's senses, and the hillsides were covered with long green grass and dainty white and purple violets. Wild strawberries grew in abundance.[48]

Some of the first outdoor moving pictures were shown on a piece of cloth that hung between two large trees. Sitting on the grassy hillside, crowds laughed at pie-tossing comedies or sat silently while mustached villains chased attractive ladies across the screen.[49] There were movies, band concerts, boxing exhibitions, and of course, boat races.

Colonel Dyer, on the other hand, eventually answered the call of the west once again. In 1911, he sold his interest in the *Augusta Chronicle* and teamed up with his good friend, William F. "Buffalo Bill" Cody, to enter the mining business.[50] Colonel Dyer would pass away a year later after a lingering illness at his summer home in Kansas. Dyer's dramatic impact on Augusta and the development of Lake View Park would not be forgotten anytime soon.[51] His influence was so impressive that Lewis Sawyer composed and dedicated the musical piece known as the "Lake View March" to Colonel Dyer.[52]

In late 1906, the regional guru of entertainment, Col. Sanford H. Cohen, took over management of Lake View Park. Colonel Cohen was well-known in amusement and business enterprises in Augusta and the southeast.

> Col. S. H. Cohen is too well-known in Georgia and Carolina to attempt even a brief sketch of his career or personality. He is possibly one of the best known, if not the best known amusement directors in this section of the South, having been connected with some of the largest and most daring enterprises ever undertaken in that line. For 20 years Cohen has been before the public gaze as a caterer to the public taste.[53]

Cohen previously managed the Masonic Theatre and the Augusta Grand Opera House. He managed theater stars including James O'Neil, Fred Ward, Roland Reed, and Mile Rhea, among others.[54] As a promoter, Mr. Cohen was associated with the first great Augusta Exposition, as well as the Cotton

States exposition in Atlanta and the Great Appalachian exposition held in Knoxville, Tennessee. He served as a general passenger agent for the Charleston Consolidated Railroad and had a substantial role in the development of the Isle of Palms as a great seashore resort. Cohen also was the traffic manager for the Mount Mitchell Scenic Automobile Highway in North Carolina[55] and wrote a valuable book known as the *Compendium of Georgia*, a legal, commercial, and industrial directory. He also served as editor of the *Augusta Chronicle*. Cohen was truly a great "booster" and a firm believer in his city.

Upon becoming the sole manager of Lake View Park, Colonel Cohen immediately celebrated by hosting the Great Carnival, Pure Food and Merchants' Holiday Exposition. He contracted with the Robinson Carnival Company to provide the carnival midway featuring the colored aristocracy, the electrical theater, the Japanese theater, fighting the flames, a Wild West show, the Katsenjammers' castle, Samson, the Ferris wheel, and even camels. Within the next couple of months, Cohen added additional amusements at Lake View Park, such as an aerial tramway and a gigantic gondola.[56] He also purchased forty new boats for use by patrons.

Figure 32. The Casino at Lake View Park (drawing by Britani Gunther)

No doubt, the theater at Lake View Park blossomed under Cohen's management. Opening the 1907 season was the musical comedy *Cinderella*, followed by *Aladdin's Lamp*.[57] Soon, a magnificent new theater, referred to as the Casino, was built at Lake View Park. It was one of the largest summer theaters in the South and had a capacity of 1,400.[58] The Casino's first floor accommodated more people than any other auditorium in Augusta at that time. It featured raised seats in the rear, box seats in the front, and a 30' × 56' stage. The theater thrived under the management of Colonel Sanford H. Cohen and Fred Wayne, recognized as one of the best in the theater business.[59]

In 1908, Manager Cohen announced that he had made arrangements with the Jake Wells circuit of summer theaters.[60] Jake Wells (1863-1927) was known as the Father of Vaudeville in the Southeast.[61] Along with his brother Otto, the Wells brothers maintained the largest theater circuit in the South with forty-two theaters in nine states. Cohen also secured the Augusta Brewing Company as the Casino's concessions operator.

Some of the plays performed at the Casino included *Hiawatha*, *The Private Secretary*, the English comedy *David Garrick*, and *Escaped from the Toils*.[62] Frequent bands included Bearden's Band, the Augusta Silver Cornet Band, the Augusta Military Band, and the Clinch Rifles Band. It was not unusual for over three thousand people to be in attendance for a particular show or dance. Of course, by the end of the night, at least one or two couples would be enticed by the romantic allure of Lake Olmstead and opt to take a moonlight excursion on its serene waters.

A new bowling alley was constructed to compliment the skating rink and merry-go-round. When the Augusta Military Band performed in the summer of 1908, three thousand people passed through the gates of Lake View Park to enjoy the music.[63] Average park attendance that year was over fifteen thousand visitors in a week.[64] Lake View Park was a considerable operation employing over eighty people. During the second week in May 1908, the payroll account for the Lake View Park Casino management was $1,050. For the season of five months, payroll was estimated to be $25,000.

Lake View Park was prospering, and boats swarmed the lake. Lake Olmstead was home to about two hundred boats and eight launches in addition to the Lake View Park boats.[65]

> Every private canoe, every one of the park boats, every private launch and the amusement company's steamer *Anita*, made up a great fleet which swept in triumphant procession up and down the channel's full length and in and out every cove along both shores.[66]

The steam launch *Anita*, with capacity for thirty passengers, was cruising around the Lake and the white Mullins' nonsinkable rowboats were in constant use. The sight must have been simply amazing.

The Mullins rowboat was a metal boat, similar to a kayak. Utilizing air chambers built into each end of the boat, the Mullins rowboat was unsinkable. The design came to W. H. Mullins when his wooden boat sank while duck-hunting in North Dakota in the early 1890s.[67] Although skeptics laughed when Mullins began manufacturing metal boats in 1896, within six years, he was selling all the boats he could manufacture.

With the finances of the Railway, enhancements and new amusements continued to be added to Lake View Park. The buildings were freshly painted, new swings installed, and a full-time boathouse keeper hired for the next season.[68] A curve-dip roller coaster was also added. The roller coaster was compared to the dru chute, which had won fame across the nation as a funmaker.[69]

Park management often took advantage of traveling exhibitions, hosting numerous thrilling acts. For instance, in 1909, Captain L. D. Blondel, well-known for his water feats, put on a thrilling exhibition. Blondel, a professional swimmer, had received much notoriety when he negotiated thirty-one miles in Chesapeake Bay in nine hours and thirty-four minutes.[70] A few of his amazing feats included cooking a meal on a raft he constructed from driftwood that he picked up while swimming around, then having an after-dinner smoke and reading the newspaper while in the water. However, his main act was the detonation of a fully rigged ship that he would build on location several days prior to his show. The ship he built in Augusta was so comely and won so much favor from those who saw it that the Railway put it on exhibition in downtown Augusta. It was even illuminated at night.[71]

Battle of 1911

A major battle ensued over the control of Lake View Park in 1911. In June of 1911, the Augusta Land Company filed a suit against the Augusta Railway and Electric Company seeking possession of Lake View Park, as well as past due rent of $500 a year since the spring of 1902.[72] The petition asserted that Colonel Dyer, then president of the Railway, and the Augusta Railway Company failed to comply with the 1895 agreement between the parties when they removed their streetcar tracks on High Street and ceased to operate the route in accordance with the agreement. Thus, the petitioners argued that the agreement was rendered void, and the property reverted back to the Augusta Land Company.[73]

The case was heard by Judge Henry Cumming Hammond (1868-1961) of the Richmond County Superior Court. Judge Hammond came from a distinguished family. He was the son of Harry and Emily Cumming Hammond. His grandfather, James H. Hammond, was a former governor and senator in South Carolina. His mother was the daughter of Henry Harford Cumming (1799-1866), father of the Augusta Canal. He learned law while living with his uncle, Major Joseph B. Cumming.

Judge Hammond ruled in favor of the Railway, finding that the belt line was put down and operated according to the agreement until the rails were removed twelve years earlier. In sustaining the Railway's demurrer, Judge Hammond held that "the failure of the land company to bring action against the company at the time the tracks were being removed and the fact that the changing of the course of the road had benefitted the petitioners by enhancing other property held by them."[74] According to Judge Hammond, not only did the Augusta Land Company acquiesce by not filing suit for over twelve years after the tracks were removed, but it had, in fact, since benefited from the Railway's actions.

The litigation did not end with Judge Hammond's ruling. The Augusta Land Company appealed its case to the Georgia Supreme Court. The Supreme Court affirmed Judge Hammond's findings, ruling that when the Augusta Land Company executed the June 29, 1900, deed to the Augusta Railway and Electric Company, it did so without any condition or restriction.[75] Therefore, the conditions of the 1895 agreement were merged into the deed and were no longer applicable.

The legal dispute, however, did not hurt attendance at Lake View Park. After nearly seven hundred people attended the movies at the Casino on July 26, 1912, previous attendance records were shattered.[76] By midyear, more people had already visited the park than the entire previous year.

McLendon and May

To ensure that Lake View Park would continue as a first-class summer resort, the Railway brought in new management in 1915. During the previous couple of years, the park evidently had obtained the reputation of being a questionable environment for unaccompanied ladies and children. The Lake View Amusement Company, owned and operated by W. E. McLendon and John C. May, became the lessees of Lake View Park.[77] McLendon and May were well-known, successful businessmen in Augusta. McLendon was renowned for his brilliant competence and popularity as manager of the Modjeska Theatre in downtown Augusta. May was a manager for the Chero-Cola Bottling Company.

McLendon and May immediately began work to convert Lake View Park into a family-friendly, swanky, high-class suburban park.

> Messrs. McLendon and May enter the venture with the firm determination above all others of operating the resort on a high plane and to make of it a place where individuals, families and their friends may mingle without the least fear of coming in contact with anything or any person the least objectionable.[78]

New management sought to ensure that families, including ladies and children, felt absolutely confident within the park's enjoyable atmosphere while receiving courteous treatment.

Figure 33. Historic Lake Olmstead (*Credit: Dayton Sherrouse Collection*)

Another one of their initial courses of action was to petition city council for permission to build a dam and spillway at the foot of the lake.[79] As the lake was not initially dammed, the intrusion of muddy water from the canal was a reoccurring problem and consequently viewed as the continuing culprit that for years had spoiled one of the region's prettiest parks. Destruction of boathouses at Lake Olmstead in 1914 had again drawn protest to prevent the flow of water from the canal into the lake.[80] The projected solution was to erect a dam at the foot of Lake Olmstead. The lake could conceivably be dammed a couple of feet below normal water level of the lake, allowing small boats to enter the canal while keeping out a good deal of the water out. Another proposal was to have the bank of the lake continued and gates installed between the two water bodies separating the canal from the lake. McLendon and May were optimistic about the dam transforming the lake from what some depicted as a large puddle of yellow muddy water into an ideal crystal-clear swimming lake.

In May of 1915, May and McClendon submitted their petition to the city council for permission to build the dam,[81] agreeing to pay the entire expense. Auspiciously, the project was endorsed by Dr. Eugene E. Murphey, president of the Richmond County Board of Health. "I can see no objection to your putting in the bathing pond you have in mind. The board will do whatever lies within its power to help you along in the work."[82] Dr. Murphey's endorsement carried significant weight. In addition to serving as president of the Richmond County Board of Health from 1908 to 1933, and the Medical Association of Georgia from 1917 to 1918, Dr. Murphey was a well-known physician and humanist, as well as a member of one of the first families of Georgia.[83] His family also owned one of the oldest remaining public buildings in Augusta, the Old Richmond County Courthouse (Old Government House), which was built around 1801.[84]

An unexpected hurdle, however, was the potential impact to the vested interest of the adjacent Lakeside Club. Although he had no objection to gates being installed at the intersection of Lake Olmstead and the canal, E. Fred Gehrken Jr., president of the Lakeside Club, opposed the dam because it would potentially elevate the water in the lake by six inches, causing Rae's Creek to back up onto the club's property. The Lake View Park interest retorted back.

> That muddy water from the canal has for years spoiled one of the prettiest parks, and what might have been one of the prettiest lakes in the country . . . . Don't let the Lakeside Club boys get in the way. I'm thinking more about the thousands of people who will use Lake View Park this summer, than I am about the hundred or so boys who may use that club.[85]

There was palpable social tension between the Lake View Park crowd and the exclusive Lakeside Club. Irrespective of opposition from the Lakeside Club, the city council adopted the recommendation of the canal committee and allowed McLendon to construct his dam and gates across the northern neck of Lake Olmstead.[86] The dam was not immediately constructed, but that did not deter the attractiveness of Lake View Park.

It was soon announced that swimming facilities, including a one-hundred-apartment bathhouse, would be in full operation and ready for patrons by June 1, 1915. The Lake View Natatorium, as it was appropriately named, formally opened on Sunday, June 20. The facilities included dressing rooms, showers and a 250-foot stretch of beach on lake's shores.[87] A sandy bottom was also installed in the swimming area.[88] For twenty-five cents, patrons could rent bathing suits and use the dressing rooms.[89] If patrons provided their own bathing suit, they could have use of the facilities for just fifteen cents. Management touted Lake View Park as better than ever.

IT'S THE BEST EVER!
OF COURSE, YOU KNOW WE ARE TALKING ABOUT
LAKE VIEW
Where the cooling breezes blow and good cheer abounds.[90]

Management couldn't resist the temptation to take a shot at its nearby competition, the highly frequented Tybee Island beach. "Let Tybee beware. We have built our own beach out at Lake View Park."[91]

Lake View Park hosted some spectacular events under the management team of McLendon and May. A spectacular exhibition of the European War during the beginning of World War I (1914-1918) was staged at Lake View Park on June 22, 1916. The live pyrotechnical production was directed by renowned fireworks expert and producer of the famous "Destruction of Herculaneum," A. Rousseau of New York's Rousseau Fireworks Company.[92] Intended to demonstrate the terrifying reality of war and merciless destruction of human life, Rousseau's production followed a time line of the war featuring European battle scenes, storming of forts, blowing up of ammunition, destruction of cities, zeppelins and airships fighting in the air, as well as battleship warfare. The explosion in the air of one huge shell over one hundred different times was the novel feature of the exhibition.

A couple of years later, Captain L. D. Blondel made a return visit to Augusta. The main event this year was the destruction of a model of the schooner *William P. Frye*. Blondel demonstrated how the ship, carrying a cargo of wheat, had been sunk on the high seas by the German cruiser *Prinz Eitel Friedrich*.[93] The loss of the ship was valued in 1915 at $228,059.54. The *Frye*, accompanied by soldiers and burglars, was exhibited on Broad Street during the day prior to the exhibition.[94] Captain Blondel also gave swimming exhibitions as part of his performance.

The Lakeside Club

Organized on May 31, 1890, the Lakeside Club was the second social club to take up residence at Lake Olmstead.[95] The club's aspiration was to become a leading social organization and a popular spring and summer afternoon club, with evening dances and card parties. Although the club was not to be a boating club, it inevitably gave impetus to boating, which would be its major draw. Membership was limited to one hundred gentlemen and social lines were strictly drawn. Although wives, sisters, and sweethearts could have an interest and role in the club, they could not enjoy the benefits of membership.

Founding Members

Many prominent Augustans were among its seventy-five charter members. Its initial officers were Thomas W. Alexander, Bryan Cumming, and William H. Barrett Jr., a virtual slate of "who's who" in Augusta at that time. Thomas W. Alexander was elected president. Alexander headed one of the largest cotton factors firms in Georgia, Alexander & Alexander, and served on the Board of Police Commissioners.[96] Bryan Cumming was elected vice president. Cumming, a descendant of Augusta's first mayor, came from a very influential Augusta family and was a local railroad attorney. William H. Barrett Jr. (1866-1941) was elected secretary and treasurer. Barrett was the city attorney from 1898 to 1904 and would subsequently be appointed by President William G. Harding to serve as a federal judge for the United States District Court for the Southern District of Georgia.

Its governing committee was comprised of L. L. Fleming, L. A. Berckmans, H. C. Lamar, W. J. Craig, E. C. Goodrich, and F. M. Butt.[97] Each of these men was a well-known community leader in Augusta.

Lafayette Lamar Fleming (1861-1934) was a prominent cotton merchant in Augusta, until he later moved to New York City, then Texas. He served as vice chairman for President Dwight Eisenhower's Commission on Foreign Economic Policy and an adviser to the Ninth General Agreement on Tariffs and Trade conference held in Geneva. Interestingly, later in life, he was bestowed the Italian Solidarity Star, the highest honor Italy can bestow upon a citizen of another country, due to his ongoing interest and work in Italy.[98]

Louis A. Berckmans was the son of infamous horticulturalist, Prosper J. A. Berckmans, who was also a founding member. Berckmans was well-known for his Fruitland Nurseries as well as numerous other projects, including the landscaping for Radio City in New York. He would subsequently be intimately involved with landscape architectural work at the Augusta National.

William J. Craig was the general freight agent and general passenger agent for the Port Royal and Western Carolina Railway, formerly the Augusta and Knoxville Railway, as well as the Atlantic Coast Line. While serving with the Atlantic Coast Line, Craig was responsible for publication of seventy-five thousand promotional brochures containing pictures of Augusta's tourist hotels, the Country Club and other local scenes, as well as an eloquent description of Augusta's superiority as a progressive city and winter resort.[99]

Dr. Edward C. Goodrich, an Augusta native, was a prominent physician in Georgia. He served as secretary of the Board of Health.[100] His wife, Lillie, was the sister of Edward and Henry Platt, who had won the honor of launching the first boat in Lake Olmstead. She also served as the organist and choir director of St. John's Church.

Frank M. Butt was a well-respected insurance agent, recognized as "the best-posted underwriter on the handling of cotton and marine covers in the Southern field."[101] He served as the special agent for the Phoenix Insurance of London, operated a general fire and marine insurance business, and was manager of the Cotton Insurance Association in Augusta. He subsequently moved to Atlanta where he was selected to act as manager of the Cotton Insurance Association, an association made up of fifty of the leading fire insurance companies.[102]

The last member of the governing committee was Henry C. Lamar. Lamar had acquired national fame while at Princeton University, not only in class but on the football field as well. He will always be fondly remembered by Princeton for his infamous "Lamar's run." Lamar's run occurred in the fall of 1885 at the annual Yale-Princeton football game when he ran over half of the Yale field and scored the first touchdown ever scored during a championship game behind a Yale goal post since the present system of scoring was introduced, leading Princeton to a 6-5 victory.[103] After his graduation from Princeton in 1886, Lamar had been involved in international trade. On one of his trips in 1890, Lamar visited Nicaragua for six weeks exploring commercial trade possibilities. In those days Lamar chose as the most direct and expeditious return route from Central America to voyage by boat around South America to New York and then by railway from New York to Augusta.[104]

Tragedy struck Augusta when Lamar died the following year on the canal next to Lake Olmstead. He and his lady friend, Ms. Louise King Connelly, drowned on the canal at the Warwick Mill gates on March 11, 1891.[105] Henry's classmates at Princeton University (Class of 1886) thought so much of him that they passed a resolution of respect in his honor. The following is an excerpt from the esteemed resolution:

> No formal expression can do justice to the many lovable qualities which Lamar possessed, but all who knew him fell under the inexpressible charm of them. His life was manliness itself; manliness and courtesy, kindliness and gentleness, touched with the warm sympathy of a generous Southern nature.
>
> His life was gentle; and the elements
> So mixed in him, that Nature might stand up,
> And say to all the world, this was a man.[106]

Ms. Connelly, the granddaughter of the late John P. King, former US senator from Georgia, was one of the most popular young ladies in Augusta. Just five days earlier, Ms. Connelly had been elected as a vice president of the Widow's Home to represent St. Paul's Church.[107]

Regattas and Water Carnivals

Pursuant to its organizational plan, the Lakeside Club erected a $2,500 clubhouse on the shore of Lake Olmstead. The clubhouse, erected on pillars over the water with space underneath for the club's fleet of boats, was positioned to be the focal point of driving, riding, and boating parties.[108] It was open annually from April through October.

The club also purchased naphtha and electric launches and rowboats for its members to use on Lake Olmstead. Designed by F. W. Ofeldt in 1885 and manufactured by the Gas Engine and Power Co. of New York, the naphtha launch, typically 20'-24' in length, became popular in the late eighteen hundreds as an affordable alternative to the steamboat.[109] Due to problems with boiler explosions in steamships, it was unlawful for anyone other than a qualified marine engineer to operate a steamboat. The naphtha engine was an external combustion engine powered by naphtha, a low-grade form of gasoline.

Within years, the Lakeside Club began featuring amazing regattas and water carnivals. The annual spring regatta was an exceptional festival of the Lakeside Club and an event eagerly anticipated by Augustans. The clubhouse would be gaily decorated with electric-colored lights and Japanese lanterns. The boats, occupied by members and their lady friends, were also elaborately decorated with Japanese lanterns and garland in imaginative designs. Both the beautifully decorated electric launches and charming rowboats would sashay by in the clear waters of the lake, led by a launch of musicians.[110] It was "indeed a triumph of art and evokes frequent applause from the appreciative spectators."[111] The scene was reminiscent to the traveler of a Mediterranean bazaar.

The Lakeside Club regattas were so spectacular that the public would often turn out in droves to witness the stunning events. For example, the 1898 annual regatta held on May 23, 1898, attracted several thousand nonmembers to Lake View Park to view the spectacle. There was no moon that night, making the sky idyllic for the water pageant. Thousands of glimmering Japanese lanterns, fairy lights, and hundreds of brilliant arc and incandescent lights from the boats and clubhouse lit up the night sky with amazing colors and beauty.

Laughing and singing, members sped over the rippling waters in their boats and canoes. "There were some thirty dainty canoes and rowboats, bearing as freight the loveliest women in the world."[112] The fleet of boats gathered together, each boat securing its tow line to the boat in front of it, all in tow of *Nan*, the steam launch. Amid the firing of Roman candles, at the sound of a whistle, the procession started. As the procession began, numerous boats fired hundreds of Roman candles in rapid succession. Red and blue lights flashed forth from the candles, and when done, only the reflection of the light upon the smoke of the fireworks could be seen. "No more brilliant scene has ever been witnessed in this section of the country and it is doubtful if anywhere it could have been surpassed."[113]

Membership in the Lakeside Club was exceedingly desired and increased so rapidly that within ten years, the club built a larger clubhouse. The membership list included many prominent Augustans.[114] In 1899, the club acquired 120 feet of land along the waterfront from Colonel Dyer to enhance its improvements, planning to build a dance pavilion and enlarge its current building.[115] Within a year, bids were received, and the clubhouse was expanded.

The newly enlarged clubhouse was a beautifully constructed two-story building fronting on the Lake. The clubhouse was 317 feet long and had two wings. The first floor was used for club purposes, while the second floor was a private open-air dancing pavilion limited respectively to club members and friends. It had long verandas running the length of the building, a cozy sitting room, dressing rooms, and a "splendidly appointed" boathouse including accommodations for a hundred boats and launches.[116]

Every year, it seemed the regattas became larger and more impressive. The 1901 regatta was reported to be one of the greatest social successes ever attained by a social club in Augusta.[117] Perhaps that was due in part to the throngs of visiting beauties and the "fairest young ladies" in Augusta crowding the club's striking new reception parlor. The regatta began at the firing of the starting gun. The lead launch commenced with a sequence of boats from the lower end of the clubhouse around to the far bank of the lake half a mile then turning back on the opposite side. The water spectacle was one of the most beautiful ever witnessed.

The annual opening of the Lakeside Boat Club of 1902 was yet another extravagant event in Lake Olmstead's history. Description of the affair cannot be replicated any better than the *Chronicle's* accounting.

> The long promenades were—outlined in myriads of red, white and blue electric lights, while the spacious dancing pavilion was draped in smilax and further adorned by Japanese lanterns. The height of beauty was attained in the lawn decorations. As one gazed from the promenade down on the velvety lawn, darkness seemed converted into glorious day by a couple of thousands of exquisitely tinted Japanese lanterns arranged a few feet above the ground in the intricate meshes of a perfectly formed spiderweb. Walks, trees and reception hall were literally ablaze with lanterns, the rays of which were reflected again and again in the placid waters of picturesque Lake Olmstead.[118]

Members vied for an opportunity to win the cherished silver trophy cups awarded to the most fabulously decorated rowboat or canoe. The boat adorned with the most unique decorations, and sporting the most unusually festooned launch, would take home that title. Capping off the regatta, fireworks were detonated from floats stationed in the lake garlanded with colorful balloons. Beautiful arrays of colors and smoke filled the night sky.

Merger with the Augusta Tennis Club

Within the next several years, however, membership waned, and therefore, facilities began to decline. The Augusta Tennis Club began exploring the prospect of buying the rights and property of the club. In May, the Lakeside Boat Club and the Augusta Tennis Club entered into an agreement whereby the members of the Tennis Club became members of the Lakeside Club.[119] The two clubs were merged, and within two months, the membership of the reorganized club had reached its limit of 150 members.[120] Work began immediately on renovating the clubhouse and constructing two tennis courts on the edge of Lake Olmstead. The new club formally reopened with a dance on August 5, 1908.[121]

Lake Side Club, Augusta, Ga.

Figure 34. The Lakeside Boat Club

To the delight of many, the rejuvenated club soon planned to reinstate its annual regatta. The 1909 regatta, held on Friday night, August 11, was described as the largest and most beautiful regatta ever held on Lake Olmstead. A myriad of electric lights shone like diamonds against the background of the soft summer night darkness, as hundreds of Japanese lanterns hung in garlands around the pavilions and down the club plazas. The ladies wore light lingerie gowns, and the men were predominantly in flannels or white linen suits. "Surely the bosom of no lake has ever been more gorgeously adorned than Lake Olmstead, when the sparkling jewellike craft was spread out upon its smooth, dark waters. And overhead the moon seemed trying to outdo the brilliancy of mortals with a bewildering radiance."[122]

The opening regatta of 1911 was also a spectacle. With over five hundred young people present, the regatta featured a grand boat parade with members vying for numerous prizes. The team of John McAuliffe, Will Lester, and Frank Bussey won the prize for best boat. Their boat, the most expensively decorated boat at the regatta, was made to represent a Chinese dragon. Apparently, Mr. Lester's sister, Ms. Emma Lester, a missionary, sent the pattern for the boat from Suchow, China. The dragon's "large shining eyes were illuminated with small lights, and the whole wide open mouth carried with it all of the hideousness of the dragon."[123] As the boat's two side wheels propelled it across the water, smoke poured out from a smoke stack in the boat. Receiving most unique rowboat was Dr. Roper, whose boat represented a lighthouse. Second best launch was won by L. C. Levy, his boat representing a Japanese tea garden.

Beginning in 1909, after the merger with the Augusta Tennis Club, the annual city tennis tournament took up residence at the Lakeside Club. Tournament matches were played on the club's two courts.[124] Women were also accorded membership in 1909. The initiation fee was five dollars, which included the first year's dues. The popularity of tennis increased dramatically, leading the club in 1911 to announce the addition of another tennis court.

Aquatic Carnivals

Swimming had yet to be officially embraced at Lake Olmstead. In fact, section 339 of the city code forbade bathing in any part of the canal or sluice thereof due to the city obtaining its drinking water below Lake Olmstead. That would soon change. Swimming was first officially embraced at Lake Olmstead in 1909, thanks mostly to the work of R. Roy Goodwin, president of the Lakeside Boat Club.

Roy, a Wofford College graduate, realtor, and city councilman, was a prominent and well-thought-of Augustan. In April 1909, Roy, on behalf of the Lakeside Boat Club, brought a petition asking that the city council allow the members of the club and their friends the privilege of bathing within a radius of one hundred yards in front of the boathouse.[125] The petition was granted and section 339 of the city code repealed.

Roy would later die in the prime of his life from a lightning strike. While playing golf at the Augusta Country Club on the afternoon of June 8, 1919, a violent storm arose. Roy and his fellow golf party sought shelter in a small wooden toolshed near the tenth hole. Unbeknownst to them, the toolshed proved to be inadequate shelter against the intensity of the storm. Lightning struck the shed, killing Roy and two other people, as well as injuring twelve others.[126]

In 1912, the Lakeside Boat Club and the Young Men's Christian Association (YMCA) collaborated in sponsoring the first annual aquatic meet at Lake Olmstead. The event was a huge success, attended by over two thousand people. The meet held in late August featured boys and men vying in swimming, diving, canoe, and novelty races. Amusingly, one of the grammar school boys lost his bathing suit during his event and had to linger in the water until his "roundabouts" were located. Although that might seem like bad luck, he ironically won his event.[127] The most anticipated moment of this event was a relay race between the Augusta firemen and policemen. The race was excitingly close, but the firemen earned the honor of taking home the silver trophy cup. Mr. George Newberry won the one-mile race, which he swam in thirty-five minutes and thirteen seconds.

Although a judicial race was not on the program, toward the end of the swim meet, Judge Henry C. Hammond, wearing all his clothes, sprang from the diving platform to perform a backward somersault into the water. He was followed by Judge Jos. Ganahl, who also jumped into the water fully clothed. The two then swam the allotted course with Judge Hammond eventually winning the impromptu race. It appears that the two judges had engaged each other in a "daring" contest and neither gentleman wanted to be called a feather-log.[128] Perhaps Judge Ganahl did not know about a previous wager accepted by Judge Hammond eighteen years earlier. In 1894, a local gentleman had offered $50 to anyone who could swim across the Savannah River five times without resting. Judge Hammond, a twenty-five-year-old lawyer at the time, accepted the wager. With a swarm of onlookers crowding the banks of the river, he completed the swim in little over an hour.[129]

Judge Hammond was eccentric and never married, devoting his retirement years to growing camellia plants. He set aside fifteen acres on the Hill to grow over 275 varieties of camellias. One of the highlights of his life was his visit to Italy where he studied the camellias in the Vatican gardens and had several audiences with the pope.[130] Every March when his camellias were in full bloom, he would place an announcement in the newspaper inviting the public to visit his gardens. In 1943, his ad was a little different, taking into account that we were engaged in World War II.

> All my Friends and Enemies, German, Japs and Italians excepted, are cordially invited to my place today and next day, rain or shine, but not freeze, to see more Camellias than you thought was in the world. A nickel bus fare and a leg-stretching mile—I'll give you back your nickel when you come. Everyone can walk back by Oliver General Hospital and carry a wounded soldier a flower.[131]

Judge Hammond's wit was also legendary. He even threw a birthday party for comedian Charlie Chaplin at the Augusta Country Club for Chaplin's twenty-ninth birthday.[132] No doubt, Judge Hammond was a colorful character in Augusta history.

In the second year of the aquatic event, a twenty-five-yard swim contest and fancy diving contest were added for the girls and young ladies. As in the previous year, races ranged from fifty yards to a mile, as well as diving and canoe races. The highly anticipated event drew a huge crowd of over two thousand spectators.[133] In addition to the normal races, contestants competed in a novelty race and canoe tilting. The highlight of the event was to be the relay race between the firemen and police, but the police did not show up for the contest. Instead, the novelty race highlighted the events. Contestants had to swim to a canoe fifty yards from the landing, put on a full suit of clothes, and return to the landing swimming fully clothed.

Due to scheduling conflicts, the fourth annual meet was canceled and later held at Lanke's Pond, located below the Bon Air Hotel. The event returned to the Lakeside Club the following year. Held on August 10, 1915, the afternoon events of aquatic sports were open to the public and included many different water sports such as swimming, diving, sailing, rowing, and novelty canoe races. Sponsors advertised the aquatic meet to include every sporting event that could be performed on a body of water like Lake Olmstead.[134] The highlight, however, was little Martha Jenkins, who at seven years of age astonished the crowd with her swimming and diving performances. Martha apparently was the daughter of Charles Jenkins, the manager of Lanke's Pond.[135]

Devastation and Rebuilding

Catastrophe struck the Lakeside Boat Club on the night of December 5, 1912, when its clubhouse was completely destroyed by a raging fire. Originating in the ladies' dressing room, the fire began from faulty wiring and quickly engulfed the clubhouse. Ten motorboats moored at the clubhouse were included in the devastation: the *Wahwahnoah*, owned by Howard Carpenter; *Humming Bird*, owned by Dr. Cleckley; *Poo Poo*, owned by Joe Herman; *Snipe*, owned by Pete Stafford; *Mudcat*, owned by Frank Bussey; *Wildcat*, owned by John McAulifie; *Shingler*, owned by I. C. Levy; *Maybel*, owned by Warren Moran; and *Lithia*, owned by Coles Phinizy.[136] There were also eighty-seven canoes within the ruin, only ten of which were able to be pushed safely out into the lake. The loss was estimated at $12,000, almost four times the insurance coverage held by the club.

The fire, however, would not deter the Lakeside Club for very long. Although the club soon experienced a brief decline in membership, it converted one of its undamaged buildings into a temporary clubhouse and continued expanding membership.[137] It also rebuilt the three tennis courts that had been damaged by recent flooding. The Lakeside Club was gaining strength, and once again in 1913, the annual city tennis tournament was played at the Lakeside Club.

A new clubhouse was imminent. In early April of 1914, the Lakeside Club entered a contract with the firm of Mobley & Crooks for construction of its new clubhouse.[138] The new $3,200 clubhouse was formally opened during a gala event several months later on June 16, 1914, with an estimated 450 members and guests in attendance.[139] The clubhouse, located twenty feet from the water, was a handsome two-story structure. The first floor was designed for boat storage with a capacity for more than two hundred boats. Boats were moved to the water through use of a little trolley car running on a small track. On the second floor, a 40' × 60' dance hall was erected with what was considered the finest dance floor in Augusta at the time. Directly outside of the dance hall was a ten-foot balcony overhanging the front entrance to the clubhouse. The brick foundation extended up to the second floor. From there up to the roof was white lattice, allowing the breezes from the lake to fan the dancers. The roof was bungalow style and painted dark green. The locker room and showers remained in the chalet located at the gate of the clubhouse grounds. Within a year, the club also added glass windows around the dance hall to accommodate cool weather dances during the winter months.[140]

By 1915, the club already had more than one hundred members.[141] President Fred G. Gehrken Jr. (1885-1941) took a great interest in the club, and under his leadership, it took on new life. Gehrken was a well-known realtor in Augusta. His German roots were deep. His father had served as president of Augusta's Deutscher Scheutzen Club for four consecutive terms.[142] Young twenty-three-year-old Henry Burnside headed Gehrken's entertainment committee.

After several years of absence due to destruction of their clubhouse, the members of the Lakeside Club revived their annual regatta on the night of August 13, 1915.[143] Expanded from previous years, the event was a multiple-day affair. As a precursor to the regatta, the club held a water carnival and aquatic meet with a special invitation issued for lady swimmers. The regatta itself featured a parade of fifty or more merrily decorated and lighted canoes, followed by a colossal regatta dance.

Terpsichore or dancing was a beloved pastime of the Lakeside Club members. Terpsichore in the pavilion perpetually concluded the grand regattas. The "sailors and their lassies" would come ashore and dance until after midnight. Music would be provided by numerous orchestras, such as Bearden's Orchestra and Balk's Orchestra.

Even if one was not a skipper or commodore, the parties were elaborate events that provided entertainment for all. "Those who do not care for dancing in warm weather may enjoy boating on beautiful Lake Olmstead and listening to the music, the strains of which sound sweeter floating over water than any other place. But the breezes will keep the dancing room cool enough for those who enjoy dancing."[144]

Well preserved are descriptions of the grand parties of 1915. The clubhouse was illuminated with hundreds of gleaming electric lights, "their brilliant illumination reflected in the depths of the water like so many submerged diamonds."[145] Within the pavilion was the perfume of spring, from the hundreds of honeysuckle vines, which completely covered the ceiling overhead and formed almost a canopy of bloom and beauty. The midsummer dance was highlighted by a number of charming visiting girls. The dance continued well into the night, finally coming to an end at 1:30 a.m. with the playing of "Home, Sweet Home."

In 1919, Lakeside was the first club in Augusta to take up arms against the latest dance craze, the shimmy. All over the country, there had been a growing wave of protest against the shimmy. By many, the shimmy was seen as a vulgar and horrible mutilation of the fine art of terpsichore. Numerous cities adopted special ordinances prohibiting the shimmy and imposing fines for violations. In Georgia, a reformation movement started in Macon to abolish the shimmy, cheek, and tickle-toe dances. Frank Hodges, manager of the Lakeside Club, posted an edict against such dances on the wall of the dance pavilion. During the first evening the notice was posted, four couples were ruled off the floor.

Property Sold

The Lakeside Club profited from remarkable success and was a celebrated entertainment venue to its members. It promoted the growth of athletic and outdoor sports in Augusta and was the scene of many gala regattas and dances as well as the site of more than a little romance. As World War I came to an end, so went the Lakeside Boat Club. Hard times took its toll on the club by 1918. On August 6, 1918, the Lakeside Club property was sold at sheriff's sale to satisfy a $1,500 mortgage on the property held by Mrs. Anna Wolfe.[146] Sam Baron, a local realtor and hotel investor, purchased the property at auction for $550. Baron was also well-known as the owner of Baron's Variety Farm, located between Martinez and Evans on the Washington Road. Baron's Elberta peaches won national fame for their uniform size and fine flavor.[147]

Although 1918 was the official end to the Lakeside Club, its clubhouse was still used for some time. Several young men leased the clubhouse for a period of time sponsoring dances for soldiers and civilians on Monday, Wednesday, and Saturday nights.[148] The dances were held under the supervision of Mrs. Bass. The club was also used on Sundays as a resting spot for the soldiers where they could read and relax. In 1921, several well-known young men organized a dancing club at the Lakeside Clubhouse.[149] The new dancing club would only last a short time. Soon thereafter, Sam Baron sold the property to the city.[150] The Lakeside Club was now but an artifact of history.

VIII

Holiday Celebrations and
an Augusta Legend

Augusta has a storied history of fantastic summer holiday celebrations, especially Fourth of July festivities. For years, Augusta has celebrated Independence Day with events such as fireworks and large barbecues at Lake Olmstead. The overwhelming war sentiment that pervaded the country during the Spanish-American War of 1898 resulted in a patriotic demand for a general observance of the Fourth of July all over the South. In Augusta it was only the third annual observance locally, as Augusta had just reestablished the patriotic custom in 1896.[1] Irrespective, it was an enormous party. Augusta celebrated with fireworks by day on Broad Street and fireworks by night at Lake View Park.[2]

From the gaily dressed "Fantastics" to colossal barbecues, Augusta celebrated with style. Holiday celebrations included such events as boat races, sack races, aquatic events, and fireworks. Lake Olmstead was the central site for many of the area's holiday celebrations. Horse racing and motorcycle racing at the adjacent fairgrounds were planned to spill over between events at Lake Olmstead.

The Labor Day program of 1899 was spectacular. Festivities began with a parade downtown, followed by a program of activities and speeches at newly erected stands at Lake View Park.[3] Activities included a root race, tug-of-war, wheelbarrow race, three-legged race, a greasy pole climb, barrel race, sack race, standing long jump, running long jump, and shot put, as well as a walking contest for the ladies. There was also a ten-round boxing match. To the most attractively dressed lady union member, a pair of fine ladies' union-made shoes donated by Great Eastern Shoe Company was awarded.

By 1911, Augusta had declared Independence Day a legal holiday, with all public offices and virtually all businesses closing for the day. The mayor's office was besieged with requests for barbecue permits within the city limits. Fireworks at Lake View Park capped the long day of events, with eight beautiful sparkling designs, beginning with the "Fourth of July," and ending up with the "William Howard Taft."[4]

A Barbecue King Is Born

Perhaps, the most anticipated facet of Augusta's celebrations was good ole Southern pig roasting. Some of the largest barbecues in Augusta and Central Savannah River Area were held on the shores of Lake Olmstead in the early nineteen hundreds. Augusta may not have been the birthplace of barbecue, but it is the birthplace of the Barbecue King, Clement Lamar Castleberry. Although Clem was recognized as an outstanding public servant, serving on both city council and the county commission, his claim to fame was his notorious barbecues. Clem was known as the greatest of hog and sheep roasters, bar none.

For many years, Clem operated a wholesale and retail merchant grocery business, but his hobby of preparing down-home Georgia barbecue quickly grew into legendary prominence. Clem was the master of copiously large barbeques, making Augusta famous for barbecue. Clem's barbecues were prepared for thousands and fostered community spirit and appreciation from numerous dignitaries, including presidents Roosevelt and Taft.

One of his famous city 'cues occurred in September 1919, when he served over six hundred ex-service men who had recently returned from duty in World War I.[5] The barbecue, sponsored by the American Legion, was held at Lake View Park on the shores of Lake Olmstead. The mouthwatering menu included not only pork barbecue but veal, hash, tomatoes, rice, corn, peas, and lemon tea. The service was excellent as well. It was said that you could travel the world over and not find a hundred women as pretty, as capable, or as good-natured as those who served the returned ex-servicemen at the American Legion barbecue.

Less than a year later, on July 9, 1920, Clem, along with hundreds of helpers, prepared barbecue for over eight thousand people at a community 'cue staged by the Augusta Board of Commerce at the fairgrounds adjacent to Lake Olmstead. In addition to the fifty hogs and lambs roasted, a ton of potatoes were prepared, as well as 3,300 pounds of hash, 1,400 pounds of tomatoes, nearly ten thousand ears of corn, five hundred cans of peas, and sixteen thousand rolls. Tables for the 'cue were constructed, stretching three quarters of a mile. The service staff included five hundred waiters, 125 Boy Scouts, and seventy-five cooks. The description of the preparations imparts an intimate picture of Augusta's rich barbecue tradition.

> Just to see such a sight at night to smell the tantalizing hunger-inspiring odor that permeates the whole atmosphere, one unconsciously sniffs and then feels pangs of hunger.[6]

Clem Castleberry was quoted after the 'cue to say,

> I never saw so many people in my life before. We had prepared for over
> 6,000 but I thought there were about 15,000 people in that line. If the
> Kaiser ever saw them he would never have started the war.[7]

The event was so large that it took the fifteen dishwashers a week to clean up.

The Barbecue King's fame continued to grow. In the early '20s, Clem prepared barbecue on behalf of the Augusta Rotary Club for the Detroit Tigers baseball team. The 'cue was so good that a sports writer from Detroit informed Charles Phelps, advertising agent for the Dodge Brothers, that Augusta had the finest barbecue cook in the world. Thus, Clem was invited to prepare a 'cue for the Dodge Motor Company in Detroit. He was told to name his price. Clem accepted, and he, along with Charlie "Streets" Gover, his old reliable cook and the best "cue artist in Georgia," went to Detroit.[8] Clem was treated to a car and chauffeur and given quarters in the Detroit Athletic Club. Not to outdo the barbecue, the setting for the eighth annual district managers' dinner was extraordinary. The dinner was served in specially constructed log cabin built entirely for the purpose of serving that one-barbecue dinner. The cabin was furnished with handmade rustic chairs and tables, and cowboys were even brought in from Texas to ensure the event had a Western flair to it.

In May 1923, Clem served another mammoth barbecue event at the fairgrounds for over seven thousand employees and their families from the Augusta Factory, Enterprise Mill, and Sibley Mill. One hundred and fifteen pigs and lambs were barbecued, as well as four hundred pounds of rice and 3,500 pounds of hash cooked. Six hundred pounds of sugar were required just to sweeten the lemonade.[9] Although reportedly preparing barbecue for crowds as large as twelve thousand, one of Clem's largest barbecues occurred in 1924 for the Sand Bar Ferry Bridge Opening Celebration. A pit 130 feet long and covered by a shed was constructed to cook the 135 to 150 hogs.[10] Over one thousand benches were set up to accommodate eight thousand people.

Clem also prepared an annual 'cue for the Kiwanis Club of Augusta at Carmichael's Fishing Club. The guests of honor in 1926 were the Detroit and Augusta baseball teams. The managers of the Detroit team were none other than Ty Cobb and "Gabby" Street. Cobb was recognized by the Kiwanis Club for bringing so much fame to the city where he first started his Hall of Fame baseball career. When Cobb was introduced as the greatest baseball player of all time, he received thunderous applause. It was told by those who had the chance to hear Cobb speak at banquets and informal affairs that he had the ability to speak in a most agreeable manner that was most pleasing and with the modesty of a great man that would rather be left in the background than be placed before a flattering public.[11]

Clem's hobby subsequently grew into one of the largest industries in Augusta. In 1925, Clem founded Castleberry's Food Company Inc. Although Clem conceived the idea of canning barbecue and hash and selling it to food stores, it was his son, Clement Stewart Castleberry Jr., that turned his father's small Broad Street grocery business into the nationally known Castleberry Food Company. In 1926, Clem Jr. started canning Castleberry's barbecue and Brunswick stew at a small shed on Fifteenth Street. By 1985, Castleberry's had become a business with sales over $50 million and employing over three hundred employees.

Figure 35. Castleberry's Barbecue

Clem Castleberry will be fondly remembered in Augusta's history as the King of Barbecue. "If the inventor of the 'cue is unknown, the man who can prepare the best one is not. Clem Castleberry, the peer of barbecue generalissimos, the champion hog roaster, hash maker, rice cooker, corn boiler, lemon tea concocter in the universe today."[12]

Fantastics

Plausibly not as tasty as its barbecue tradition, Augusta also boasted one of the most unusual Independence Day celebrations. Although July 4th is now a federal holiday, one of Augusta's most extraordinary Independence Day traditions has faded away. Unbeknownst to many Augustans, Augusta's revelry used to rival that of major party cities. The Fourth of July in Augusta was known as Fantastic Day, when adults and children roamed the streets in oversize, outrageous clothes, singing and playing.[13]

Beginning as early as 1860, the Fantastics comprised of men, women, and children with painted faces wearing fantastic gay clothing and carrying walking sticks or brooms who roamed the streets of Augusta on the Fourth of July banging their sticks on fences and doors.[14] According to one accounting of the ritual, children would garner their costumes and go to neighbors' houses, chanting, "Fantastic, fantastic, come to stay. Give us cake and we'll go away." If no cake was provided, the children would retaliate by playing tricks on the inhospitable neighbor, such as turning over swings and freeing the horses from the barns. It was unquestionably an extraordinary and festive occasion.

Boys would adorn whiskers and wear long pants, while girls would borrow clothes from mom, stuff pillows in their clothes, and wear oversize shoes that flapped on their feet. The girls also tried to find the most elaborate hat they could wear. Little children would carry baskets and receive all kinds of food from their neighbors. All day long, the Fantastics roamed the streets of Augusta, banging their sticks and setting the dogs to barking and the babies to howling.

Figure 36. Children dressed as Fantastics, ca. 1950s
(*Georgia Regents University, Reese Library Special Collections*)

Augusta is the only known place in the country where Fantastics paraded the streets on Independence Day. How Augusta's curious celebration started is not known. What is known is that some time in the eighteen hundreds, July 4 became Fantastic Day in Augusta. One guess as to where the Fantastic tradition started is linked to an old English holiday tradition known as Guy Fawkes Day in England. Fawkes was a British conspirator who wanted to blow up Parliament.[15] When the king found out, he had Fawkes put to death and ordered the execution day, Nov. 4, to be a day of celebration.

Appearances by Fantastics provided much flair to Augusta's Fourth of July celebrations. Black-faced men and men dressed as women provided entertaining comedy to the festivities. Fantastics stole the show in Augusta's delayed Independence Day festivities of 1937.

> "Fantastics," Augusta's gift to the nation's *Believe It or Not* columns, paraded the streets during the day . . . . Masked and lamp-black painted they roamed, men dressed as women and women dressed as men. Playing pranks, singing songs, prancing hither and yon, the "fantastics" enjoyed the day, even though an early-morning rain caused many of them to sport white, rain-streaked lines on their blackened faces.[16]

The highlight of the celebration occurred at Lake Olmstead. Fantastics paraded, danced, and sang, swimmers vied for aquatic honors, bathing beauties displayed their charms, all to the tune of speeding motorboats, as hundreds of Augustans lined the banks of Lake Olmstead and enjoyed the gala hold over Fourth of July celebration. Fantastics dressed as movie characters, mountain folk, and comic-strip characters. They even had their own beauty pageant. David Jackson, dressed as a blond mountain girl, walked away with first-place honors. Earl Folds, attired as a "Harlem hotshot," was awarded second place, and J. H. Levy, festooned as a hula girl, won third place.

The Fantastic Independence Day celebration was even larger in 1939. By early morning on the Fourth, Fantastics were seen scattered in groups on Broad Street in downtown Augusta. Their numbers increased as the day went on, and by late afternoon, the portion of Broad Street above Thirteenth Street looked like a masquerade ball.[17] Groups of Fantastics took to their cars, popping up all over the city. It seemed as if the Fantastics were competing to see who could wear the weirdest costume possible.

By the mid-1960s, the tradition had begun to die. Augusta announced that it would no longer sponsor Fantastics Day Celebrations. The last known Fantastics celebration took place during America's bicentennial celebration in 1976. Hosted by the Richmond County Department of Parks and Recreation, a child-friendly Fantastic celebration was held at Lake Olmstead. Included in the festivities were a bozo dunking, train rides, covered wagon rides, sack races, tug-of-war, home-run derby, pie-eating contests, flour digs, a greased pole climb, and of course, a parade of Fantastics.

The Augusta Canal Heritage Area revived the tradition in 2006, sponsoring the program "Our History is 'Fantastic.'" The program implemented at John Milledge Elementary School included a "Fantastic Day" parade in costume for the participating students.

IX

The Roaring '20s

After WWI, the United States stormed into a decade of dramatic economic and social change—the roaring '20s or the Jazz Age. Women were given the right to vote, the first Miss America pageant was held in Atlantic City, New Jersey, commercial radio broadcasts began, Charles Lindbergh made the first nonstop transatlantic flight, and Walt Disney produced the first Mickey Mouse cartoon. It was a period of good times and rebellion. Young women set themselves free. Flappers, carefree young women, wore short "bobbed" hair, heavy makeup, and short skirts. The Jazz Age, with such artists as Louis Armstrong, Duke Ellington, Benny Goodman, and Bessie Smith, resonated through the AM radio. Prohibition led to bootlegging. Hollywood and the movie industry took off, speared by slapstick comedy such as Charlie Chaplin and Laurel and Hardy. The first talking movie, *The Jazz Singer*, starring Al Jolson, hit the screens. The Jazz Age and roaring '20s had arrived.

Economic growth was remarkable. The United States moved to a dominant position in international trade and global markets. For the first time, middle-class America prospered with financial means and the automobile. Americans started investing in the stock market and using credit. Electric utilities rapidly expanded, resulting in a growth in consumer appliances. The vast majority of middle-class Americans owned cars, homes, and the newest electrical devices such as AM radios, electric irons, fans, electric lighting, and vacuum cleaners. Automobile travel began to replace passenger rail travel. Demand for paved roads and the movement to the suburbs increased dramatically. Commercial radio networks and stations came into existence. Middle-class Americans began to travel, go to movies, and embrace professional sports such as the newly formed professional American Football League.[1]

Tourism

Coinciding with the postwar economic growth, the first nationwide twentieth-century real estate "bubble" appeared in the early 1920s. Real estate speculation and investment grew throughout the country, but especially in the South and Florida. As real estate traders from the North descended upon Augusta in 1921, there was a mad race for land. Real estate sales soared seeing common monthly sales of over a million dollars. The *Atlanta Journal* commented enthusiastically on Augusta's Forward March, proclaiming Augusta as a marvelous city with golden opportunities for development and investment. Augusta was viewed as having unparalleled climatic, soil, and industrial advantages. Thomas J. Hamilton, president and editor of the *Augusta Chronicle*, declared that Augusta was destined to become one of the greatest metropolitan cities of the Southeast or the country.

> We need the faith move mountains, and we have it; we need the work to push us forward, and we are willing to do it; we must have imagination and vision and we have that; we must have cooperation to make a success of anything we undertake, and we have it; we must have enthusiasm, and we have barrels of it; we must have money to advertise and we have only a part of it. Let's get the remainder at once.[2]

The real estate market exploded.

As a result of this mad real estate frenzy, tourism became a sizzling topic of discussion in Augusta during the early 1920s. Community leaders contemplated plans to make Augusta a great polo and tourist center. In March of 1923, throngs of citizens and business people showed up for a meeting held at the Board of Commerce Hall to discuss polo, horse racing, trapshooting, and erection of an amusement park for Augusta and its large winter colony.[3] Given the success of the Bon Air-Vanderbilt Hotel, it was anticipated that with the addition of polo fields and an amusement center, tourism would flourish, new hotels would be erected, and large crowds of wealthy Northerners would flock to Augusta seeking to enjoy Augusta's unrivaled climate. Tourism growth appeared inevitable given Augusta's marvelous year-round climate.

> As most of the nation knows, there is no better place for the winter vacation than the Augusta-Aiken region, in an area of Georgia and South Carolina where the climate is mild, although bracing, in a high altitude where the air is dry and healthful and there are no interruptions to wholesome enjoyment of life in the out-of-doors.[4]

Augusta, it was said, was a marvelous southern city where

> The sun shines all winter
> And there's never any snow
> Where the peaches reach perfection
> And the watermelons grow.[5]

Moreover, thousands of potential tourists were being turned away each year because Augusta's hotel accommodations were sold out.

Along with its exceptional climate, Augusta was recognized as an up-and-coming sports center, particularly during the winter tourist season. For example, Augusta hosted the South Atlantic Tennis tournament featuring tennis stars such as William Tilden II (1893-1953), renowned as one of the greatest tennis players of all time and the World no. 1 player for numerous years, and Vinnie Richards (1903-1959) a former World no. 2 tennis player. The Augusta Kennel Club's annual dog show brought in dogs and their wealthy owners from all over the United States and Canada. Over four hundred dogs from the finest pedigrees were entered in the 1925 show held at the old J. B. White building downtown.[6] Augusta also hosted a notorious annual horse show. Augusta's annual horse show at the fairgrounds was a highly anticipated event, drawing horse fanciers and prominent society members from all over the country. Some of the organizing committee members included Thomas Barrett, W. M. Partridge, and Rodney Cohen.

Figure 37. Ty Cobb and family, ca. 1923. From left:
Shirley, Ty, Jimmy, Ty Jr., Charlie, Beverly and Herschel

One of Augusta's most legendary tourism supporters was a young major league baseball player and manager, Tyrus "Ty" Raymond Cobb. Ty Cobb was intimately associated with Augusta as a thirty-year city resident and a baseball player. Ty began his storied professional baseball career in Augusta, playing his first game with the Augusta Tourists of the South Atlantic League on April 26, 1904. Over the next twenty-four years, Cobb, often referred to as the Georgia Peach, would establish an unsurpassed .367 lifetime batting average, win twelve batting titles, and earn a spot in the first class of inductees into the National Baseball Hall of Fame. Cobb also held the record for most hits with 4,191 until Pete Rose broke it in 1985, as well as the record for most stolen bases with 824 until Maury Wills surpassed it in 1962. Indicative of his bond with Augusta, Ty was not the only member of his family to win titles in Augusta. His son, Ty Cobb Jr., along with his partner and fellow Augusta resident, Bobby Glickert, won the city tennis doubles championship in 1937.[7] Cobb Jr. was singles runner-up.

According to Ty, development of polo grounds would draw an affluent class of sport tourists to Augusta, increase real estate values, and enhance Augusta's ability to attract more major league baseball clubs to Augusta for spring training.[8] Augusta had been the home for the Detroit Tigers spring training between 1905 and 1907, as well as for five seasons (1922-1926) while Cobb was a player-manager in the 1920s. Augusta had previously hosted spring training for numerous other baseball teams including: the Boston Red Sox (1902); Cincinnati Reds (1903); Philadelphia Phillies (1905); Atlanta Braves (1908-1912); Minnesota Twins (1918-1919); Los Angeles Dodgers (1913-1914); and San Francisco Giants (1928).[9] The Toronto Maple Leafs of the International League and the Pittsburg Rebels (1914) of the Federal League of Baseball Clubs also held spring training in Augusta.

In the mid-1990s, a group of local residents would seek to rename Lake Olmstead Stadium, home to Augusta's minor league baseball team, in honor of Ty Cobb's involvement in the community as a ballplayer, manager, and citizen. Consequently, in 2004, Augusta commissioner Andy Cheek proposed naming the playing field at Lake Olmstead Stadium Cobb Field. However, opposition from local NAACP president, John R. Maben, among others, centered on Cobb's reputation as a virulent racist and led commissioners to withdraw the proposal.

Community leaders engineered a master plan in 1922 to construct numerous tourist attractions at Lake Olmstead and the adjoining fairgrounds in anticipation of creating a magnificent civic park. One of the strongest proponents of the master plan and tourism was Colonel Sanford H. Cohen, a well-known entertainment promoter and former manager of Lake View Park. Cohen had extensive managerial experience, having previously managed Augusta's Opera House, the theater at Lake View Park, Augusta's carnival, and the fairgrounds.[10] Recognizing the importance of Augusta's winter colony, Colonel Cohen often spoke in support of winter sports, especially polo, at civic clubs throughout

Augusta. He cited Aiken as a city that had successfully become a mecca of Northern visitors.

In an interview with the *Augusta Chronicle*, Colonel Cohen hyped the prospect of making Augusta the preeminent tourist town of the South.

> Augusta fortunately now has a wonderful chance. Adjoining the Lake golf course is a lake that can be arranged for clear water bathing, boating and other aquatic sport. The end of Lake View Park that adjoins the Lake can be made suitable for trapshooting and other forms of sports.[11]

Colonel Cohen's proposal was for Augusta to put on a great musical jubilee that would attract tourists to Augusta and raise sufficient funds to purchase the ninety-acre fairgrounds and convert its front building into a first-class 3,500-seat auditorium. After the jubilee, the property could then be bestowed to the city and utilized as a park, polo grounds, racetrack, and auditorium ready for conventions.

Cohen's plan coincided with the rebuilding of the Bon Air with 304 rooms. Given the reputation of the Bon Air Hotel, its adjoining Lake Course golf links, Lake Olmstead, and Lake View Park, the plan would capitalize on the energetic active class of wealthy tourists. All these wonderful tourist attractions, including the golf course, Lake Olmstead, the polo grounds, racetrack, trapshooting grounds, and the auditorium would all be contiguous.

Escalating sentiment for tourism was expressed after President Harding's visit to Augusta during the first week of April 1923. An ensuing editorial in the *Augusta Chronicle* advocated Augusta's development as a tourist destination.

> Augusta, we might say, has just closed a week which was one of the most eventful and most inspiring in her long history as a tourist resort and with hundreds clamoring to come to Augusta and who have to be turned away each year, it is inconceivable that we do not build more and more hotels. Let's provide the polo grounds, the race course and another golf course as outlined in Col. Sanford H. Cohen's plans for an amusement park at the Georgia-Carolina Fair grounds, and let's keep on building tourist hotels. Augusta has a God-given climate and if she does not provide a place to stay for those who wish to come then she is sadly lacking in the enterprise which she should have.[12]

Augusta's development as a tourist center seemed inevitable.

Another robust proponent of Augusta tourism was Thomas G. Barrett Sr. (1861-1929), also known as the Father of Modern Augusta.[13] Barrett had spent most of his life in Augusta and served as its mayor from 1910 to 1913. He assisted in securing financing for rebuilding the Bon Air Hotel after it burned, began the campaign to construct the Augusta levee, and was instrumental in the Augusta Horse Show. Barrett also campaigned for University Hospital, which established Augusta's reputation in health care.

Figure 38. Thomas G. Barrett. Barrett actually spent the last several days of his illness at the Bon Air where he passed away. (*Year Book of the City Council of Augusta, Georgia, 1910*)

Appearing before the Kiwanis Club on Thursday, March 13, 1924, Barrett advanced the idea of an amusement park for the benefit of the city and its winter visitors.[14] He also espoused the need for polo grounds and improvements for other winter sports. He spoke of this needed development as being "one of the things between Augusta and its goal as the outstanding resort place in the South."[15]

Augusta was growing rapidly as a resort center. On December 27, 1925, the *Augusta Chronicle* published a "Progress and Prosperity Edition," with more than one hundred pages telling the story of Augusta's past, present, and vision of a golden future. Development was progressive as Augusta exempted new industries from taxation for a period of five years, and at the time, Georgia also had no state or inheritance tax. Construction began on new hotels, and financing was still pouring into the Augusta market. To accommodate the lack of hotel rooms, many local Hill residents, including Harold Boardman, Thomas Barrett Sr., and Carter

Burdell, began renting their residences out to Northern visitors. Of the three planned resort hotels, only one would actually be completed. Little did anyone know, but the real estate market was about to plummet as the nation slid into the impending Great Depression.

In 1925, Benjamin Marshall, famous architect and hotel builder of Chicago, and fellow financier and founder of North Augusta, James U. Jackson, announced plans for a $10 million hotel development in North Augusta, to include an enormous four-hundred-bedroom hotel, a tourist colony, two eighteen-hole golf courses, polo fields, a riding club, and an aviation landing field.[16] The main floor would integrate a tropical garden and palm trees with the dining area and indoor swimming pool.[17] The roof and garden walls were designed so that they could be opened and closed as dictated by the weather. Although Marshall purchased a four-thousand-acre tract of land overlooking Augusta and the Savannah River Valley, the hotel was never built.

Forrest Hills

At the same time, the Forrest Hills Corporation announced the development of a six-hundred-acre area west of the Hill. Plans included an exclusive residential section, a luxurious resort hotel, golf course, and polo grounds. Investors involved in the project included Augustans John E. Reed; Willis Irvin, the architect of the new Bon Air-Vanderbilt; Blanchard & Calhoun, a local real estate company; Frank Adair, vice president of the Adair Reality and Trust Company of Atlanta and New York; and William Rockefeller Comfort, an infamous New York and Miami capitalist. The unusual spelling of the development's name, Forrest Hills, was derived from Frank Adair's father, Forrest Adair (1865-1936).

Construction of the $100,000 golf course and the Forrest Hills-Ricker Hotel began in 1926, through the financing of the Ricker family and the reputation of their grand New England hotels, including the Poland Spring House and the Mansion House. Built at a cost of $2 million, the Forrest Hills-Ricker Hotel was located on top of one of the highest points in Richmond County, overlooking pine-covered hills. The hotel opened on December 18, 1928, featuring fireproof construction with spacious verandas, beautifully appointed sunrooms and lounges, large airy guest rooms, and a beautiful eighteen-hole golf course now known as Forrest Hills Golf Course. The golf course was constructed under the supervision of renowned golf architect Donald Ross, who also was responsible for installing grass greens at the Bon Air's Hill course. Hunting rights for quail and dove shooting were available to guests on ten thousand nearby acres. There were also stables and trapshooting.

Figure 39. The Forrest Hills-Ricker Hotel

The allure and success of the Forrest Hills-Ricker Hotel would only last for a short time. In 1942, the army purchased the hotel and operated it as the Oliver General Hospital. Early in 1950, the Department of Defense closed Oliver General, and in July of the same year, the hotel property was transferred to the Veterans Administration. The property was closed in 1980 and the buildings subsequently demolished.

Figure 40. Forrest Hills Golf Course, No. 12 (between ca. 1920 and ca. 1930)

Commodore Stoltz

Largely through the efforts of Charles F. Rossignol (1908-1985), one of Augusta's great tourism boosters,[18] another imposing hotel kingpin, Miami businessman Commodore J. Perry Stoltz, arrived in Augusta in October 1925 to announce that he would open the Fleetwood Hotel of Augusta. Stoltz had created a stir in the hotel industry, especially among the young travelers, with his Miami Beach hotel. He had already built a Fleetwood Hotel in Hendersonville, known as Fleetwood of Skyland, and was erecting another hotel in Chattanooga, Tennessee, on Lookout Mountain, known as Fleetwood of Fairyland. The Augusta hotel would rise above the magnolias and the myriad shrubs and flowers offering a spectacular view and be named Fleetwood of Sunland. Rossignol and Commodore Stoltz became friends several years earlier, when Rossignol, the South's oldest pathfinder, convinced Stoltz through persistent urging to visit Augusta. Their friendship grew, and the commodore invited Rossignol to deliver a presentation promoting Augusta from his radio station WMBF, Fleetwood Hotel, Miami Beach, Florida on September 8, 1925. Rossignol spoke for over thirty minutes of Augusta's marvelous climate and her multitude of advantages. He declared that Augusta was raising $100,000 to advertise its superior advantages and marvelous future.[19]

Excitement filled the air for Stoltz's visit to Augusta in October 1925. Commodore Stoltz was given the royal treatment. Upon his arrival, he was presented a luncheon under the auspices of the Augusta Board of Commerce at the famous Fruitland Manor. Later, he was the guest of honor for the Georgia-Furman football game at the fairgrounds.[20]

In an announcement that could have changed Augusta's history, the commodore declared that his grand $2-million, fifteen-story resort hotel and golf course would be developed on the Fruitland Manor site. This incredible property, exquisitely shaped by the master landscape architect and horticultural prodigy of the late Prosper J. A. Berckmans, was destined to become one of the most renowned places in the world.

Stoltz entered into a contract with the Washington Heights Development Company to construct his Fleetwood of the Southland hotel with an option to buy four hundred acres of the former Berckmans' property on January 23, 1926.[21] Meanwhile, the Washington Heights Development Company offered subscriptions for the surrounding land for $500 an acre. Local realtors, Blanchard and Calhoun, Alexander and Garrett, Duvall and Powell, and Wm. E. Bush and Dickey predicted the land would sell for prices ranging from $700 to $1,000 per acre upon completion of the Fleetwood Hotel.[22]

Commodore Stoltz planned to raze the manor and a few other small houses on the property after construction was completed. During construction, the manor would be used to house the superintendent of construction and assistants.

The now-famous grove of beautiful magnolia trees that led from the Washington Road to the hotel site was to be preserved.

> This grove of trees, that for years have been admired by winter visitors, caught the eye of Commodore Stoltz the minute he saw them, and that they will be left to greet the visitors and guests of the new Fleetwood here means that the approach to the hotel will be the most attractive that any hotel can boast of in the country.[23]

The Augusta Fleetwood would be fifteen stories high, with the fifteenth floor to be used for an observation roof garden. Commodore Stoltz also planned to erect a radio broadcasting station with two one-hundred-foot steel towers on top of the hotel. Another interesting feature was that the dining room and kitchen would also be located on the fourteenth floor. The hotel would have three hundred rooms, each equipped with a bath and shower. A fifteen-foot terrace was to be constructed that would extend around the building. Walking eight laps around the hotel would equal walking a mile.

Having secured the property, Stoltz broke ground in February of 1926.[24] As the steel girders were raised, bathtubs delivered, and the golf course staked out, Augustans invested over a million dollars in the surrounding land, including the Lakemont area around Lake Olmstead. The hotel, however, was never completed. The Great Miami Hurricane of September 1926 left 372 persons dead, over $105 million in damages,[25] and a flattened Miami Fleetwood Hotel in its wake. The destruction to Stoltz's Miami Fleetwood Hotel would eventually lead to his bankruptcy during the depression years.

Augusta Purchases Lake View Park

During the early '20s, Lake View Park had begun to deteriorate, but significant changes were coming to Lake Olmstead in 1924. On January 1, led by Augusta mayor Julian Murphey Smith (1875-1946), it was announced that the city would begin negotiations with the Augusta-Aiken Railway and Electric Corporation for the purchase of Lake View Park.

Figure 41. Julian Murphey Smith (*Year Book of the City Council of Augusta, Georgia, 1923*)

Mayor Smith was instrumental in the city's acquisition of Lake View Park. Smith, a handsome young man, succeeded William P. White as mayor in 1922.[26] Smith, a wholesale grocer, ran on a progressive platform specifically appealing to the ladies who were voting in Augusta's mayoral election for the first time.

To the Ladies Who Will Vote for the First Time:

> We wish to say that in JULIAN M. SMITH we have a candidate who represents the best there is in the community, a man who has always taken a large part of his own time to devote to community affairs. He is former president of the Board of Commerce, former member of city council and he is a PROGRESSIVE in the true sense of the word. Mr. Smith believes in the development of schools, the abolition of all illiteracy, the development of parks and playgrounds, in community work of every sort. He is for a GREATER AND BETTER AUGUSTA. By his work you shall know him.[27]

The Nineteenth Amendment guaranteeing women the right to vote and hold office had just recently been passed by Congress and ratified by the states on August 18, 1920. Smith served as Augusta's mayor from 1922 to 1925.

Anticipation grew in hopes that Augusta's purchase and enhancement of Lake View Park would revive one of Augusta's most popular parks and playground. Well-known druggist and columnist for the *Augusta Chronicle*, N. L. Willet added his commentary on the city's expected purchase of Lake View Park.

> This park possesses some pretty ever-flowing springs of water that are quite potable. It is singularly blessed in having in it a great variety of forest trees. Its steep hillsides too, are picturesque and the park is

happily bounded on the one side by Lake Olmstead which is really a
noble sheet of water and at its base, borders the canal.[28]

Negotiations to purchase Lake View Park were successful, and Augusta bought the
park for $9,150. Julian Smith remarked, "[A]fter buying this property, in order to
make the park more useful to a large number of our people, it was decided to put
in a bathing beach and municipal swimming pool."[29]

Shortly after the purchase of Lake View Park, City Engineer W. H. Wise, in
his 1924 Annual Report, recommended that Lake Olmstead be dammed at the
mouth of the lake in an effort to transform the lake into a crystal body of water,
making it a perpetual asset for the city.[30] Although city council had previously
approved McLendon and May's petition to dam the lake, the dam had never been
erected. Gates were installed, and an earthen fill placed at the northern end of the
lake. Mayor Julian Smith received glowing compliments once the dam was finally
constructed in 1924. Upon completion, it was declared that Lake Olmstead was
now filled with the clear cool waters of Rae's Creek, reflecting only the stunning
colors of the beautiful Augusta sky and surrounding trees in its crystal waters.[31]
Lake Olmstead was now one of the largest metropolitan bodies of clear water
between Washington, DC, and Jacksonville, Florida.

The next step for Mayor Smith was to obtain cooperation from the county in
constructing a road around Lake Olmstead. Even though the city had practically
finished the road along the eastern boundary of the lake, to complete the oval, a
stretch of road had to pass through the county's jurisdiction. Mayor Smith commented,

> [A]fter building the dam I conceived the idea of building a road on
> top of the dam, and having it connected with the county's road on the
> western side of the lake, and then extended along the eastern shore
> of the lake up to the city's park, and thence back to Broad Street thus
> encircling Lake Olmstead with a boulevard.[32]

The project was endorsed not only as "a drive of scenic beauty unsurpassed in this
section of the South" but also by appreciably increasing the taxable property in the
city and the county, as a project that would more than pay for itself.[33]

Lakemont and the Oval

Another hurdle remained. To complete the oval boulevard, the road had to
traverse the Lakemont subdivision on the northwestern side of the lake. As city
dwellers began to move to the suburbs during the '20s, the beautiful wooded area
on the northwestern shores of Lake Olmstead had been subdivided for residential
lots. The Lakemont neighborhood boasted twenty-five choice lots that were

magnificent, splendid, and superbly beautiful. Of course, the marketing for sale of the lots accentuated the beauty of Lake Olmstead.

> Lakemont is the splendid property which has recently been subdivided and a paved road with a magnificent entrance just west of the lake provided.

> With the clear waters of the lake, as contrasted with the muddy Savannah River water which filled it before the canal was shut off and the waters of Rae's Creek emptied into it, with a luxurious growth of wild flowers and dogwood in profusion, the development is simply idyllic.[34]

> Here's the ideal spot—truly a paradise for home lovers. Just near enough to the city to reap its benefits, but still far enough away to give it the suburban atmosphere . . . Here, too, are the advantages of city life—a place for you and your children to breathe the pure, unadulterated air as nature intended.[35]

Lakemont truly was a beautiful location for a home complete with cool breezes from the lake. Marketing also hyped the fact that the Augusta Country Club's two golf courses were only a few hundred yards from the neighborhood.

Figure 42. Lakemont Advertisement (*Augusta Chronicle*, Mar. 2, 1925)

The beauty and charm of Lakemont subdivision made it one of the most sought-out areas in Augusta at the time. Property values in the area had increased dramatically during Augusta's real estate boom. For instance, during the morning of September 21, 1925, the Georgia Railroad Bank offered forty-nine acres of land near Lakemont for $200 an acre. The property was sold within a couple of hours.[36]

Lakemont property was high, dry, well drained, and included urban advantages such as water, lights, phone, paved drives, etc. Its location also provided opportunities for boating, fishing, and swimming in a beautiful scenic setting. Plans included the development of a lakefront neighborhood park with sidewalks leading from the water's edge to the top of the Lakemont development.

As the Lakemont area developed, completion of the road around Lake Olmstead seemed to be in everyone's interest. Local attorney Lansing Lee spoke before the Augusta Commission on behalf of the Lakemont property owners with his renowned eloquence.

> The owners of the property have voluntarily and properly indicated their willingness to assume their fair share of the public burden, and have offered to pay forty percent of the cost of the paving laid in front of their land.

> The entire cost of constructing the street on the city's side will be borne by the city, just as the cost of the construction of the dirt road on the county's side has been borne by the county.

> I have begun my statement to you by saying that this work was undertaken by the commissioners at the request and in cooperation with the City of Augusta. The mayor, who is present, has told you so. I wish also to say that the Bon Air-Vanderbilt Hotel and the Augusta Country Club, and all of the property owners in the neighborhood are deeply interested in its success and its early completion. You are earnestly requested by the owners of the property, and by these interests I have just named, not to be dissuaded from undertaking this work, but to go forward with it and to push it to as early a completion as is possible.[37]

A deal was reached whereby the owners of the Lakemont property; Henry H. Cumming and William E. Bush would pay a share of the cost with the city paying the rest. It was a substantial accomplishment, as reported in the *Augusta Chronicle*.

> One of the most important meetings of the county commission ever held in Augusta occurred yesterday at noon at the courthouse when bids were received, opened and are being canvassed for the pavement on

the Lakemont Drive, which is being jointly paid for by the owners of the
property and by the city of Augusta.[38]

It appeared that the boulevard was destined for completion.

Yet another hurdle arose the next year. The authority to construct the road
was the issue of a 1925 case of *James T. Gardner, et al. v. the Richmond County Board of
Commissioners of Roads and Revenues, Claussen-Lawrence Construction Company and the
Georgia Railroad Bank.* The petitioners led by their attorney, William H. Fleming,
sought to permanently restrain the county from constructing the section of
highway skirting Lake Olmstead.[39] They avowed that the planned section of road
was not a public thoroughfare, and therefore, the county had no legal authority
to award the contract and pay for the paving with public funds. By the time the
petitioners filed suit the paving project had already been completed. In the end
the county won the battle, and the road was finally completed.

Walton H. Marshall, president of the Bon Air-Vanderbilt Corporation, in a
letter to Mayor Smith, applauded the city's efforts.

Augusta, Ga., Nov. 24, 1924
Hon. Julian M. Smith, Mayor
City of Augusta
Augusta, Ga.

Dear Sir:

I have been in Augusta several days in connection with the business of
the Bon Air-Vanderbilt Hotel, and have had occasion to carefully observe
the work you have done at Lake Olmstead.

I congratulate you very heartily on what you have accomplished in
transforming this Lake from a mud hole into a lovely body of clear water.
Your money has been well spent, and the City will be amply repaid.

I also wish to voice my hearty approval of what you and the County
Commissioners are doing in building a boulevard around the Lake. I
urge that you and Council and the Commissioners complete and pave
this road at the earliest possible moment.

My work takes me into many parts of this country and abroad, and I have
no hesitation in saying that that drive around the Lake will create for the
use of your people and for the Winter tourists a roadway of such beauty

as is rarely equaled. It is my confident belief this work will do more to advertise Augusta as a Winter Resort than anything which has been done in a long time, and I am sure that it will cause a great many people to buy and build their Winter homes here.

Very truly yours,
Walton H. Marshall,
President[40]

Not only had the city made the waters of Lake Olmstead clear of the muddy canal water, the new boulevard around the lake was one of unsurpassed scenic beauty.

As a consequence of Mayor Smith's actions, the city's permanent assets increased approximately $1,500,000 during his mayoral term.[41] The increase in assets was largely the product of street paving, new sewers, new water mains, Julian Smith Park, the clarifying of Lake Olmstead, and the building of a road across Lake Olmstead's dam. In appreciation of the mayor's leadership, members of city council, led by Councilman Clem Castleberry, appropriately renamed Lake View Park to Julian Smith Park.

X

Decline and Depression

The boll weevil set the stage for the Great Depression in Georgia. Although Augusta was one of the largest inland cotton markets in the United States, much of that market fell apart after the boll weevil arrived in 1915, ravaging Georgia's cotton fields. It became impossible for small farmers to endure life on the farm. By 1940, the rural farming population in Georgia had shrunk from two-thirds of the population to less than one-third.

As if the arrival of the boll weevil was not bad enough, the stock market crash in the waning days of October 1929 began the worst economic depression in US history. The Great Depression struck Georgia and the South harder than other regions of the country, exacerbating an economic downturn that had begun a decade earlier. Although the urban population tended to fare better than the rural population, the impact on Augusta was significant. Dr. Edward Cashin, renowned Augusta historian, explained the impact on Augusta.

> For the first time since this story of Augusta began, the zest went out of things. The mart no longer bustled, enterprise was discouraged, the vision of empire was lost, the Old South was a legend and the promises of the New South sounded hollow.[1]

No doubt, the boll weevil and depression took much of the wind out of Augusta's push to transform itself into a tourism center.

Acknowledging the hard economic plight of its residents, the city declared that it was stocking the lake with five thousand to eight thousand largemouth bass in 1927. Stocking of the lake served two essential purposes. Fishermen without the financial means to go out of town would have a place to fish. More importantly, it would also provide food for families in need.[2] Several months later, the lake was stocked with an additional five thousand bream.

To ensure a healthy fish population, officials recognized the need to regulate fishing in Lake Olmstead. In 1928, Augusta enacted Ordinance No. 543. The ordinance prohibited certain methods of fishing in the lake and provided

Robert A. Mullins

penalties for violations. More specifically, it prevented the setting of trout lines, the baiting or catching fish with nets, shooting, trapping, dynamiting, or using of lime or other poisons in Lake Olmstead.[3] Local residents took little heed of the ordinance.

By 1928, the state of Julian Smith Park had declined significantly. The shrubbery was not kept, and benches and swings were in a state of decay. Demands to beautify Julian Smith Park emphasized the natural beauty of Lake Olmstead and that the park, if beautified, would be one of the finest municipal parks in the South. "With clear water in Lake Olmstead, instead of the muddy river water, the park is prettier than ever, there is no finer place on hot summer afternoons and evenings."[4]

Irrespective of its state, Julian Smith Park was swamped with crowds described as exceeding twenty-five thousand people from all over Georgia for an open forum political debate for candidates in July 1928. The political candidates spoke in the "open air and under the inspiration of the cooling breezes that come from Lake Olmstead."[5] Barbecue was served to the throngs. The dance pavilion, similar to days of old, was "gaily festooned with Japanese lanterns, colored ribbons, and a ton or two of serpentine."[6] The crowd attending the dance that evening was reported to be one of the largest crowds ever attending a dance in Augusta.

XI

The Augusta National

Commodore Stolz's misfortune and the hilly topography around Lake Olmstead ensured the development of one of the world's most beautiful and famous golf courses, the Augusta National. The tract of land, which would become the famous Augusta National golf course, began less than seven hundred yards from Lake Olmstead. The Berckmans Manor Estate, as it was known, bounded Washington Road along Berckmans Road, nearly adjoining the property of the Augusta Country Club with its famous Hill Course and Lake Course. Situated by the mouth of Rae's Creek and the headwaters of Lake Olmstead, the land is rolling, steep with hills, wooded glens, ravines, and hallows.

> It is virgin forest, with towering pines and huge oaks that were standing when General Oglethorpe sat about a cheery fire of pine knots and smoked the pipe of peace with the Cherokee Indians.[1]

The property was one of extraordinary beauty.

On the north side of the Berckmans tract was Fruitland Manor with "natural beauty of the landscape enhanced by over sixty years of architectural landscaping, with magnificent cedars, pines and magnolias that would require two-third of a century to grow if the place were to be duplicated."[2] Planted years ago, hundreds of azaleas and camellias also adorned the grounds.

Figure 43. Fruitland Manor, 1936 (*Historic American Engineering Record*)

The property had a storied history as a world-class nursery and botanical gardens. Fruitland was the name Dennis Redmond gave the nursery he started upon purchasing the 315-acre tract from Judge Benjamin Warren of Augusta in 1853. A year later, Redmond built his residence on the property, a large house designed to incorporate features of a Louisiana plantation house with West Indies architectural elements.[3] Redmond grew apples, peaches, figs, grapes, strawberries, and ornamental shrubs but also experimented with growing indigo plants. Redmond, however, only owned the property for five years, when he sold it in 1858 to renowned Belgian horticulturalist, Baron Louis Mathieu Edouard Berckmans (Louis M. E., 1801-1883), his son Prosper Jules Alphonse Berckmans Sr. (Prosper J. A., 1830-1910), and Prosper's wife, Mary Craig.

Figure 44. Louis Alphonse Berckmans, Robert Craig Berckmans and
Sam McGourhey, ca. 1885 (*Georgia Regents University, Reese Library Special Collections*)

Prosper was born near Brussels, Belgium, was educated in France, and studied botany at the Botanical Gardens of Brussels. He and his father had moved to Augusta, Georgia, in 1856 and established a nursery adjacent to Redmond's property, known as Pearmont. After purchasing the Fruitland tract, Prosper and his father partnered together, forming P. J. A. Berckmans Company, and expanded the Fruitland Nursery by combining both the Pearmont and Fruitland nurseries.

Fruitland Nurseries was a huge success, selling plants throughout the world. In their nursery, the Berckmans grew many different plant varieties, including Japanese wisteria, Spanish cork oak, Japanese persimmon, camellias, azaleas, and Chinese pines. Many of the azaleas and camellias were imported from Europe and Japan.[4] Berckmans tirelessly perfected the peach, planting more than three million peach trees and earning the title the Father of the Peach Tree Culture in the South. The Berckmans also planted magnolias along the entrance to the Redmond plantation house creating a special ambience. By 1900, the nurseries encompassed over five hundred acres.

Figure 45. Montrose Dramatic Club (*Georgia Regents University, Reese Library Special Collections*). The Montrose Drama Club formed in the late 1800s included T. J. Hickman, Miss Sarah Hardwick, Miss Mary Cuthbert, Mrs. W. L. Martin, Mrs. James Paul Verdery, Bryan Cumming, Miss Ann Smith, Mrs. Bryan Cumming and Miss Hattie Ganahl. Louis A. Berckmans (bottom left) and Robert C. Berckmans (bottom right) were both members of this popular drama club.

When Prosper Sr. died in 1910, his three sons, Prosper Jr., Robert Craig, and Louis Alphonse Berckmans continued to manage the business. However, at his death, control of Fruitland was transferred to his second wife and stepson, Alonzo Purdy. The Fruitland Nursery would only last several more years until it was shut down around 1918 and the trade name sold.

After Commodore Stoltz's business demise, the Bon-Air Vanderbilt Company paid $5,000 for an option to buy the Fruitland property so that it could be obtained by the Fruitland Manor Corporation, composed of Thomas Barrett Jr., Clifford Roberts, Walton H. Marshall, Fielding Wallace, and Col. Robert P. Jones (the father of Bobby Jones).[5] The Berckmans' tract was destined to become the most famous tract of property in the world. One of the world's greatest golfers was retiring at the age of twenty-eight to focus on building his own golf course, and it was on this property that he would build his infamous course. On July 15, 1931, Robert Tyre Jones Jr., "Bobby," made the following announcement.

I am joining with a group of friends as one of the organizers of a new club to be known as the *Augusta National Golf Club*. It is a private undertaking and in no sense a commercial project. Although my time is now largely devoted to the practice of law, golf will always be my hobby, and having retired from active competition, my ambition is to help build something that may be recognized as one of the great courses of the world.

Augusta, which is in my home state, *has been selected for the location because it offers such a splendid winter climate and a golf setting that I consider unsurpassed for the idea we have in mind.* The property has already been purchased and the architects have commenced the designing work.

The membership will be national in character. In addition, a number of Canadians and Englishmen will be invited to join. I expect to give liberally of my time to the club, especially during the formative period, and I hope that certain ideas of my own will be useful in creating what we wish to achieve, *a golfers' paradise.*[6]

Bobby Jones's announcement rattled the golf world, bringing immediate prestige and recognition to the Augusta project. Apparently, Jones had dreamed about the Berckmans' tract, after his friend Tom Barrett Jr. (1894-1934), former president of the Bon Air Hotel Corporation and vice president of the Bon Air-Vanderbilt Hotel, suggested it as the most ideal spot for a golf course, particularly from the standpoint of terrain, climate, and soil.[7] The rolling terrain, Rae's Creek, Lake Olmstead, ancient oaks, tall pines, and the toils of previous landscape artists presented exciting possibilities to even the most exacting golf architect.

Figure 46. Bobby Jones, Atlanta, Georgia, ca. 1921

Bobby Jones, a lawyer by profession, had won thirteen major golf championships in the last seven years. Jones is still the only golfer to ever win the four major golf tournaments known as the Grand Slam in the same year. Remarkably, he never turned professional. His entire career in competitive golf was as an amateur. Upon retirement from golf, Jones served as legal counsel for the Bon Air-Vanderbilt Hotel for a period of time but largely focused his energy on building the ideal golf course.[8]

Coinciding with Jones's announcement was the declaration that the 365-acre Berckmans tract had been purchased for $70,000. Dr. Alistair Mackenzie, world-famed Scottish golf-course architect, also arrived in Augusta to saunter the Berckmans' tract and discuss plans for the golf links. Mackenzie, although practicing medicine in his earlier years, was renowned for the famous golf courses he had designed such as Cypress Point in California and the famous Jockey Club course in Buenos Aires, as well as four hundred other golf courses in Europe and America.

In addition to Bobby Jones and Mackenzie, other notable people involved in the development included Fielding Wallace,[9] president of the Augusta Country Club; Alfred Bourne,[10] winter resident of Augusta and millionaire sportsman; Tom Barrett Jr., perhaps the principal organizer; General Manager Kent Cooper, famous journalist and executive director of the Associated Press; President M. H. Aylesworth, of the National Broadcasting Company; and Grantland Rice, the world's premier newspaper golf authority. Rice's column appeared in well over 150 daily newspapers, and his audience easily reached millions of golf fans. With the support of these gentlemen, Bobby Jones was set to build his dream course. O. B. Keeler, prominent golf writer for the Atlanta Constitution and golf authority, projected that the Augusta National "will constitute the leading golf club in this hemisphere," and the golf course "in all probability is to be the most famous layout in North America, if not in all the world."[11] "It is fitting that the world's most perfect golf course should be built by the world's most perfect golfer."[12]

Bobby Jones was elected president of the Augusta National Golf Association at the first organization meeting held in the Augusta law offices of Cohen and Gray.[13] An executive committee and board of governors were created to govern the organization. Included on the board of governors were William C. Breed, president of the New York State Bar Association, and Eugene G. Grace, president of the Bethlehem Steel Company. The bylaws provided for two thousand shares of capital stock without nominal or par value and provided for two thousand members subject to amendment by the board. The initial membership fee was $385, plus the annual dues.

Wendell Miller and the Miller Engineering Company of New York were placed in charge of construction. Olmsted Brothers, a Boston landscape engineering firm, headed by John Charles Olmsted and Frederick Law Olmsted Jr., the sons of renowned landscape architect Frederick Law Olmstead, were hired to design the elaborate landscaping of the grounds. Prosper J. A. Berckmans Jr. was appointed as general property manager and keeper of the greens, and his brother Louis "Lewie" Berckmans was appointed as the director of landscaping and beautification.[14]

Figure 47. Thomas Barrett Jr. *(Year Book of the City Council of Augusta, Georgia, 1934)*

Thomas Barrett Jr. served as the local representative for the club's sponsors. Barrett was a handsome man who had fought during WWI at the Battle of Argonne. Barrett, following in his father's footsteps, was elected mayor of Augusta by one of the largest majorities in local history in 1933. He also succeeded his father, the late Thomas Barrett Sr., as president of the Bon Air Hotel Corporation and later became vice president of the Bon Air-Vanderbilt Hotel. He lent his support as mayor to the first Augusta National Invitation Tournament. Unfortunately, his reign as mayor terminated after five months and ten days in office, shortly after the first Masters golf tournament. On the day of his funeral, the county courthouse closed at 2:00 p.m. and thousands of people overflowed historic St. Paul's Church for his funeral.[15]

Henry Parson Crowell (1855-1944), a winter resident of Augusta, acted as chairman of the beautification committee of the Augusta National Golf Club. Crowell was the founder and chairman of the board of the Quaker Oats Company.[16] Through aggressive marketing strategies, he successfully marketed his Quaker Oats brand of oatmeal into a nationwide breakfast cereal.[17] Crowell's charge was to meticulously select the plants and shrubs in making the grounds the most beautiful spot in the universe. Crowell was well-known as an expert on plants and shrubs and maintained exquisite gardens known as the Crowell Gardens at his winter home on the Hill, which were annually opened to the public. Mr. S. A. Thompson, secretary of the National Rivers & Harbors Congress, made the following comment when he visited Mr. Crowell's gardens in 1931: "[W]hy any man who lives here would want to go to any other heaven, I can't see, for he has heaven at home."[18]

Although plans for a new clubhouse had been designed, it was soon determined to utilize the Fruitland Manor, the former residence constructed in 1854 by horticulturist Dennis Redmond. The renovated clubhouse was designed for the comfort and convenience of golfers. Great thoughtfulness was paid to the locker room. Lockers were to be placed in small groups of a dozen or more and arranged around tables, chairs, and lounges. Deep bay windows in the locker room were designed to give views of the course so that play could be comfortably watched from the clubhouse.[19]

The clubhouse would become symbolic of the Augusta National, as would Magnolia Lane, one of the most celebrated and oldest sites on the property. Planted from seed by the Berckmans in the late 1850s, sixty large magnolia trees line the 330-yard-long entrance from Washington Road to the clubhouse.[20] Steve DiMeglio, writing for *USA Today*, captured the allure of Magnolia Lane through the eyes of three-time Masters winner Gary Player and his first drive up Magnolia Lane in 1957.

> "A player once said years ago that The Masters is the only tournament where you start choking when you pass through the gates at Magnolia Lane," Player said last year. "I remember my first drive on Magnolia Lane as if it happened yesterday. I drove as slow as I could. I met Bobby Jones that day, too, and the next day I met President Eisenhower. It was all a bit overwhelming."[21]

The grounds were further beautified with dogwoods, azaleas, and more than fifty different shades and japonicas artistically grouped about the holes.

Every hole at the Augusta National represents a plant or tree that preexisted on the grounds from its days as a nursery. The greens were covered with Italian ryegrass and Bermuda grass used for the fairways.[22] Presumably, the sand for the sand traps was obtained from the seashore. The course also had a ninety-yard nineteenth hole for use in case of ties.[23]

On May 20, 1932, less than a year after Bobby Jones's announcement, Clifford Roberts, chairman of the executive committee, announced that construction crews and machinery would be withdrawn, leaving only the permanent maintenance crew at the Augusta National golf course. The cost to construct the golf course was estimated at $100,000, the clubhouse approximately $100,000, and the landscape work between $100,000 and $200,000.[24]

The golf course was officially opened with formal ceremonies on December 24, 1932.[25] The first official rounds took place on January 13-15, 1933, with Bobby Jones and Grantland Rice greeting players at the first tee.[26] Over eighteen thousand prominent governors, golf stars, USGA members, newspapermen, bankers, and others were invited for the official opening. Clifford Roberts and Grantland Rice went so far as to charter a train from New York to Augusta to recruit members for the Augusta National. Guests arriving by train were taken directly to the National for golf and Southern-style barbecue, while their bags were carried to the Bon Air Vanderbilt Hotel, where the majority of the guests stayed. Although the opening round was played in cold and blustery conditions with the high temperature only reaching thirty-eight degrees, the occasion was jovial. When asked for a comment, Clifford Roberts said, "[Y]ou can't print what I think about the weather, but the entire affair is splendid. All we can ask for."[27]

Augusta was moving forward with its goal of becoming the winter golf capital of the nation. A couple of years earlier, led by Hal R. Powell and T. Y. Rabb, the municipal golf course, commonly referred to as the "Patch," was developed David and Alex Ogilvie on the Hill through the raising of capital by subscriptions. With four golf courses, Augusta was destined to become the winter golf capital of the country.

The first Masters Golf Tournament, at that time known as the Augusta National Invitation Tournament, was held in March 1934. The tournament was "a fitting climax to the history of Augusta's growth as a golfing center from the humble beginning of a small 9-hole course to its present position as a recognized winter golf metropolis with courses and equipment which cannot be surpassed anywhere in the world."[28]

Five years later, the tournament officially became known as the Masters. The first Green Jacket awarded by the Augusta National went to Sam Snead, who emerged victorious in 1949 Masters Tournament. Originally, Bobby Jones and Clifford Roberts initiated the wearing of matching blazers for members so they would be easily identified by patrons.[29] Since the 1949 Masters, the Green Jacket has become synonymous with the tournament with the winner of the previous year's tournament customarily presenting the Green Jacket to the new winner.

Figure 48. Ike's Cabin at the Augusta National (*Historic American Engineering Record*)

One of the Augusta National's most infamous members was five-star general and thirty-fourth president of the United States, Dwight D. Eisenhower. President Eisenhower visited Augusta and the Augusta National on at least forty occasions. Soon after he was elected president, the Augusta National built Ike's Cabin, or the Eisenhower Cabin, near the tenth tee. Built to Secret Service standards, the three-story cabin was also commonly referred to in the press as the Little White House.

Some of the other notable members of the Augusta National include Bill Gates, cofounder and chairman of Microsoft; Arnold D. Palmer, professional golfer; Frank Broyles, former football coach of the University of Arkansas Razorbacks; Lou Holtz, former college football coach and sport commentator; Pat Haden, former NFL player and athletic director at the University of Southern California; Sam Nunn, former United States senator from Georgia; Condoleezza Rice, former United States Secretary of State; Carl Sanders, former governor of Georgia; Pete Coors, former chairman and CEO of Coors Brewing Company; George P. Shultz, former US Secretary of State; Melvin R. Laird, former US Secretary of Defense; and Lynn Swann, former NFL player with the Pittsburg Steelers.[30]

Clifford Roberts served as the first chairman of the Masters, a position he would hold until 1976, pouring his heart and soul into improving tournament golf and making the Masters the most famous golf tournament in the world. Unfortunately, riddled with cancer, Roberts took his own life on the grounds of the Augusta National in 1977.

Today the Masters Golf Tournament is one of the most renowned and infamous tournaments in professional golf. The tournament, one of four annual major professional golf tournaments, brings thousands of visitors to Augusta every spring.

XII

Municipal Beach and Julian Smith Casino

In 1931, Augusta officials turned their attention toward improving Julian Smith Park and providing swimming facilities. Led by Councilman Lon L. Fleming, city councilman from 1929 to 1931 and chairman of the Trees and Parks Committee, the proposal of creating a municipal beach finally came to realization. On Friday, July 3, 1931, Councilman Fleming and city engineer W. H. Wise rounded up a gang of city employees at Julian Smith Park and began clearing out the underbrush and weeds to create a beach on the shore of the lake. The Municipal Beach, also known as the Lon Fleming Beach, was situated on Lake Olmstead near Washington Road and Broad Street. Promoted as a way to provide swimming for thousands of children in the western section of the city, the beach stretched for approximately fifty yards with a score of nearby willow trees providing shade for the beach.[1]

With fervor, lights were installed for night swimming, ropes to delineate the depth of the water, a diving platform, a pier, and a lifeguard tower. Two diving boards were installed on the diving platform. One diving board was positioned three feet above the water and the other one ten feet above the water. Yet above these diving boards was another platform for high divers. Eight days after the project began, Councilman Fleming announced that the deep water had been roped off and the electric lights turned on for the first time.[2] Policeman Irvin Connor, a former navy officer, was stationed at the park as a lifeguard along with two assistants.

Municipal Beach was a huge success with hundreds of swimmers converging on the beach on a given afternoon. The impact of the beach was reported in the local newspaper.

> To go by the bathing beach in the afternoon and see the hundreds of children playing in the water, swimming, making sand piles on the beach and having a good time generally is an inspiration and we begin to realize how little is the cost to the municipality, and how little is the cost to us a individuals, to make a great many people happy.

> Certainly, with so much splendid water within easy reach of a sweltering
> people it is almost criminal not to utilize it.[3]

To see the many children swimming and building sand castles on the beach must
have been an astonishing sight.

Within a month after the Municipal Beach opened, the YMCA sponsored an
Inter-Park Swim meet at Lake Olmstead. Buster Bohler won first place in the principal
event sponsored by Councilman A. D. Tobin, swimming the five-hundred-yard course
at Lake Olmstead in eight minutes and twenty-nine seconds.[4] Bohler took the lead
in the first hundred yards of the distance swim, reaching the 250-yard buoy in three
minutes and fifty-five seconds. On the return trip, however, he was pushed by young
seventeen-year-old Maurice Steinburg who won second place.[5] Prizes of $7.50 and a
carton of cigarettes, $5, $3.50, $1.50, and $1 were given.

During the same year, the former Lakeside Club property was acquired from
Sam Baron, increasing the size of the park.[6] The new property adjoined Julian
Smith Park on the north side of Broad Street. There was hope of extending the
beach for at least a half mile on the eastern shores of the lake and construction of
a large bathhouse by the following year.

Lake Olmstead's reputation as an entertainment venue continued to escalate.
The completion of the new beach spurred the city's capability to promote special
events at Lake Olmstead. In May 1931, Augustans who visited Lake View Park had
the thrill of experiencing a two-day visit by the Pinecastle Boat Company. The
Pinecastle Boat Company placed several of its passenger boats, especially designed
for thrill seekers, on Lake Olmstead for rides from morning until darkness. There
was professional and amateur aquaplaning, as well as ski gliders making flights
over two hundred feet in the air towed behind a high-powered motorboat.

As the popularity of the Municipal Beach grew, so did demands to renovate
Julian Smith Park, which had fallen into a state of disrepair.

> It is one of the most beautiful natural parks possessed by any city and
> has been sadly neglected. The large grove of trees on the slope of
> a great hill, with the waters of Lake Olmstead below, makes this place
> susceptible to beautification and this work is certainly important to the
> pleasure and convenience of the people of Augusta.[7]

Although plans had been in place to beautify and improve the park since it was
purchased by the city, available funds were not. Fortunately, as part of President
Roosevelt's New Deal recovery from the Great Depression, funds became available
through the Federal Emergency Relief Administration (FERA).

In an attempt to curb the effects of the Great Depression, President Franklin
D. Roosevelt initiated the New Deal economic relief and recovery programs after
his inauguration in 1933. The New Deal's Social Security program offered income

support for the workforce, and the National Labor Relations Act (1935) facilitated unionization of the state's textile mills and factories, establishing minimum wages, working conditions, and working hours for industrial workers. Child labor, infamously common in Georgia's factories and mills, was eliminated; while the school year was expanded to seven months, new schools were constructed and textbooks provided free of charge to students. New Deal programs like the Civilian Conservation Corps and the Works Progress Administration (WPA) helped put thousands of Georgians back to work.

Led by Mayor Richard E. Allen Jr. and Lester S. Moody, secretary of the Augusta Chamber of Commerce, Augusta utilized resources accessible under Roosevelt's New Deal to improve Julian Smith Park. Augusta furnished the necessary materials while labor was provided through FERA and the Works Progress Administration (WPA), another New Deal program employing millions of unskilled workers to carry out public works projects.

Mayor Allen was a popular mayor coming from a long family line of politicians dedicated to community service. Not only was his father a former mayor and councilman, but his great-grandfather was Mayor Joseph V. Henry Allen (1830-1883), who had supervised the enlargement of the Augusta Canal. Allen typified the new spirit in Augusta and was a strong proponent of Savannah River transportation.

Acknowledging Lake Olmstead's scenic splendor, Mayor Allen sought to make Julian Smith Park and the lake into a showplace of the South through a beautification project of landscaping, the planting of four thousand shrubs, the building of a casino and bandstand, and other improvements. He was thoroughly aware that Lake Olmstead, with its beautiful waters, tall pines, and sweet gum trees, had previously been a mecca for thousands of Augustans.

Figure 49. Julian Smith Casino

Plans called for building a striking new casino, restaurant, boathouse, administrative offices, and paving the street around the lake. Architect Edward Lynn Drummond (1890-1950) and his firm, Drummond & Drummond, were hired to design the buildings.[8] Plans also incorporated landscaping with distinctive trees and shrubs under the supervision of Prosper J. A. Berckmans Jr. Rock for the paving came from the city quarry, while numerous garden clubs eagerly provided trees, shrubs, and flowers.

Augusta also purchased an additional three to four acres of property from William J. "Red" Grammer,[9] a wrestling promoter, and Mrs. Sara Watkins, owner of Watkins' Store, resulting in the extension of Julian Smith Park to Broad Street and the Washington Road Bridge. Intentions for the newly acquired property included a segregated playground for children, tennis courts, volleyball courts, a wading pool, and other playground facilities.[10] Optimistically, Augusta hoped the improvements would attract thousands of annual visitors to enjoy Augusta's winter climate and golf links. "We feel that Julian Smith Park will become one of the showplaces of the Southeast when the beautification program is completed."[11]

The most costly improvement was the new casino. The rustic casino was a rambling structure built of rubble stonework with a wing of log construction. Inside the casino was a large dance floor made of polished maple, an octagonal lobby, and concession area.[12] A three-story observation tower topped off the casino, affording an unobstructed view of Lake Olmstead. A prominent orchestra shell, fashioned as a classic garden temple with a tile roof, crested by an ornamental copper finial, was erected on the second of four terraces, "commanding a view of the lake through a wooded ravine at the foot of which stands an exedra, or long semi-circular seat, or rubble masonry." Additional improvements included a bathhouse, a boathouse, and a barbecue pavilion all in a harmonious architectural style. The project employed one hundred laborers assigned by the Work Progress Administration, as well as another 125 workers laboring in landscaping and beautification.[13]

Figure 50. Laurel Lane (*Robert A. Mullins Collection*)

Improvements at Lake Olmstead were not limited to Julian Smith Park. There were also plans for a seven-acre park known as Laurel Park on the opposite side of the lake in the Lakemont subdivision. The enchanting park features an elevation drop of seventy feet over a distance of two thousand feet from its highest point to the lake. In the middle of the old-growth ravine flows a stream that emerges out of the bedrock at the top of the park and gently cascades down to the lake. Augusta planned to make the park more beautiful by a succession of waterfalls that would tumble down through the rocks and the woodland ravine.[14] Mayor Allen projected that the improvement of Julian Smith Park, in conjunction with Laurel Park, would provide Augusta with a scenic garden superseding the famous Magnolia Gardens at Charleston, South Carolina, in beauty and size.

Julian Smith Park and its newest improvements were formally dedicated on the evening of April 28, 1937, with a ceremony and dance. Former mayor Julian Smith was honored and his name forever linked to Augusta's acquisition of Lake View Park. At the dedication, Smith emphasized the restoration of Lake Olmstead to its former prominence. The freshly renovated park now boasted five distinct recreational features: a swimming area, an area for dancing and other social events, an outdoor music pavilion, a boating area, and a barbecue and picnic area. The final cost of the improvements was roughly $120,000.

Once again, hundreds of Augustans flocked to Municipal Beach for the opening of Lake Olmstead's summer season.[15] Rental fees for the casino were $2 for private parties and $5 for commercial events.[16] Given the park's enormous success, additional plans were again drawn up by the city engineer's office for construction of a new stone and log boathouse, bathhouse, and playground.

Continuing in the celebrated tradition of Lake View Park, the city sponsored numerous splendid events at Julian Smith Park. In September of 1938, the dramatic production of the "Legend of Silver Bluff" was presented on a mammoth stage constructed on the lakeshore. The colossal pageant conveyed the story of the adventures of Fernando DeSoto and his Portuguese and Castilian soldiers in their travels from Spain to Silver Bluff, South Carolina, near Augusta. Legend has it that DeSoto traveled to Silver Bluff, approximately twelve miles downriver from Augusta, looking for gold. Upon arrival, he was greeted by an Indian princess who ruled the area offering food, shelter, and canoes. Having not found gold, DeSoto soon left but took the princess hostage to ensure his safe travels. She later escaped and returned to her Indian village, Cofitachique. Told through song and dialogue, the show featured sixty-five principal characters, 175 ensemble and chorus members, and twenty singers. With Lake Olmstead as a background to the stage, the vivid sets made for a dazzling pageant.[17]

Bill Goll, a former championship swimmer and high diver, presented an exhibition on October 17, 1940. Goll was a marathon swimmer and posthumous inductee to the International Marathon Swimming Hall of Fame.[18] Among his amazing feats was swimming a quarter mile with his hands and feet tied. Another incredible feat was Goll's underwater escape from a straitjacket while in an alligator tank.

Julian Smith Park would continue to prosper over the next years. With the Municipal Beach and new casino, the park was frequently packed with throngs of patrons. The city actively brought in entertainment, such as theatrical performances and traveling exhibitions. Little did anyone know, but dramatic change was just around the corner.

XIII

Municipal Beach Closed

Julian Smith Park was in full swing during the spring of 1949, offering a variety of facilities, including the casino where couples often danced the night away and a barbecue pit and dining hall where several thousand people were served every year. The city operated a nursery at the park and invited high school bands to give concerts every Sunday at the bandstand.[1] Motorboat races and ski events attracted thousands of spectators. Everyone was anticipating the opening of Municipal Beach on May 8.

Although the year of 1949 began with much enthusiasm, it would be a year of lasting change for Lake Olmstead. Instead of welcoming swimmers to Municipal Beach for the opening of the season, the city, in a May 7 announcement, delayed the opening of the beach due to contamination of Lake Olmstead's waters.

> Opening of the city's bathing beach and bathhouse at Lake Olmstead, scheduled for today, has been postponed due to a contamination of the water in the lake . . .[2]

While Mayor William D. Jennings, a third-generation medical doctor, posted policemen at the lake to warn people of the dangerous conditions, Dr. Abe J. Davis, Richmond county health commissioner, conducted a detailed stream pollution survey of all tributaries discharging into Rae's Creek.[3] According to Dr. Davis, the main source of pollution originated in the upper reaches of Rae's Creek, the infamous creek that flows through the Augusta National Golf Course.[4]

Rae's Creek wound through an area of Augusta that had seen significant development over the previous twenty years. As the upstream areas of Rae's Creek continued to develop with Augusta's increasing population, so did issues with urban runoff, lawn fertilizers, and litter and siltation. Due to the length and size of Rae's Creek drainage basin, it was a continual threat of flooding and pollution. The creek's headwaters spring from the ground near Frontage Road and Interstate 20 in Columbia County and travel approximately ten miles through rapidly emerging urban development to Lake Olmstead.

Named after John Rae, an Irish Indian trader who came to the Augusta area in 1734, the creek was historically home to numerous grist mills, a lumber mill, and a foundry. In addition to a grist mill established by Rae, there were numerous other mills located along the creek. Lake Aumond, a ten-acre lake off Walton Way Extension, is a remnant of one of the former millponds.[5] It is located approximately three miles upstream from Lake Olmstead. The extensive Rae's Creek watershed drainage area covers over fifteen thousand acres or twenty three and a half miles or about one-sixteenth of Richmond County.

Dr. Davis's unscientific survey revealed two key sources of pollution. The main culprit was located seven miles upstream of Lake Olmstead. Apparently, several families in the vicinity of Sue Reynolds School had placed outhouses across the creek, and others had septic tanks that drained into the creek.[6] The second source was discharges from Oliver General Hospital, formerly the Forrest Hills-Ricker Hotel, located in the Forrest Hills area. Oliver General responded swiftly, announcing that it would do everything possible to eliminate discharges of any polluted water from the hospital, which might be contaminating swimming areas in Richmond County. The sewage discharges from the families in the Sue Reynolds School area, however, were more problematic as it was outside the city's jurisdiction. Before anything could be done, Mayor Jennings requested city attorney Edwin D. Fulcher to provide an opinion as to which entity, the city or the county, was the proper agency to take corrective action.[7]

In an act of unification, officials from Augusta and Richmond County conducted a series of efforts to identify and correct the pollution in the Rae's Creek Water Basin. At a combined meeting on June 9, county officials proclaimed that five minor sources of pollution between Lake Aumond and Flowing Wells had been corrected. The city also announced that it had repaired two sanitary sewers, which were discharging raw sewage into a tributary of Rae's Creek.[8]

As the ongoing pollution at Lake Olmstead persisted, Mayor Jennings declared that a new culprit had been identified. It was now believed that residential sanitary sewer lines had been illegally connected to the main storm sewer line in the Forest Hills area.[9] As a further attempt to discover the source of pollution, city, county, and state officials decided to inject dye into the sewage line in the Fox Springs Road section of Forrest Hills. Workers also visited residences whose sewage lines were presumed to be illegally connected with the storm sewer line instead of the sanitary sewer line. Meanwhile, the city and county proclaimed that if the dye method failed to identify the problem, both the city and county would share the cost of excavating the storm sewer to ascertain if sanitary sewage was flooding over into the storm sewer system.[10]

In July, Dr. Davis cheerfully proclaimed that through joint investigation and corrective measures, all human pollution had been eliminated from Lake Olmstead. On July 7, 1949, the Richmond County Board of Health authorized reopening of the Municipal Beach at Lake Olmstead, with the caveat that if the bacterial count increased beyond a safe level, the lake would be immediately closed to swimming.[11] Dr. Davis cautiously emphasized that pollution in Lake Olmstead would likely be a continuing problem and urged that plans be considered for building a swimming pool at Julian Smith Park.

Concern over pollution, however, would not prevent Julian Smith Park from having a banner year in 1949. In addition to the spring events, the city hosted dances for teenagers and soldiers every Friday night at Julian Smith Casino, except during football season. Officials estimated total attendance at Julian Smith Park for the first ten months of 1949 at 139,721.[12]

Although ongoing efforts were made to keep the lake safe, Municipal Beach did not open the next year due to dangerously high bacteria levels. Dr. Davis stated that the bacterial count in Lake Olmstead's waters was over ten times the public safety. Davis could not explain the high bacteria count other than its connection to increasing population creating sanitary hazards.

As predicted by Dr. Davis, 1949 would be the last year swimming was allowed in Lake Olmstead. Signage was placed around the lake the next year, notifying the public that the lake was unsafe for swimming. City officials, however, had their hands full as residents refused to honor the no-swimming ban. Officers were even placed at the park in an attempt to enforce the no-swimming order.

Although swimming was no longer allowed at Municipal Beach, Augustans were not daunted from the other recreational offerings of Lake Olmstead. Lakeview Gardens, a new amusement area, was opened along the shores of Lake Olmstead in 1950. Attractions included pony rides, a miniature train, a bowling alley, a small dance floor, and boats for rent. In between activities, hungry patrons could feast on various types of food, including barbecued chicken, pork and lamb hash, cold soft drinks, and ice cream. Eddie Lewis managed the park under contract with the city council.

Figure 51. Last Boathouse on Lake Olmstead, 2007 (*Robert A. Mullins Collection*)

As the years went by, water sports became more and more popular in the Central Savannah River Area (CSRA). Boat owners and ski fans were rapidly multiplying. Motorboats were so numerous on Lake Olmstead that in 1950, safety signs were posted around the lake reminding speedboat operators to observe the rights of smaller craft, being careful not to swamp them. To help avoid accidents, other signs were posted on the sides of the Lake Olmstead Bridge, instructing all boats to keep to the right when passing under the bridge.

Trendy during this time period were free concerts by the Augusta Civic Orchestra at Julian Smith Casino. Classical music would fill the air around Lake Olmstead, drawing crowds exceeding a thousand listeners.[13] During the concerts, the casino's windows were opened so that listeners could choose to hear the concert inside the casino or while sitting or strolling outside in the park. The concerts were so popular that people would often come to Julian Smith Casino with their families to listen to the orchestra practice.[14] Loudspeakers were even used to make it easier for listeners to hear while strolling around outside.[15]

XIV

A Call for Cleansing

As the lake remained closed to swimming, discussions of reopening Lake Olmstead was a hot topic of discussion for Augusta's then mayor Mayor Hugh Hamilton. Hugh Lamar Hamilton (1921-1974) was elected as one of Augusta's youngest mayor in 1952. Running as an Independent, he was only thirty-one at the time. "He was a man whose devotion to principle rose above the expediency of the moment, and was a primary factor in making his service to this city a memorable chapter in its political history."[1]

Mayor Hamilton, during a meeting with city officials and health authorities, emphasized the desire to have Lake Olmstead open for swimming by the summer of 1957. With the amount of grazing on the adjacent lands decreasing, the mayor contemplated that purification of the water might finally be possible. "If we could get the water in Lake Olmstead rendered safe for bathing, we could make the park and beach one of the finest facilities in Augusta's entire recreation setup."[2] Acknowledging that the lake was one of the city's most attractive recreation spots, the *Augusta Chronicle* emphasized the great benefits to the community if Lake Olmstead could be decontaminated for swimming by the summer of 1960.[3]

City, county, and health authorities initiated a joint effort of experimentation in hopes that the water could be cleansed. On August 14, 1956, the city appointed a committee to study ways of making the water suitable for swimming. City engineer M. P. Phillips and Dr. Abe J. Davis, Richmond county health commissioner, were tasked with leading experimentations with several methods of water purification.

Lake Olmstead was given little hope of getting its clean bill of health. A reoccurring proposal was the chlorination of Lake Olmstead. Inevitably, city officials announced that it was not practicable or feasible, moneywise or healthwise, to attempt to purify Lake Olmstead. Phillips explained that the city had explored a plan to run pipes under the lake to dispense chemicals into the water. The expense, however, was too high due to the enormous amount of chemicals necessary to keep up with the constant flow of water.

Dr. Davis offered insight into ongoing evaluation of possible solutions:

> Consultation with competent public health and water engineers has
> brought us the opinion that chlorine or its compounds would not long
> be effective in our case and they cited experiments in similar goodies of
> water, these experiments having been dismal failures.[4]

Chlorine, he pointed out, was ineffective against viruses and is so unstable that its benefit is short-lived. It is rapidly broken down by sunlight and is toxic to animals and plant life in large quantities. Other methods mentioned but deemed implausible were aeration and quaternary ammonium compounds.

In August of 1959, the Augusta League of Women Voters, led by Dr. Martha McCranie, a local child psychiatrist and professor at the Medical College of Georgia, released findings from its study of sewerage disposal in Augusta. The study indicated that the source of pollution stemmed from Rae's Creek. Engineer Phillips concurred, believing that much of the contamination was instigated by livestock grazing on pastureland above the lake on Rae's Creek.

The condition of the lake continued to deteriorate. By the 1960s, Lake Olmstead was being compared to the Brown Danube. Warning signs were posted around the lake informing residents that the water was unsafe and swimming was prohibited.

In an effort to help promote an upcoming State Water Ski Tournament on Lake Olmstead, Mayor Millard A. Beckum designated the week of August 22-28, 1960, as Water Sports Safety Week.[5] Despite warnings by County Board of Health officials, the Jaycees, under cooperation of the Augusta Ski Club, continued with the tournament. As a cautionary measure, contestants were insured for medical care arising from illness due to contaminated water.

The following year, the Augusta Junior Chamber of Commerce, led by its director and future representative in the Georgia House of Representatives, Dick Ransom, canceled its annual water ski tournament because of high bacteria levels in Lake Olmstead's waters. Instead, the Junior Chamber of Commerce opted to file a decontamination plea with governmental authorities. Dr. Davis was quoted saying, "As we have often said before, the march of civilization has long since caught up with Lake Olmstead and it is one of the minor penalties we pay for all the other blessings we now enjoy."[6] Reportedly, the police department was inspecting Lake Olmstead four to five times a day for illegal swimming.

In conjunction with their call for decontamination and civic investigation, the Jaycees issued a report detailing the lake's contamination. The report identified six sources of pollution: water from the canal back flowing into Lake Olmstead; broken sewer lines; surface disposal of human waste several miles upstream on Rae's Creek in the Pleasant Home Road Extension area; septic tank overflows in the vicinity of Lake Olmstead; dumping of septic waste tanks from service vehicles; and common waste from drainage of the watershed terrain, such as waste from livestock and pets, fertilizer, and miscellaneous refuse.[7]

A three-point solution was presented. The first recommendation was for the city of Augusta to maintain water in the canal below the level of the lake and conduct periodic inspections on the condition of sewer lines, especially those in the Rae's Creek and Lake Olmstead area. Second, the Jaycees requested Richmond County officials to eliminate surface disposal of human waste and periodically check septic tanks compliance in known trouble areas. Third, the Jaycees requested residents to report broken sewer lines, septic tank overflows, and surface disposal of human waste to the Health Department, as well as any dumping of septic tank waste by service trucks or other refuse in the watershed streams to the Sheriff's Department.

In response, city engineer Phillips was instructed by the city council to evaluate the Jaycees' recommendations and report back to the council within thirty days. Michael J. Padgett, chairman of the county commissioners, agreed to seek "wholehearted cooperation and assistance of the County Commissioners."[8] After reviewing the Jaycees' study, Phillips recommended

1. Complete sanitary sewer lines in the 12 areas around the lake that now use septic tanks. The cost to complete the sanitary sewers in the 28.8 miles was estimated at $700,000.00.

2. Clean all debris from Rae's Creek upstream from Lake Olmstead to Jackson Road.

3. Maintain constant inspection and vigilance in the watershed area to prohibit accumulation of pollution.

4. Continue checking bacteria counts at six established points and draw charts showing major points of pollution.

5. Pursue finding chemicals for treatment of the lake water.[9]

Phillips cautiously emphasized that three-fourths of the lake's drainage area was located in Richmond and Columbia Counties, outside of the city's jurisdiction. Moreover, Julian Smith Park was located on the city-county boundary. Because of these jurisdictional issues, the Jaycees requested joint participation by the city and county governments.

Recommendations were also made for the improvement of Julian Smith Park, such as restoring the band shell, adding picnic tables, landscaping, and requiring owners of boat docks and boathouses to either repair them or tear them down. Other recommendations included hiring a night watchman or increase police coverage to twenty-four hours a day for surveillance of the park, clear and maintain the wooded areas, establish gardens, cover unsightly fill material, beautify the north shore road bank, and prohibit dumping of trash on the lakeshore. Several months later in March 1962, the city council launched a baby step toward beautifying the park by approving $3,800 for installation of a sprinkler system.

In 1964, the Junior Chamber of Commerce released yet another report on Lake Olmstead and Julian Smith Park. In its 1964 report, the Jaycees accentuated the spectacular potential of Lake Olmstead. Augusta had the raw materials for a park and tourist attraction paralleling Cypress Gardens. The eventual result would not only be a productive business investment but a haven of beauty and recreation for Augusta area residents. Mr. Ransom declared that even greater promise for early improvement lies in the areas of park beautification and water-ski-show development.[10] The Jaycees proposed that the city or Chamber of Commerce subsidize weekly or biweekly ski shows by the Augusta Ski Club.

After a local television station, WJBF-TV, successfully pulled off a 1965 ski show, earning rave notices from the thousands of viewers who lined the shore, accusations flew at city officials for not taking a more aggressive stance on remedying the city's no. 1 eyesore. "That ugly word, pollution, has made the headlines in Augusta again and as usual, officials with authority have turned their heads the other way."[11] Even with the knowledge that Lake Olmstead was polluted, unsafe for skiing or swimming, city officials took a "swim, boat, and ski at your own risk" attitude. Dr. Davis reportedly shrugged his shoulders and said, "The water does not meet accepted standards for swimming and skiing. In fact, the standards miss acceptance by a mile—by 10 miles."[12]

In 1966, Augustans identified the overgrowth and pollution of Lake Olmstead as one of the three most chronic situations in the city.[13] Even in 1967, there were reports that a storm sewer was discharging into the lagoon between the old and new Washington Road bridges.[14] By the next decade, Lake Olmstead was described as "a king-size commode and garbage disposal." Earl A. Burch Jr. commented,

> There are places where human waste and garbage can be seen floating toward the lake. Augusta likes to think of itself as the "Garden City," but as long as Lake Olmstead remains in its present condition, I'll refer to Augusta as the "garbage city."[15]

Even with swelling public interest in cleansing the lake during the last twenty years, water quality continued to deteriorate. Lake Olmstead was disgracefully trashy.

XV

Motorboat Racing

I t wasn't long after Ford's Model T or Tin Lizzie arrived in 1908, making the automobile affordable for middle-class Americans, that motorboats arrived on the scene. One of the first Augustans to own a motorboat was Frank Bussey. In 1911, Frank Bussey and Will Lester set off in Bussey's boat, the *Wild Cat*, powered by an eighteen-horsepower gasoline engine for a three-week hunting trip down the Savannah River in route to Charleston, South Carolina.[1]

Ole Evinrude revolutionized the motorboat industry when he designed one of the most successful early outboard motors in 1909. His wife, Bess, helped launch his advertising campaign with the slogan "Don't row! Throw away those oars! Use an Evinrude motor!"[2] Between 1909 and 1912, Evinrude sold thousands of his outboard motors.

Louis C. Edelblut and Eugene Murphy, a.k.a. Edelblut and Murphy, began selling Evinrude motors in Augusta by 1919.[3] Within years, Lake Olmstead had become a motorboat haven, hosting frequent speedboat races. In October 1927, two speedboat racers synonymous with Lake Olmstead launched their speedy craft on the lake. Carl Edelblut (1898-1979), son of Louis Edelblut, set a record for light watercraft on Lake Olmstead, piloting his fourteen-foot hydroplane at a speed of thirty miles an hour.[4] Terris Christie, a local mechanic, demonstrated Scooter, his twelve-foot hydroplane equipped with a four-horsepower motor, at a speed of twenty-two miles per hour.

Augusta Outboard Motor Club and Early Racers

A year later, in 1928, local motorboat enthusiasts organized the Augusta Outboard Motor Club and joined the Chicago-based American Outboard Motor Association.[5] Shortly after organizing, the club rented a clubhouse from one of its members, Hollis Boardman, on nearby Bath Lake, a 285-acre lake in Aiken County, South Carolina. The club sponsored racing and trips on several water bodies, including the Savannah River, Lake Olmstead, and Bath Lake.

Carl Edelblut was elected as the first president of the Augusta Outboard Motor Club.[6] As previously mentioned, Carl was the son of Louis Edelblut, one of the earliest retailers of outboard motors in the Augusta area. Carl worked with his father and subsequently took over his Evinrude franchise. Edelblut had a fun-loving disposition and was notorious for thrilling children at Camp Kiwanis when he would appear with his motorboat and surfboard to pull campers up and down Lake Langley.[7] He also had the remarkable opportunity to have his photograph taken with baseball great Ty Cobb. When Ole Evinrude came out with a new motor in 1921 named the Champion, it sought to have current sports champions endorse the new product. Ty Cobb, dressed in hunting togs and carrying a shotgun, posed with Edelblut for the endorsement photograph.

Herman G. Sheats (1883-1955) was elected vice president. Sheats was a graduate dentist and managed the first sports department in J. B. Whites before going to work with his brother-in-law Thomas Y. Rabb at the Augusta Sporting Goods Company. Along with Simpson O. Houck, Rabb founded Augusta Sporting Goods in 1926. Augusta Sporting Goods would be a significant sponsor of motorboat racing in Augusta.

Augusta native Charles W. Bowen Jr. (1902-1974) was elected as secretary and treasurer. Bowen was a commercial real estate broker and served as president of his family's business, Bowen Brothers Hardware. Called to civic duty, Bowen was a member of the Bell Auditorium Commission, City Tax Board, and the Zoning and Appeals Commission. Bowen Brothers Hardware and Charles Bowen Jr., similar to Augusta Sporting Goods, would also play an important role in motorboat racing in Augusta.

In addition to the officers, Edgar Raines, Terris Christie, and George W. Tidwell were elected as directors of the club. W. Edgar Raines was elected chairman of the board of directors. Raines came to Augusta from Jefferson County, Georgia, to enter the contracting business. He was an extremely active young man, who at the age of twenty-six was elected president of the Augusta Christian Endeavor Union and the statewide Georgia Christian Endeavor Union in 1928. Raines was subsequently elected from the Independent Party platform to the city council in 1949, where he chaired the waterworks and finance committees. Raines was also a leader in the Red Cross, serving as the big business chairman, and an executive board member of the local YMCA.[8]

George W. Tidwell Jr., after moving to Augusta with his family from Tennessee, wound up in the printing business as a cofounder of Ridgeley-Wing-Tidwell Printers in 1913. The business would survive over ninety years. Tidwell was a frequent early motorboat racer in the late '20s and '30s and spurned a long line of motorboat enthusiasts. Years later in 1951, George's son, Ted Tidwell, who learned how to race on Lake Olmstead, would capture the South Carolina State B Hydroplane Championship.[9] Ted's son, Martin Tidwell, would carry on the family tradition as a major contender in regional and national motorboat racing.

F. Terris Christie, a local mechanic, was also an avid racer. He was one of the first motorboat racers to display his racing skills on Lake Olmstead. Christie, piloting his speedy craft, *Chief*, would win numerous local events during the late '20s and early '30s.

There are numerous other racers synonymous with motorboat racing on Lake Olmstead. Fred B. "Barney" Smith was one of the most successful early racers. Barney grew up hunting and fishing on the Savannah River. Over time, he made friends with Captain Rouse, the steamboat pilot for the Altamaha that traveled between Augusta and Savannah. Barney would often share his spoils with Captain Rouse, and Rouse would reciprocate by giving Smith a ride back to town from his downstream adventures. Barney started racing in his early twenties. After winning several major races, Evinrude awarded Smith the franchise for the Augusta area.

Another of the early racers was Augusta native and all-around athlete Reggie M. Dales. In high school, Reggie was the city champion all-around swimmer of the public schools. Dales also won the gold medal in the local Senior International Hexathlon Athletic Contest in April 1922.[10] Reggie worked as a general manager for the Merry Shipping Company and operated a sand and gravel company on the Savannah River for years, hauling materials on his barges up and down the Savannah River.[11] He was a pioneer and leading figure in the utilization of the Savannah River.

Walker Inman, another member of the Augusta Outboard Motor Club, was a frequent racer. Inman was also an avid golfer. Walker Inman and golf legend Bobby Jones were not only in college together at Georgia Tech, but they were fraternity brothers. Inman's son, Walker Jr., was just the second Augusta native to compete in the Masters golf tournament, which he did after being invited by Bobby Jones. Walker Jr. remembers exactly where he was standing when he first saw Jones. Jones said to his dad, "Is this your son, Walker?"

Jones put his hand on Walker's head and said, "Walker, are you going to be a golfer like your daddy?"

Walker said, "No, sir, Mr. Jones. I want to be a golfer like you."[12]

Walker Jr. went on to compete in nine US Opens and six PGA Championships.

Then there were the Holman brothers, Marsden F. Holman (1902-1963) and W. Herbert Holman (1905-1959). Both grew up in Augusta, sons of William Fessenden Holman, who operated one of the oldest retail meat markets in downtown Augusta. Herbert worked as a salesman for Armour and Company and was a leader in the Exchange Club. Marsden worked for the power company and later served as chairman of the Jenkins County Defense Council, utilities committee. Both were active in early motorboat racing in Augusta.

Another set of brothers would be active in later years, Harold Bateman and Charles W. Bateman. Harold was active in motorboat racing until he finally called it quits at age 58. Harold recalls, "My brother, C. W. Bateman, got me started in it while he was racing. I'd always been a pretty good mechanic, so one day he asked me to work on his outboard. I asked him, 'Where's the manual?' Of course, there wasn't one for his souped-up motor, so I learned to work on them from scratch."[13]

Figure 52. Harold Bateman (*Travis Bateman Collection*)

Racing Classifications

Early motorboat races were divided into several different motor classifications and racing divisions. The rules governing outboard motor competition defined Class A motors as under fourteen cubic inches piston displacement, Class B as fourteen cubic inches and under twenty piston displacement, and Class C as twenty cubic inches and under thirty piston displacement. Class B motors were typically capable of speeds up to thirty miles per hour. Class C motors were typically able to achieve speeds of thirty-five miles per hour. Class D motors were defined as thirty cubic inches and under thirty piston displacement. Class D motors were larger and heavier and able to achieve about thirty-eight miles per hour. There was also a larger size "E" motor, a Johnson Giant Twin with a forty-nine-cubic-inch piston displacement capable of obtaining speeds of forty-five miles per hour.[14]

In addition to the motor classifications, motorboat racing was typically divided into at least two different racing divisions. Division I, or the Amateur Division, required the boats and motors to be owned and driven by an amateur using a stock motor. On the other hand, Division II, or the Free-for-All Division, had no ownership restrictions. The usual restrictions as to piston displacement, stock motors, and nonspecial parts, however, still applied. A stock motor was defined as one that has been advertised and offered for sale to the general public at least thirty days prior to a race. At least twenty-five motors of identical design and assembly must have been manufactured and delivered prior to the race to qualify as a stock motor.

Savannah River Marathon Race

The most infamous motorboat race in Augusta history was the 1928 Savannah River Marathon Race, which took place on Aug. 15, 1928. The 202-mile race from Augusta's Fifth Street dock to the Bull Street dock in Savannah received widespread national publicity. A newsreel company sent representatives to take pictures of the racers as they left the Municipal Wharf in Augusta and followed the progress of the race downstream from an airplane.[15] The race, sanctioned by the American Outboard Motor Association, featured fifteen entries, including four Class B entries, nine Class C entries, one Class D entry, and one Class E entry. At Cohen's Bluff, approximately halfway, the racers were required to make a thirty-minute compulsory stop.[16]

Augusta entries in the race included a number of well-known racers. Augusta native Hollis Boardman Jr. (1899-1943) entered the race with the *Bullet* powered by a Johnson Giant Twin motor. Hollis was sponsored by the People's Oil Company, Augusta's first independent oil company, which was started by Hollis's father in 1904. Hollis would carry on the family tradition, and later the People's Oil Co. would grow into Boardman Petroleum and own a chain of over seventy Smile gas stations.

Carl Sumerau, another Augusta native, was a daring speedboat racer. He entered the race piloting the *Spirit of Augusta*, equipped with a Johnson Giant Twin engine. Sumerau was sponsored by his employer, Bowen Brothers Hardware.

Barney Smith entered the race with his boat, a thirteen-foot mahogany-hulled Boyd-Martin step-plane, which he aptly named *Lightning*. The boat was powered by an ELTO Quad engine, another motor designed by Ole Evinrude. The ELTO motor was made extensively with lightweight aluminum and weighed one-third less than Evinrude's best-selling (single cylinder) model and produced 50 percent more power. Smith made a deal with Augusta Sporting Goods to carry its name on his boat if the store would underwrite his entry fee. Smith's entry was aptly named the *Augusta Sporters*.

W. J. Griffin entered the race piloting the *Spirit of Atlanta*. Griffin worked for the Johnson Motor Company, so naturally, his boat was propelled by a new model Johnson Giant Twin. Marsden Holman drove *Miss Quaker State*, sponsored by

Quaker State Oil Company. Holman's boat was powered by an Evinrude motor. Terris Christie piloted *Chief*, equipped with a Lockwood motor and sponsored by the Augusta Outboard Motor Club. Reggie Dales also entered the race, sponsoring himself.

The weather for the race was anything but perfect. The front-page headline in the *Augusta Chronicle* the next day read FLOODS MENACE GEORGIA.[17] The remnants of a tropical storm were making their way through the area and were the second major storm to hit the area within a week. The heavy rain was so bad the morning of the race that the race began almost an hour after the scheduled 6:00 a.m. departure from the municipal wharf. Pilots were covering their engines to dry them out so they would start. Heavy rain fell throughout the morning, and a stiff wind out of the east made a choppy sea out of the Savannah River. The river, which had been swollen by recent rains, was littered with logs and driftwood.

A little after 7:00 a.m., the official race announcer and newly elected officer of the Augusta Outboard Motor Club, Charles "Charlie" Bowen Jr., waved the start flag. The Class B boats, with motors wide open, sped beneath the Fifth Street Bridge, followed shortly by the Class C boats. Last but not least came the Free-for-All high-powered boat entries, piloted by Barney Smith and W. J. Griffin.

Smith and his rival Griffin raced down the river at breakneck speed for about eighty miles, with both boats running neck and neck. Smith, however, had trouble at Shell Bluff when he sheared a pin. While he stopped to fix his motor, Griffin forged ahead gaining a two-mile advantage. Smith followed behind Griffin for nearly an hour before catching him near Cohen's Bluff. Leaving the mandatory midway stop location, Smith again experienced trouble when he reached Little Hell, about eighty-five miles down the river. In an attempt to avoid a huge floating tree, he dived into a bunch of willow trees, and his boat plunged into a muddy bank and sheared yet another pin.

Smith, however, would not lose the lead. Griffin suffered fatal engine trouble when his motor struck a log about seventy-five miles down the river, breaking the gear unit and putting Griffin out of commission. Griffin, conscious of potential mechanical problems, carried a small backup motor just in case of such trouble. Although he was unable to finish the race, he put the backup motor on his boat and assisted another racer, Lucius Whittle of Brunswick, Georgia, who also experienced mechanical problems, towing Lucius and his distressed boat to Cohen's Bluff. Griffin and Whittle would slowly continue to make their way to Savannah in Griffin's crippled craft, the *Spirit of Atlanta*.

Smith remained on task. On arriving in Savannah, Smith narrowly escaped being thrown into the water when his little race boat was nearly swamped by the wake from several passing tugboats. Smith recalled, "[T]here was a tugboat running full speed and I was caught by its wake. I bounced past and my boat took on some water, but not enough to swamp me. I had been running that motor wide open since I left Augusta, stopping only to change shear pins and props twice."[18]

Smith crossed the finish line in Savannah at 2:10 p.m. Smith, not being certain where the race terminated, circled the river as far down as the Atlantic Coast Line Wharf, a mile and a half seaward of the finish line, to be certain he had passed his goal. Not expecting that any of the boats would be in before three thirty or four o'clock, only a handful of people were on hand when the leader flashed by the wharf. Smith recalled that there was a flag on a mast marking the finish line, "but it had rained hard that day and the flag was drooping. I never saw it. But as I roared past, I saw a lot of folks waving, so I turned around and came back to where they were standing."[19]

Twenty-five-year-old F. Barney Smith of Augusta had not only won the Augusta-to-Savannah race by completing the 202-mile run from Augusta's Fifth Street dock to the Bull Street dock in Savannah in six hours and three minutes, he had also set a world record that still stood as late as 1972. His average speed was reported at 32.6 miles per hour.[20] Smith, a onetime professional hunting guide, captured the silver trophy offered by the *Augusta Chronicle* for crossing the finish line first.

The next boat to cross the finish line was *Miss Quaker State*, piloted by Marsden Holman, one hour and seventeen minutes after Smith crossed the finish line. Holman won first place for the Class C entrants with an average speed of 26.8 miles per hour. The Savannah entry, *the City of Savannah*, finished in second place. C. R. Culler of Orangeburg, South Carolina, piloting the *City of Orangeburg*, finished in third place at 3:45 p.m. He captured first place for the Class B entries with his boat powered by a Johnson motor. Terris Christie was second in the Class B division, followed by Pete Culler, also of Orangeburg, South Carolina. Unfortunately for Augustan E. A. Kelly, he and his boat, the *Pan Am*, were unable to complete the race when he burned out a spark plug.

During an interview published forty-four years later in the *Augusta Chronicle*, Smith shared his recollection of his marathon run. Prior to the race, Smith had tested various propellers to see which would push the boat the fastest. He mounted a Dodge twenty-five-gallon gasoline tank on his boat and equipped it with two hand-operated pressure pumps. Therefore, if one broke, he had a backup. He also removed the muffler from the motor, increasing the noise but giving his boat a little more speed. Smith practiced until he became adept at changing shear pins while sitting in the narrow cockpit of his craft. After the race, Dick Pope, vice president of the American Outboard Association, telegraphed Smith that his time "was a world record for the distance." Consequently, Evinrude and Elto awarded Smith a franchise for the Augusta area.

Racing on Lake Olmstead

On Labor Day, September 3, 1928, a couple of weeks after the Savannah River Marathon, the Augusta Outboard Motor Club held its first reported motorboat race on Lake Olmstead. The races included four events on the half-mile lake course and were presented in combination with two baseball games between the Augusta Tygers and the Ashville Tourists. Leonard Bassford, a founding member and officer of the Richmond County Game and Fish Conservation Club and once head of the old Georgia Game and Fish Commission, won the 1928 Labor Day Race.[21] Perhaps similarly exciting, Bassford once took golfing legend Bobby Jones out on Lake Olmstead in his cruiser.

Motorboat racing was firmly entranced during the '30s. Typically, racing events coincided with the summer holidays of Memorial Day, Independence Day, and Labor Day. In 1933, motorboat races were held at Lake Olmstead on July 4, August 6, and Labor Day. The Independence Day races, however, had to clash with what was the coldest July 4 in the history of Augusta.[22] The morning low was sixty-one degrees, and thirty-miles-per-hour gale winds blew in from the Northeast. The cool weather, however, did not dampen the electrifying races. Drivers such as Rut Whaley, Charles Goodwin, Buck Ergle, John W. Collier, Jimmy Stafford, Frank Peters, Bum Holliday, and Terris Christie competed in a three-mile Class B event and a ten-mile Free-for-All race in hopes of taking home the Bowen Brothers Hardware and R. L. Sumerau & Son awards.[23]

The August 6 races were advocated as a buildup to the upcoming Labor Day races in the *Augusta Chronicle*.

> While thrill piled on top of near-collisions and spills yesterday afternoon at Lake Olmstead, Carl Edelblut and Terris Christy led more than 20 speedboats under the wire in two 10-mile races to give Augusta a taste of what it can expect in the way of aquatics entertainment from the coming Labor Day races.[24]

At the August 6 races, Carl Edelblut won the opening Class B ten-mile event by a half-length over Charles Goodwin, who barely managed to nose out J. W. Collier for second place. In Class C, Terris Christie, driving the original *Rocket*, scored a close first over Barney Smith in his *Wildcat*. Jimmy Stafford placed third. Bum Holliday was in the running until he rounded a turn and nearly collided with Christie.

As billed, the Labor Day races were the major race of the summer, featuring both amateur and professional racers. Some of the best-known racers in Augusta entered their boats. Prior to the races, the drivers did not know how much prize money the winners would take home. Prize money was partially raised from the competitors' entrance fees with the remainder of the prize money collected from the race day crowd. The contestants, however, were so fervent about the upcoming races that virtually every competitor ran trial runs on the race course just prior to the big Labor Day races.

Four of the top local speedsters registered for the Class C ten-mile race: Barney Smith, winner of the recent Savannah River Marathon Race; Bum Holliday, who made a strong bid for the July 4 Free-for-All at Bath Lake until he almost wrecked; and two Fourth of July winners, Terris Christie and John W. Collier. Eight competitors entered the Class B ten-mile race, including Barney Smith, Bum Holliday, Terris Christie, Jimmy Stafford, Charles Goodwin, Frank Peters, Pew Martin, and Carl Edelblut.[25]

When race day arrived, Holliday seized first place in the Class C ten-mile Free-for-All. Smith grasped second place, and Christie third place.[26] Charles Goodwin (1909-1944), employed by the McGowen Printing Company, came in first in the Class B race, with Barney Smith close behind. Charles, also a gifted skeet shooter, was the son of R. Roy Goodwin, former president of the Lakeside Boat Club.[27] Pew Martin thrilled the crowd when his powerful craft overturned as it rounded a buoy at full speed, throwing Pew into the water.

In between the morning amateur races and the professional races in the afternoon, renowned professional speedboater and fireman from Barnwell, South Carolina,[28] Lloyd Plexico, staged two impromptu demonstrations of the world's fastest speedboat, with a capacity of traveling eighty miles per hour.[29] Although he did not enter the races, Plexico installed an identical motor in his special-designed hull to that of the world's record holder. Plexico skimmed the waters of Lake Olmstead faster than anyone else had previously done, at more than thirty miles per hour.

Spectators crammed Julian Smith Park and the Municipal Beach for next year's July 4 races. Sponsored by the American Legion and the Augusta Outboard Motor Club, many of the same racers competed, but perhaps the most fascinating historical aspect was the list of prizes, including items such as

- $1 in trade (Marks Drug Company);
- one gallon of Gladdin Aladdin Jar (Bowen Brothers Hardware Company);
- one quart of Spar varnish (Whaley Brothers Building Material);
- one stylish leather belt (C. C. Farr and Company, Clothiers);
- free barber service for one month (McDaniel Barber Shop);
- oil change and grease job (Everyready Battery and Tire Service);
- a set of four Champion spark plugs (Motor Supply Company);
- valuable prize to be announced later (Bearing and Parts Company);
- one hundred raised-letter visiting cards (R. G. McGowan and Company);
- two memberships, one for all summer and the other for one month (YMCA); and
- one wash, one grease, and five gallons of Woco Pep (Reesex Service Station).[30]

Winners of some of these priceless prizes included Bum Holliday, winner of the Class C Free-for-All ten-mile race and James A. Stafford, victor in the Class B ten-mile race.[31] Barney Smith was a crowd rouser, enthralling the lake-lining spectators when his boat actually left the water during some of his dramatic turns.

Popularity of motorboat racing continued to escalate. An estimated 6,500 spectators witnessed the 1935 July 4 races.[32] Frank Peters, an early racer on Lake Olmstead, recalled that large crowds would engulf Lake Olmstead each Sunday afternoon when the Augusta Outboard Boating Club held races.[33] Crowds were so large that people would be parked all the way around the lake. With the huge crowd lining the shores of Lake Olmstead, Charles Goodwin took first place in the Class B race followed by Bum Holliday.

The crowd was not as large, but next year's event was a tremendous success. Approximately two thousand persons celebrated Augusta's Independence Day Aquatic Carnival at Municipal Beach. The carnival included swimming and diving events, a swimsuit contest, and boat races, giving Augustans an afternoon of excitement, thrills, and pleasure.[34] The day-long activities began with a swimming competition for boys and ended with an eight-mile race between six of Augusta's fastest speedboats. Anxious excitement filled the air when Terris Christie, zipping across the water at thirty miles per hour, overturned on the last lap while rounding a buoy. Auspiciously, Christie had to be rescued by his fellow contender John W. Collier. Far in the lead when his rivals overturned, Bum Holliday continued the race, oblivious of the calamity and easily secured first place. Trailing Bum by several lengths was Duke Goodwin. Otis Hitt captured third place.

While baseball, motorboat racing, and golf headlined Augusta's Memorial Day sports program in 1937, the July 5 Independence Day celebration was headlined by aquatic events and speedboat racing. Hundreds of Augustans witnessed the belated festival at Lake Olmstead.[35] An array of thirteen of the area's preeminent outboard motorboat pilots sped around the one-mile lake course in three different races. Jimmy Brown captured first place in the Class B event followed by Frank Peters, James Livingston, and J. C. Thomas. In the Class C event, Barney Smith finished first, followed by Dan Henderson, Morris Rock, and J. C. Thomas. Charles Goodwin was the big winner of the day, winning the Free-for-All event. Robert Goodwin finished second, pursued closely by Barney Smith and Bum Holliday.[36] In between the races, hundreds of spectators escaped the heat by cooling off in the lake's chilly waters. The annual bathing beauty contest climaxed the day of stupendous events. Fifteen-year-old Evelyn Bennett was unanimously chosen as the most beautiful.

Several months later, Lake Olmstead was again turned into a choppy sea during the Labor Day races of 1937. Out-of-town racers, including several professional speedboat racers, competed for a share of the substantial cash purses offered. Perennial local speedboat veterans competing included Barney Smith, Bum Holliday, and Charles Goodwin. Claude Smith of Atlanta, Georgia, took first

place in the Professional Class C race.[37] Bum Holliday won the Class C event for
locals, followed by Robert Goodwin, and Morris Rock. Bum also won the Class B
event with Wyman Tyler securing second place and Dan Henderson, third place.
The Free-for-All event between local and professional drivers was dominated by
Augusta's out-of-town guests.[38]

The crowd at the July 4 races in 1939 was larger than ever. The estimated
eight thousand spectators were electrified by the thrilling, spilling boat races and
stunts. Traffic jams around the lake and in the surrounding neighborhoods were
so numerous that hundreds of spectators were unable to find parking in time
to see the races. Wyman Tyler captured first place in the Class C event, followed
by Gordon Beard, Morris Rock, and Barney Smith.[39] J. C. Thomas, who had just
recently established a new speed record on Lake Olmstead, triumphed in the
Free-for-All race. Several months earlier, J. C. Thomas navigated the mile course
at Lake Olmstead in sixty seven and a half seconds for the new record.[40] His speed
was clocked at 53.5 miles per hour.

Numerous daring speedboat exhibitions, such as speeding through a hoop
of fire and a tricky boat leap by veteran pilot Frank Peters, supplemented the
electrifying races. The crowd also enjoyed aquaplaning, a runabout race, and a
parade of speedboats. Perhaps the most attention-grabbing event, however, was
the balloon race. Gordon Beard's feat of bursting eight of the fourteen inflated
balloons buoyed in the lake as his craft zoomed by gave him first place. Bum
Holliday took second place, popping six of fourteen balloons.

Another memorable Fourth of July was enjoyed by thousands of Augustans
at Lake Olmstead the following year. Highlighting the day, as was becoming
customary, were the motorboat races. The races, sponsored by the Augusta
Jaycees and Junior Chamber of Commerce, again incorporated numerous events
for thrill-seeking spectators. Following the races monopolized by three veterans,
Bum Holliday, Wyman Tyler, and Morris Rock, the crowds were elated by a stirring
air show produced by Buck Newton, the local Southern Airways manager.[41] As
nightfall settled in on Lake Olmstead, an enormous two-hour fireworks display
entertained the crowd, followed by a dance at Julian Smith Casino to round out
the program.

Figure 53. The Weasel, built by the Studebaker Company, was introduced in 1942
as an all terrain military vehicle and could travel four miles an hour in water.

Due to World War II, the annual boat races were canceled in an effort to
conserve gasoline for the war program. Instead, Lake Olmstead became home to
numerous military exhibitions. As a way to raise capital, the Third Cavalry Unit
stationed at Camp Gordon gave rides in amphibian jeeps and military vehicles
during the weekend of July 25, 1943, to each of the 1,400 people who had
purchased war bonds during the previous week's drive conducted by the Exchange
Club and the Third Cavalry. The crowd was so large that the Third Cavalry
returned the following Sunday to ensure everyone got a ride. Demonstrations were
also given by a fully armed troop. A couple of years later, the local army recruiting
detail presented demonstrations of army tanks and amphibious personnel carriers,
commonly known as weasels.[42]

Motorboat racing returned to Lake Olmstead in 1948. The July 11 motorboat
races must have been a spectacular sight, featuring over fifty motorboats and
crowds estimated in the thousands. Leonard Casella walked away with the main
event, a three-mile Free-for-All race.[43] Leonard Casella, a jeweler by trade and an
owner of Casella Jewelers, had been on the speedboat racing circuit for years.
Interestingly, when he started his jewelry business, he leased space at Bowen
Brothers Hardware Company, another staunch advocate of motorboat racing.[44]

Figure 54. Motorboat racing on Lake Olmstead during the 50s (*Joe Casella Collection*)

In February 1952, the Augusta Outboard Boating Club voted to join the South Carolina Power Boat Federation, and within the next couple of months, Lake Olmstead hosted its first Southern Power Boat Association race on April 13, 1952. Lake Olmstead saw competitors from Georgia, South Carolina, Florida, and Alabama racing over its waters in the first race of the season.[45] Even though the races were dominated by out-of-town entries, hometown racer Arthur Blitch made an enthusiastic showing for Augusta, winning both the Class A and Class B Hydroplanes events. Augustans Billy Murphy and Albert Gormley finished behind Melvin Little of Newton, North Carolina, in the Class A Runabouts. Joe Dykes and Earl Barton of Augusta finished second in both of their respective Class D Runabout and Class D Hydroplane events.[46] Another racer from Lenoir took honors in the Free-for-All event, Abe Ellis. Joe Dykes took bronze.

The second race of the season was held in July. Races were featured in the Class A, B, and D utility runabouts and hydroplanes classifications, plus a free-for-all dash. John Danner emerged victorious in the Class A Runabout event.[47] Alfred Gormley captured the Class B Runabout race,[48] while H. G. Rosier took gold in the Class A Hydroplane race.[49] In the Class B Hydroplane race and Free-for-All Dash, it was Billy Sligh who took first-place honors.[50]

The June 14, 1953, races were even larger. The event, sanctioned by the American and Southern Power Boat Association, and cosponsored by the Augusta Outboard Racing Association, the Augusta Recreation Department and the civic clubs of Waynesboro, included approximately one hundred boats competing on Lake Olmstead in a seven-race program.[51] Waynesboro hoped to raise money to build a community swimming pool, and the association wanted funds to build a small clubhouse on Lake Olmstead.

Motorboat racing on Lake Olmstead would soon dwindle with the completion of nearby Clark Hill Lake and advent of river racing. Racing on Lake Olmstead soon became an artifact of history.

Fastest Recorded Speed

The honor of the fastest recorded speed on Lake Olmstead was earned by Rick Magretto when he and his 1961 eighteen-foot Brendella River Race Flat Class Drag Boat hit speeds of 119 miles per hour. Magretto negotiated several quarter-mile exhibition runs at Lake Olmstead in preparation for the US Drag Boat Association Miller Southern Nationals held June 1-2, 1961, at Wildwood Park on Clark Hill Lake. During one of his runs at Lake Olmstead, he took the *Augusta Chronicle* outdoor editor, Bill Baab, on a ride of his life. Baab described the ride as nothing but exhilarating.

> The veteran drag racer put the engine in gear and with a slight jolt, started off at a slow pace. He pressed the foot pedal to the metal and I felt an incredible surge of power. At 200 feet down the lake, most of the front end of the boat was in the air.
>
> Gravity pushed my body into the padded seat, my eyes into their sockets and the rush of air distended my cheeks like an overfed chipmunk's. My right hand clutched the handle. I am not certain what my left hand was doing. My eyes focused through a misty blur partly caused by a light rain and saw Broad Street moving toward me at express train speed. Magretto throttled back, abruptly ending my debut on the fast lane.[52]

Magretto apologized to Baab that he couldn't push his boat wide open, but there just was not enough room on Lake Olmstead.

XVI

Water Skiing

Figure 55. Bobby Harbin (*Spears Family Collection*)

Lake Olmstead boasts a rich history of water skiing and was home to several of Augusta's professional water skiers. Augusta's skiers were fierce competitors and outstanding performers. Water ski shows and competitions became extremely popular in the '50s, as water skiing transitioned from a hobby into a national sport. Between the late '40s and early '90s, Lake Olmstead would host numerous ski shows and competitions. The lake also served as a training location for members of the Augusta Ski Club, often seen rehearsing on Lake Olmstead.

The most renowned ski event on Lake Olmstead, still remembered by Augustans, was the Coors Light Augusta International Water Ski Classic held in

157

1986. The tournament was one of eight on the pro ski tour and was taped by ESPN for delayed national showing. To understand the rich history of water skiing on Lake Olmstead, one needs to meet several of the skiers and recount some of the astonishing ski shows.

Although skiers are occasionally seen on the lake today, in the early 1990s, most of the water skiers and clubs relocated from Lake Olmstead due to shallow waters and sandbars created from flooding from Rae's Creek. Subsequent dredging of the lake helped the situation, but silt buildup continues to occur. It is hopeful that with additional dredging, skiing might return to Lake Olmstead. For now, however, we have memories of the past.

Ski Shows

For years, Augustans were treated to spectacular water ski shows during the summer months at Lake Olmstead. Shows ranged from local ski clubs to nationally touring water ski shows.

Guy Scott and Marie Bohler

One of the first water ski shows in the Augusta area took place on Lake Olmstead in 1949. In late May, Augustans were treated to Guy Scott and his Guy Scott Water Ski Follies in a show sponsored by the Augusta Shrine Club and City Recreation Department.[1] The Follies were a nationwide traveling water ski show that included six bathing beauties and eight male skiers performing tricks and amazing demonstrations. During their two-hour performance, the skiers performed ballets and tango dance routines, ski pyramids, and leaps through flaming walls of fire while skiing at sixty miles per hour. Wherever they performed, fans flocked to see them. For instance, the Memorial Day weekend performance by the Guy Scott Water Ski Follies packed in an estimated five thousand spectators for two performances at Cross Lake in Shreveport, Louisiana.[2] Augusta was prepared for the anticipated throngs of spectators with police sheriff deputies and MPs from Fort Gordon on hand to assist with crowd control. The crowd was so enormous that officials prohibited automobiles inside the park or boats anywhere on the lake.

A big break came to one local skier, Marie Bohler, during the Guy Scott Water Ski Follies. Ms. Bohler, a recent graduate of Mt. St. Joseph Academy, worked at the Augusta Chronicle writing a "Society Chatter" and "Shopping with Cecelia" column. Bohler was sitting at her desk at the Richmond Hotel, performing her duties as secretary for the Kiwanis Club, when Guy Scott and his entourage checked in before their show. Overhearing Scott inquire whether any local girl could water ski, Ms. Bohler spoke up and said she knew how. Although she lived on Lake Olmstead, she had only started skiing a year earlier when her uncle, George "Buster" Bohler, anchored his boat on the lake. Mr. Scott invited Bohler to exhibit her skills during the Follies practice routines. Not only did Ms. Bohler show off her skills, but she also performed so well that Scott signed her up as a member of his Ski Follies Troupe, and out on tour she went.

Buster Bohler's Water Ski Troupe

A year after Ms. Marie Bohler had been discovered by Guy Scott and the Guy Scott Water Ski Follies, Augustans were treated to her uncle's water ski troupe. Buster Bohler's Water Ski Troupe was often referred to as one of the best amateur water ski troupe this side of Cypress Gardens.[3] Buster was not only an expert skier but also a champion swimmer. As mentioned elsewhere, he swam the five-hundred-yard course at Lake Olmstead in eight minutes, twenty-nine seconds in 1931, winning first place in the main event of the swim meet sponsored by Councilman A. D. Tobin at the Municipal Beach.

Bohler's troupe performed exciting exhibitions, including a repertoire of three water gymnastic acts during the annual motorboat races.[4] Featured in this group was the cute Connie Tabb, who was quickly emerging as one of the most skilled female skiers in the Augusta area.[5] Like Buster, Connie also lived on Lake Olmstead and had other amazing talents. For example, Connie, along with Butch Mulherin, won the prize waltz at the Southern Belle Ball for high school social dancing classes in 1948.[6]

The first act featured a review of the colors by Jim Hodge, Lillian Bohler, Connie Tabb, Lib Hodge, and Ruth Sheppard, followed by crisscrossing of Buddy Hunter, Jim Hodge, and Richard Bowles. The second act consisted of precision plus routines featuring Lillian Bohler and Connie Tabb. The thrilling routine included a ski salute, a water ballet on one skis, no-hands skiing on one ski, and holding towrope with foot. It also featured a Gorgeous George clown act. The final act featured a topside tandem featuring Buddy Hunter and Connie Tabb, a one-hand, one-foot exhibition featuring Jim Hodge, and a backward swan on one ski featuring Connie Tabb.[7]

Figure 56. Ski Pyramid on Lake Olmstead (*Spears Family Collection*)

Tommy Bartlett Water Ski and Jumping Boat Thrill Show

The Guy Scott Water Ski Follies and Buster Bohler's Water Ski Troupe had previously performed on Lake Olmstead, but in 1958, Augustans were thrilled by performances from the Tommy Bartlett Water Ski and Jumping Boat Thrill Show. Bartlett, a former radio and television host from Chicago, began his ski and boat show several years early. Although the show's home base was Lake Delton in Wisconsin Dells, the show traveled all over the country performing in front of capacity crowds. Sponsored by local television station WRDW, the free Water Thrill Show at Lake Olmstead featured an exhilarating program of over twenty acts, including a sixty-foot boat jump, a one-hundred-foot water ski jump, barefoot water-skiing, and an airborne skier suspended from a kite while being towed by a motorboat. In between performances, spectators enjoyed entertainment provided by Channel 12's "Sundowners" and WRDW Radio's "Bud Anderson and His Downbeats."[8] Janie Simms, WRDW-TV's Water Ski Queen, was also present for the event.

Water Skiing and Barbecue

Beginning in 1962, the Augusta Optimist Club sponsored an annual Fourth of July celebration including a barbecue and water ski show at Lake Olmstead. The "old-fashioned Fourth of July outing" at Julian Smith Park drew a crowd upward of six thousand people.[9] The day's events included boat rides, softball games, a pie-eating contest, sack races, and an evening dance. The main attraction, however, was a water show featuring some sixteen acts. Among those skiing included Edna Hungerpiller, Sarah Thompson, Leo Ghitter, Darlene Long, Astrid George, Bobby Harbin, Nancy Philpot, Helen Young, Mike Harbin, Louie Connell, Cippie Spears, George Mutimer, Jimmy Holloman, Gene Sanders, Steve Hungerpiller, Gloria George, and Leilani Usry. Louie Connell and his kite act were the highlight of the water show.[10]

The third annual old-fashioned Fourth of July celebration was actually held on Saturday, July 3, to accommodate the Georgia-Carolina Boat and Ski Club's July 4 celebration at newly formed Clark's Hill Lake. Rodney S. Cohen Jr., cochairman of the water show committee, summed up the two objectives of the Augusta Optimist Club's celebration.

> First, we hold the barbecue to raise money for our youth work, and second we observe the Fourth by having some entrainment for the public, in this case, a water show.[11]

The Optimist Club celebration included a twenty-two-act water ski show staged by the Georgia-Carolina Boat and Ski Club and barbecue served by the plate for $1.50. Skiers from seven years of age and older participated, but the show was highlighted by a kite act and the barefoot skiing of Chip Spears of North Augusta.[12] The enthusiastic crowd was mesmerized when Chip Spears performed a barefoot beach takeoff.

McCulloch World Champions

In 1965, Lake Olmstead was host to a nationally touring water ski show billed as the McCulloch World Champions, Water Skiing USA, featuring a twenty-act water ski show, as well as a dozen world and national ski champions from California.[13] The show sponsored by local television station WJBF-TV was highlighted by a kite act, trick skiing, ski jumps, and ski ballet.

Labor Day 1971

Figure 57. Ski ramp at Lake Olmstead (*Spears Family Collection*)

In 1971, the Sportsman Ski Club of Augusta presented a free twenty-act Labor Day water ski show at Lake Olmstead.[14] Clown acts, tricks, pyramids, barefoot skiing, and jumping were part of the program. Winding up the show was a kite-flying stunt by show director Jimmy Spears, who piloted his patriotically colored red, white, and blue giant delta-wing kite into the air via high-speed boat before gliding back down. It was reportedly the first time that such an act had occurred in the Augusta area.

Augusta Water Ski Club Fourth of July Show

The Augusta Water Ski Club and members of the Callaway Gardens Ski Team performed July 4 shows in 1984 and 1985. The shows were compared to the same caliber of similar shows at Cypress Gardens and Calloway Gardens. The show included shoe skiing, ballet, barefoot skiing, swivel skiing, jumping, tricks, skiing clowns, kite acts, and pyramids. Three members of the Augusta Water Ski Club— Drew McCroan, Kenny Saitow, and Eddie Beverly—were also members of the

Callaway Gardens Ski Team. Augustan Drew McCroan performed the rare stunt of skiing backward barefoot on one foot.[15] Georgia representative Dick Ransom, a longtime Augusta Water Ski Club member, performed the kite at the Fourth of July show in 1985.[16]

Figure 58. Kenny Saitow (*Spears Family Collection*)

Jerry Saitow, onetime president of the Augusta Water Ski Club, affirmed Lake Olmstead's attraction as a professional water ski venue. "A lot of people don't know this, but Lake Olmstead is considered one of the best lakes in the Southeast to ski."[17] Jerry also trained his son, Kenny. As a competitor in boys' skiing, Kenny Saitow shattered the Georgia State ski jumping record by two feet with a 130-foot jump in 1983.[18] He finished fifth out of thirty-four in the National Water Ski Championships, with a jump of 129 feet.

Meet Some of the Water Skiers

Augusta has been home to numerous professional water skiers and regional and national champions. To obtain an understanding as to the rich water-skiing tradition in Augusta, it is helpful to meet a couple of the skiers.

Figure 59. Janie Sims performing on Lake Olmstead (*Spears Family Collection*)

Janie Sims—Water Ski Queen

Janie Sims of Jackson, South Carolina, was well deserving of her title as Water Ski Queen. Several months after the Water Thrill Show, Sims amazed water-skiing fans when she completed a four-hundred-mile nonstop ski trip from Augusta to Savannah and back in August of 1958. Sims, a petite twenty-eight-year-old ninety-six-pound housewife and mother of a seven-year-old daughter, completed the trip in thirteen hours, forty minutes.[19] Upon her arrival in Savannah, Sims delivered a letter from the Augusta Chamber of Commerce via a coast guardsman, who plucked the parcel from her hand. Forced to make an estimated eighty miles of the return trip in a rainstorm, Mrs. Sims said she experienced some pain in her left knee but otherwise felt fine.[20] Remarkably, Janie had just started water skiing a couple of years earlier.

Edna Hungerpiller

Edna Hungerpiller headed the July 19, 1959, show performed by the Augusta Ski Club.[21] The show featured five female skiers, headed by Edna Hungerpiller, who had completed six weeks of performances at the Cypress Gardens prior to the show. Edna was not only a housewife but a professional skier for the Cypress Gardens Water Show, where she was at one time the top swan girl. She started skiing in 1956, but prior to that, she was a champion long-distance swimmer. She swam across Clark Hill Lake and back at its widest point at the Fishing Village, completing the five-mile trip in about four and a half hours. Hugerpiller, a five-foot, six-inch, well-tanned light brunette also attempted the 1958 Augusta-Savannah trip with Janie Sims.

Dudley Bowen Jr.

Competitive water skiing came to Lake Olmstead the following year when the Jaycees sponsored a water ski tournament in August. Winners were eligible to compete in the State Jaycee Tournament in Savannah. John Jopling and Leola Dunlop dominated their divisions. There was competition in tricks and slalom. Dudley Bowen Jr., with seconds in both events, led the senior boys with 1,636 points.[22]

Dudley Bowen Jr. was no ordinary skier. In 1965, his picture adorned the *Augusta Chronicle* holding a Winchester Model 63, .22 long rifle in connection with the Georgia-Carolina Gun Show he was directing at the Julian Smith Casino.[23] He was an avid gun collector, and Dudley's father, Dudley Sr., operated the family business, Bowen Brothers Hardware Co., where he patented a locking device for gun racks and originated the Trig-O-Lock Manufacturing Co., producing more than thirty five thousand locks worldwide.[24] Dudley would subsequently graduate with an LLB from the University of Georgia School of Law, serve as a lieutenant in the United States Army from 1966 to 1968, and serve as a bankruptcy referee and judge in the Southern District of Georgia, before being nominated by President Jimmy Carter and commissioned as a federal judge on the United States District Court for the Southern District of Georgia. Dudley served as chief judge from 1997 to 2004 before assuming senior status in 2006.

Jimmy Spears—King of Lake Olmstead

No discussion of skiing on Lake Olmstead would be complete without talking about James Edward "Jimmy" Spears (1948-2005). Spears was synonymous with skiing and Lake Olmstead and was often referred to as Augusta's Mr. Water Skier.[25] Jimmy Spears learned to water ski at the young age of ten. "We lived near Lake Olmstead and the lake attracted me and a bunch of friends."[26]

Figure 60. Jimmy Spears on Lake Olmstead (*Spears Family Collection*)

Jimmy was a second-generation owner of Spears Signs, a business started in 1941 by his father, Chester Spears. After Jimmy became ill in 2001, Jamie Spears took over operations as a third-generation owner. Still standing on a board at the sign shop are the letters PMA written by his father, which stand for Positive Mental Attitude, a motto that he believed would help his son go a long way.[27]

After his friend Harold Bateman sponsored Jimmy's kite flyer, Spears practiced relentlessly until he became an acclaimed kite flyer. Jimmy was a pioneer in delta-wing hang-glider flying and wowed many at Lake Olmstead while being towed by a high-speed boat. Jimmy first began flying a flat-winged kite, which depended solely on a motorboat to pull it fast enough to go aloft and slow down to descend. Subsequently, he graduated into a new delta-winged kite, which the skier controlled by the means of a trapeze-type bar. As the kite reached a position over the motorboat, the skier would let go of the towrope and fly free through the sky. A picture of Jimmy Spears skiing with his kite welcomed spring on the pages of the *Augusta Chronicle* in 1972.[28]

Jimmy Spears was a competitive water skier, show skier, judge, and boat driver for over thirty-five years. He was invited to compete in five National and World Championship events. In 1974, Spears, sponsored by Sea Pines Plantation of Hilton Head Island, South Carolina, competed in the World Delta Kite Championships at Cypress Gardens, Florida, in 1974. During the competition, the kite skier was required to perform certain acts, such as completing a 360-degree turn and a reverse 180-degree turn. Eventually, after performing the required acts, the skier had to pilot his kite into a target area of one hundred feet and attempt to land on top of a small bull's-eye.

Jimmy served as president of the Augusta Water Ski Club for fifteen years. As president, Spears was instrumental in bringing ski shows and tournaments sanctioned by the Georgia Water Ski Association to Lake Olmstead from the 1960s through the 1990s. Jimmy was also instrumental in bringing the professional Coors Light-Augusta Water Ski Classic to Augusta.

Spears even practiced on Lake Olmstead after it became infamous for pollution in the late 1970s and early 1980s. He had the lake to himself, as his boat often stirred up submerged garbage.

> "The pollution kept everyone else away," said Mr. Spears, 51. "I'd say to people, 'Oh yeah, Lake Olmstead is pretty dirty. I wouldn't go down there if I was you.' "It was great."[29]

But the stigma eventually subsided, and boaters returned to Lake Olmstead, creating the water traffic he had avoided for so many years.

Figure 61. Jimmy Spears on Lake Olmstead (*Spears Family Collection*)

Spears loved to introduce and teach water skiing to Augusta-area youngsters, including his three sons. His son Charlie started skiing when he was seventeen months old and entered his first national ski tournament by the time he was eight. In 1997, Charlie won the Slalom Skiing Title in the 1997 Southern Regional's at West Palm Beach, Florida, and competed in the Fifty-Fourth National Water Ski Championships.[30] His son Jamie began water skiing when he was a toddler of only twenty-two months. Jimmy's other son skied as well, but Travis was more interested in riffles and shooting and became an all-state marksman for the Aquinas High School rifle team, which Jimmy helped start and coach.

In 2002, Jimmy was inducted into the Georgia Water Ski Hall of Fame. Jimmy served on the Master Craft Boats Promotional Team for twenty years and was an American Water Ski Association Senior Driver, the highest rating a boat driver can achieve. Among the awards he received were the Love, Service, and Devotion Award from the Georgia Water Ski Association in 1986 and the GWSA Family of the Year Award in 1994.

Tournaments

From local tournaments to collegiate tournaments, Lake Olmstead has hosted an assortment of water ski tournaments. The following events allow the reader to relive some of the past tournaments.

Central Savannah River Area Water Ski Tournament

Lake Olmstead was host to the Central Savannah River Area Water Ski Tournament on July 23-24, 1960. Thirty of the top skiers in the area competed in three different divisions: slalom, trick skiing, and jumping. Frank Fortune won top honors in the men's division, taking first place in the slalom and tricks events.[31] Fortune, a former halfback on Augusta Richmond Academy's state championship football team and high school shot putter, was deemed the CSRA Ski King. Petite Janie Sims won the women's slalom, women's tricks, and jumping. Sixteen-year-old Bobby Harbin triumphed in the boys' competition. He cleared fifty-six feet on his final jump. Highlighting the Sunday ski show was a "flying the kite" stunt by Yacht Mitchell, who soared over thirty feet above the water at an estimated speed of forty miles per hour. Other events included a flag routine, mixed doubles, shoe skiing, ballet, crisscross, pyramid, baton, barefoot, and sauces by Janie Sims.

Georgia State Jaycee Water Ski Tournament

The next ski tournament, the third annual Georgia State Jaycee Water Ski Tournament, was scheduled to occur a month later on August 27-28, 1960. The Jaycees would have to jump a significant hurdle. Dr. Abe Davis, Richmond County Health department director, issued a proclamation to Mayor Millard Beckum that the bacteria count in the water at Lake Olmstead was so high that he didn't think it was safe.[32] As invitations were already out, Dick Ransom, director of the Junior Chamber of Commerce and chairman of the Water Ski Tournament, obtained permission from Mayor Beckum on the condition that the Junior Chamber of Commerce had to insure all the water ski contestants. The contestants also had to sign a release releasing the city and the Jaycees from liability.

To help promote the event, Mayor Millard A. Beckum designated the week of August 22-28 as Water Sports Safety Week. Despite a warning by County Board of Health officials that Lake Olmstead was polluted, the Jaycees, in cooperation with the Augusta Ski Club, proceeded with the tournament. The highlight of the tournament was an eighty-foot ski jump by sixteen-year-old Earls Sauls Jr.[33]

Sportsman Ski Club Regional Water Ski Tournament

Figure 62. Frank Ransom at Lake Olmstead, 1978 (*Spears Family Collection*)

The popularity and size of the ski events continued to grow. The Sportsman Ski Club's regional water ski tournament on August 21, 1977, attracted 125 entries from all over the Southeast and an estimated three thousand to four thousand spectators. Fourteen-year-old Frank Ransom of Martinez took home the honor of overall winner of the tournament.[34] Ransom had just won all three events in the boys division of the Greater Atlanta Water Ski Tournament a month earlier.[35] Frank began learning the art of trick skiing and slalom when he was only five years old and started jumping within the next year.[36] He set the Georgia State boys' slalom record on two different occasions.[37]

Busch Open Water Ski Tournament

The Sportsman Ski Club hosted an annual Busch Open Ski Tournament on Lake Olmstead beginning in the late '70s. The two-day event, sponsored by Busch beer and Augusta's A-B Beverage Company, included competition in events such as slalom, jumping, and tricks. University of Georgia graduate Marty Flournoy won the overall Men I title at the 1980 Busch Open on Lake Olmstead, picking up first place in tricks and second in slalom.[38] Rick Anderson of Anderson, South Carolina, won the overall title at the 1981 Busch Open Water Ski Tournament.[39]

Carl Campbell Memorial Novice Water Ski Tournament

For several years during the '70s and '80s, the Augusta Water Ski Club held an annual novice water ski tournament at Lake Olmstead. It was subsequently renamed the Carl Campbell Memorial Novice Water Ski Tournament in honor of Carl Campbell, a past president of the club, who had recently died in an automobile crash. The tournament gave local skiers an opportunity to qualify for the Southern Regionals and featured competition in slalom, tricks, and jumps.

In May 1984, the Carl Campbell Memorial Novice Water Ski Tournament held at Lake Olmstead was a two-day ski tournament. The event was cosponsored by the Augusta Water Ski Club and the Richmond County Recreation and Parks Department. In 1985, the big winners were ten-year-old Jamie Spears scoring first in slalom and second in tricks and jumping and his eight-year-old brother Charlie who finished second in slalom and third in jumping.[40] Three years later, young Charlie won the junior boys' ski jumping with a jump of fifty-nine feet, besting his jump of twenty-two feet in 1985.[41]

Michelob Light Open Water Ski Tournament

During the '80s, the Augusta Ski Club hosted numerous events on Lake Olmstead. One event that was highly anticipated was the Augusta-Michelob Light Open. Dick Ransom, Frank Ransom's father, won the overall championship at the Michelob Light Tournament in 1984, narrowly beating out Chris Spears and Jeff Beck.[42] Jamie Spears earned victory in the junior boys' jumping competition at the 1985 Michelob Light Open Tournament on Lake Olmstead.[43]

Figure 63. Gusto at Augusta, 1987 Augusta International Water Ski Classic
(*Spears Family Collection*)

Georgia Water Ski Championships

The first ever Georgia Water Ski Championships were held at Lake Olmstead on August 8 and 9, 1981. Hosted by the Sportsman Ski Club of Augusta, the slalom event was won by local skier Frank Ransom while Columbus, Georgia, resident Marty Flournoy won the jumping event, setting a new Georgia jump record of 154 feet.[44] The overall men's winner and winner of his second straight state title was Steve Raybourne of Milledgeville, Georgia. Rosemary Robitzsch from Fitzgerald, Georgia, won her second straight state title as well.

South Atlantic Conference Water Ski Tournament

Similar to the early football games between Clemson University and the University of Georgia at the fairgrounds, both schools hosted intercollegiate water ski tournaments at Lake Olmstead during the '80s. In 1983, it was the University of Georgia that hosted the South Atlantic Conference Water Ski Tournament. Two years later, Clemson University would host the South Atlantic Conference-Clemson Intercollegiate Water Ski Tournament at Lake Olmstead. Charles Aurich, a Clemson skier and then coholder of the national intercollegiate ski jump record of 135 feet, captured first-place honors. Kenny Saitow of Auburn University and Drew McCroan of the University of Georgia, both Augustans, took second and third place respectively.[45]

Coors Light Augusta International Water Ski Classic

The most renowned ski event, still remembered by Augustans, was the Coors Light Augusta International Water Ski Classic held on May 10-11, 1986, on Lake Olmstead. Jimmy Spears was named general chairman of the tournament. The tournament was one of eight on the pro ski tour and featured a $21,000 purse donated by Coors Light. The tournament was taped by ESPN for delayed national showing. Other than the Masters Golf Tournament, this was the first time a sporting event in Augusta received national broadcast. Only skiers who had performed in an American Water Ski Association sanctioned tournament within the last twelve months were eligible to participate. A minimum leap of 170 feet was necessary to qualify for men's jumping, while qualifiers for men's freestyle jumping had to display proficiency in at least one of the following tricks: front flip, backflip, 360 helicopter, or 720 helicopter.[46] The event was hosted by the Augusta Port Authority, City of Augusta, Richmond County and the Augusta Ski Club. Coors Light, Yamaha Outboards, Mastercraft Boats, the Ford Motor Co., and Ski Supreme Boats were among the national sponsors. Cluese Blanchard, rated as one of Augusta area's finest competitors in the sport during the 1960s, built the ski jump in his backyard.[47]

One of the last known water ski shows on Lake Olmstead was the Coca Cola Novice Slalom Ski Tournament and Lake Olmstead Water Ski Classic held on May 17, 1997. Wake Board competitors also competed on Lake Olmstead during the Georgia Games in July of 1999.

The ski tournaments have ceased, and the ski jump has been removed from Lake Olmstead. All that remains today is the occasional skier seen gliding across the lake. Unfortunately, that view is often distracted by the litter lining the shores of the beautiful lake.

XVII

Fishing Lake Olmstead

Lake Olmstead was a good fishing spot, and of course, any accounting of the history of Lake Olmstead must include coverage of fishing and some of the colorful stories of years gone past. Fishing at Lake Olmstead has had to cope with numerous challenges, including the intrusion of muddy water from the canal, motorboats, and pollution.

Although fish were spotted in the lake merely months after it was formed, a year later, observers remarked that Lake Olmstead was devoid of fish.[1] However, by that time, federal and state governments were beginning to embrace the concept of stocking fish not only for recreation but also as a way to furnish food to thousands of people. Hence, a proposal was advocated to stock the lake with fish of various kinds, including perch, bream, and trout.

Stocking of the lake would be the easy part. Once the lake was stocked, the hard part would be stabilizing the fish population. An ordinance imposing severe penalties upon anyone fishing the lake for two years was proposed to ensure that by the third year, the lake would be teeming with fish. It is unclear whether the 1874 proposal was heeded, but by 1885, Lake Olmstead was referred to as the resort of Augusta's "dude fishermen."[2]

Subsequent stocking of fish is documented during the Great Depression in September 1927, when between five thousand and eight thousand largemouth black bass were placed into Lake Olmstead by Augusta's Trees and Parks Committee. Several months later, the lake was also stocked with five thousand bream. Acknowledging the hard economic plight of many in the Augusta area, the city declared that the stocking of the lake served a twofold purpose: it would provide fishing for those fishermen not able to take fishing trips away from home, and it would also provide food for families in need.

Figure 64. The Lakeshore Loop Bridge is a popular fishing spot
(*Robert A. Mullins Collection*)

To ensure a healthy fish population, Augusta enacted Ordinance No. 543. The ordinance prohibited certain methods of fishing in the lake and provided penalties for violations. More specifically, it prevented the setting of trout lines, the baiting or catching fish with nets, shooting, trapping, dynamiting, or using of lime or other poisons in Lake Olmstead. Local residents took little heed of the ordinance. Almost twenty years later, Oka T. Hester, director of the Augusta Recreation Commission, issued an appeal to fishermen to discontinue setting trout lines in Lake Olmstead, stressing that such practice had been prohibited by state statute. Moreover, he emphasized that the local game warden would be keeping a watchful eye with the intent of prosecuting offenders.

Fishing in Lake Olmstead had already declined in the early 1930s because of the scarcity of fish, leading one commentator to remark that such scarceness accounted for the statement "Boy, he took my line, minnow and all!"[3] Numerous efforts were made to increase the fish population. In 1935, fifty thousand to seventy-five thousand fish from the Magnolia Springs fish hatchery in Millen, Georgia, were released into in Lake Olmstead.[4] Another seventy-five thousand fish, including bass, red breast, and bream were added the next year.[5]

It seemed like there were never enough fish in Lake Olmstead. When fishermen have an unproductive outing, they customarily look to blame not themselves but external conditions. At Lake Olmstead, the same culprit that kept the water from being clear was a weighty thorn for fishermen. It seemed like the intrusion of muddy canal water was a persistent problem. Decades after a dam was installed to keep the muddy water out, fishermen still continued to complain about the muddy water. Apparently, at the time, the canal water was only kept in check by a heavy piece of timber at the point where the canal and lake intersected.

As late as 1949, then game warden Bob Spears blamed the lack of fish to muddy water intruding the lake from the canal and motorboats. Spears opined that muddy water intruding from the canal into the lake discouraged the fish population. If the muddy water could be kept out, Spears declared that Lake Olmstead could be the best fishing spot for fifty miles around.[6]

The proposed solution recommended by the State Game and Fish Commissioner was to lower a six-inch curb into slots of concrete at the entrance of the canal from Lake Olmstead to keep out muddy water and thereby safeguard the fish. The proposal was brought before the city commission in 1947. Enacting such a proposal, however, concerned J. O. Davis, Richmond County supervisor of Malaria Control. Davis had inspected the shorelines of the lake and reported that, if the lake's water level was raised, it would result in two new flooded areas, which would become mosquito-breeding grounds. Due to the malaria epidemic, he condemned rising of the water level as a health menace.

John Battle, the city editor for the *Augusta Chronicle*, had additional thoughts on the subject. Battle was well-known for his fishing prowess, having pulled fish out of mud holes, creeks, lakes, and rivers since long before World War I. Battle believed Lake Olmstead was an ideal spot for still-water fishing, except for the turmoil caused by motorboats. Even so, he said, the angling was uncommonly good.[7]

The conflict between motorboats and fishermen persisted. A reoccurring question, however, was whether the city could legally prevent residents on the west side of Lake Olmstead from operating motorboats, as it was located outside of the city limits.[8] Asserting that a ban on motorboats was needed to improve fishing and turn the area into a first-class picnic site, in 1964, Councilman Hugh Eugene Tudor (1917-1981), a staunch opponent of motorboats in Lake Olmstead, sought to introduce an ordinance to prevent boating on the lake. A perennial candidate for political office, Tudor operated a wholesale sandwich business. Although he traced his roots to Henry VIII of England, that did not help him with his political aspirations. He first ran for political office in 1949, when he ran a seat on the county school board. He ran for office another twenty-three times before he was successful in earning a seat on the city council. His first victory made national news. Appearing on the nationally televised show *I've Got a Secret*, Tudor revealed that his secret was that he had finally been elected to office after twenty-four attempts.

Councilman Tudor garnered the support of Phillip Pierce, fishery biologist for the State Game and Fish Commission who also recommended the ban. Irrespective, Tudor's efforts were futile, and he took the heat for his proposal. The conflict was so intense that Tudor was mocked in the *Augusta Chronicle*.

Ode to a City Councilman

Augusta's perennial candidate, Hugh Tudor, who raised enough cain with city fathers to at least open to the public the question of Lake Olmstead's future, is having troubles with his fight to bar the lake to all but fishermen.

With advance apologies and the reminder that spring, not fall, is the season most suitable for poets, we offer this rhyming resume of Tudor's apparently futile efforts:

Hugh Eugene Tudor with a long cane pole
Wants Lake Olmstead for a fishing hole,
But boaters and skiers like it too,
So what is the city gonna do?
J. M. Howard says leave it as it is,
With anglers and skiers both in bix.
But letters will decide the issue, Tudor claims,
Whichever side sends the most gets its aims.
It'll come to a head next week, he declared.
When a committee meets and the subject is aired.
So those who care, write Tudor today.
His mind is open, all the way.[9]

Needless to say, Tudor's proposal could not obtain any significant momentum and died out.

Alternatively, Councilman Willis Irvin had a plan to rid the lake of "rough" fish and restock it with bream. The lake would be poisoned in the fall and restocked in the spring. Heavy motors would be prohibited during spawning periods. Irvin also proposed establishing a boat rental service and a small charge for fishing. Irvin's proposal, estimated to cost $800 to $1,000, was attacked by Councilman John T. Chesser, who when told the proposal didn't include purifying the lake for swimming, said, "[I]f swimming can't be provided, there is no need to spend that much money."[10]

Although the plight of fishing in Lake Olmstead had its challenges, there was undoubtedly some good fishing. In the old days, it was not uncommon for fishermen to catch stringers full of fish. Fishing stories were common, with one fisherman catching as many as thirty-eight speckles and John Henry Zorn catching a seventeen-pound carp with a cornmeal ball and fly tackle.[11] It was also said that some of the largest trout or bass ever caught in this section were hauled in from Lake Olmstead. Sometimes a pole was not even needed to land a trophy fish. While dusting for malaria mosquito control in 1939, a four-and-one-half-pound trout jumped into the boat of A. J. Kirby.[12] Strings of largemouth bass up to ten pounds were frequently pulled from the waters of Lake Olmstead in the 1940s.

Fishing rodeos or contests were popular in the '50s. The Augusta Recreation Department held an annual fishing contest for kids at Lake Olmstead. It was not uncommon to see herds of youngsters fishing on the lake's banks. Boys and girls from seven through fifteen years of age were eligible to take part in the activities. Contestants could partake in three fishing classifications: still-fishing, casting, or fly-fishing. Prizes were given for the largest fish caught by using each of the three methods. Fishing rodeos for senior citizens were also popular.

Over two hundred Augusta youngsters participated in the 1956 annual fishing rodeo sponsored by the City Recreation Department and Better Fishing Inc. The largest fish caught was an "enormous" eleven-and-three-quarter-ounces catfish, caught by fifteen-year-old Buddy Applewhite. The prizes for the most fish caught were captured by nine-year-old David Wren, with four bream, and Vivian Clark, who caught seven bream.

Concerns over the fish population led the Georgia Department of Natural Resources (DNR) to conduct an investigation in 1976. The DNR fish probe was conducted by a team of fisheries biologists using a "shock" machine to probe the fish populations. The results were unexpected by some local fishermen. According to the fish probe, the lake had plenty of fish, including black bass weighing three pounds and more. Of course, other fish such as carp and long-nosed garfish were also identified. Don Johnson of the Walton County Fish Hatchery near Social Circle, Georgia, and part of the DNR team suggested that a Garfish Derby be held at the lake to help reduce the gar population.[13]

The record fish caught in Lake Olmstead was an amazing 1,127 pounds. A picture of the mammoth fish lying on the back of a utility truck was published in the *Augusta Chronicle* confirming the fish was a world record. Unfortunately, it was merely an advertising ploy.[14] On the other hand, Lake Olmstead was home to a $10,000 fish.

In 1986, Parts Plus and local radio station WBBQ sponsored a fishing tournament attracting 466 anglers to Lake Olmstead.[15] Fish were tagged with certain prizes. One fish bearing tag number 338 was worth $10,000. Other fish were tagged with prizes including a sailboat, a minicar, a trolling motor, as well as additional cash prizes. The fishing tournament raised over $11,500 for the benefit of the Medical College of Georgia Children's Center for Cancer and Blood Diseases.

Irrespective of contamination and the ban on swimming, Lake Olmstead is frequented by fishermen daily, fishing mostly for largemouth bass, bream, and shellcrackers. Contrary to popular belief, the Georgia Department of Natural Resources has not identified any concerns with the consumption of fish caught from Lake Olmstead. A fish study conducted by the Georgia Wildlife Resources Division's Fisheries Section in 2012 year indicates that the lake is "in really good shape. The fish are plump and the sizes are dominated by larger, catchable-sized fish."[16] The most frequent spot for fishing is around the bridge on Lakeshore Loop. Under the bridge is a weir above which water spills over from the lake to enter the canal.

Figure 65. Clarks Hill Dam (*U.S. Corps of Engineers*)

XVIII

Changing Factors

In addition to the persistent contamination, Lake Olmstead would face additional challenges as a recreational and social venue. Although the lake had been the place to go for boat racing, fishing, and water skiing, that soon changed with the creation of Clark Hill Lake. Authorized by legislation in 1944, Clark Hill Lake was constructed on the Savannah River approximately twenty-two miles upstream of Augusta by the US Army Corps of Engineers as flood control measure and a source for hydropower during the early 1950s. Its dam is over two thousand feet long and two hundred feet high and is comprised of over one million cubic yards of concrete. The seventy-one-thousand-acre lake with 1,200 miles of shoreline reached full pool of 330 feet above sea level on April 25, 1953.[1] It is the third-largest artificial lake east of the Mississippi River and one of the ten most visited corps lakes in the nation. Today, the lake, recently renamed Lake Thurmond in honor of Strom Thurmond, is also managed for recreation, water quality, water supply, and fish and wildlife management.

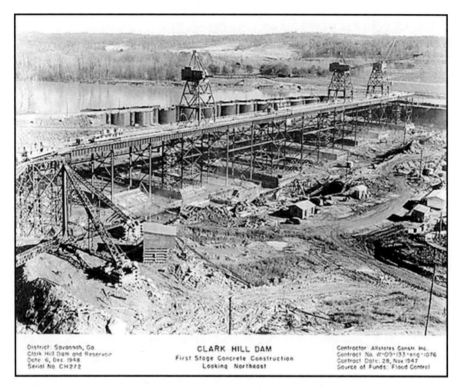

District: Savannah, Ga.
Clark Hill Dam and Reservoir
Date 6, Dec. 1948
Serial No. CH272

CLARK HILL DAM
First Stage Concrete Construction
Looking Northeast

Contractor Allstates Constr. Inc.
Contract No. W-09-133-eng-1076
Contract Date: 28, Nov. 1947
Source of Funds: Flood Control

Figure 66. Construction of Clarks Hill Dam in 1948 (*Courtesy of the Augusta Chronicle*)

In addition to Lake Thurmond, the boundaries of Julian Smith Park were forever changed during the '50s, as a result of the construction of Calhoun Expressway. The giant new superhighway bridge cut through Julian Smith Park and crossed over part of Lake Olmstead. Built on the east side of the Broad Street, the new bridge consisted of a six-lane span. Washington Road was moved across a Texaco service station and garage at Old Broad Street and across a small section of Lake Olmstead on the south side of Washington Road, which was subsequently filled in during the project.[2]

Partially due to the leadership of Councilman Sam C. Waller, the city struck a deal with the state. Augusta exchanged gravel for the new bridge across Lake Olmstead in return for clearance of a new park and playground by the Georgia State Highway Department.[3] The Highway Department was given gravel from a tract of city-owned land just east of Milledge Road Extension, north of the Julian Smith barbecue pavilion, in exchange for clearing and grading the land. Milledge Road Extension was also relocated further east, resulting in additional play and picnic grounds between the road and the lake's edge. Calhoun Expressway opened on February 24, 1976.

The John C. Calhoun Expressway

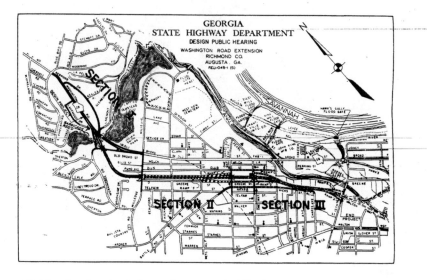

Figure 67. Map showing the Calhoun Expressway Bridge (*Augusta Chronicle*, Oct. 26, 1969)

Coinciding with the detrimental impact of Clark Hill Lake and the Calhoun Expressway was the continued deterioration of Julian Smith Park. In 1971, the Augusta Jaycees demanded the city to address the condition of Julian Smith Park. The park's buildings and improvements, especially the bandstand, fountains, and boat docks, were in a state of general disrepair; the grounds were partly barren, partly grown over and in poor condition, and few facilities had been added to the park to encourage public use. The Jaycees pushed for renovation. With its lengthy shoreline and potential beach areas, the lake and adjoining park could be developed into a large, attractive recreation area that would be a major asset to the city and a significant contribution to its citizens. Unlike other progressive cities that go to great length to beautify such spots, Augusta had only made minor improvements around Olmstead.

Figure 68. Augusta Canal Headgates (*Historic American Engineering Record*)

XIX

Battle for the Augusta Canal

The history of Lake Olmstead has always been intertwined with the Augusta Canal. Its future is also closely tied to the canal. By the mid-twentieth century, the canal had entered a period of neglect. Numerous textile mills along its banks had closed down due to economic conditions. It was seen as a polluted eyesore. Similar to the plight of Lake Olmstead, sewer lines still emptied into the canal, and trash was seen floating in its waters. At one point in the 1960s, city officials candidly considered draining the canal and using its dry bed for a superhighway. The most significant and plausible proposal, however, was the construction of a power plant on the canal, thus putting the polluted eyesore to beneficial use.

Power Plant

Historically, there were numerous proposals to use the canal to generate electricity. For example, as early as 1929, a proposal was advocated to build an electrical power plant opposite the canal overflow at the foot of Lake Olmstead.[1] By the middle 1960s, the idea of constructing an electrical plant near Lake Olmstead had progressed significantly. Augusta's fiftieth mayor, George Albert Sancken Jr. (1919-2005), would play a large role in the ongoing discussions. An Augusta native, Sancken was a decorated World War II veteran earning the Bronze and Silver Star for bravery in the European Theatre and participating in the initial D-Day landing on Utah Beach.[2] After military service, he worked with his family's dairy, Georgia Carolina Dairies, until it was sold to the Borden Company. Sworn into office on January 7, 1964, Sancken enthusiastically implored Augustans to adopt as their slogan for the coming year,

> A little more in '64 from each of us means more for Augusta in the future . . . Let us forget personal differences and work together for our mutual benefit.[3]

Sancken was an ardent supporter in efforts to build a hydroelectric plant on the canal.

In 1966, Georgia Power Company and Mayor Sancken announced plans for a $2.5-$3 million hydroelectric plant on the canal at Lake Olmstead. Endorsed by the city council's Canals, Rivers, and Wharves Committee, Augusta and the Georgia Power Company filed a joint license application with the Federal Power Commission (FPC) to build a power dam on the canal.[4] The proposed installation consisted of an outdoor powerhouse with turbines expected to generate at least twelve thousand kilowatts of electricity. Water discharged from the turbines would flow back to the Savannah River via a tailrace along the existing Rae's Creek streambed.

Mayor Sancken emphasized that the plant would generate annual revenue of approximately $130,000 from its customers. After operational costs, the city would receive annual revenue of approximately $65,000. The power plant dam, however, would result in a dry canal bed from Lake Olmstead to Thirteenth Street in downtown Augusta. Although it sounds culturally and environmentally destructive today, during the mid '60s, perceptions were different.

Figure 69. View of the Savannah River from the Augusta Canal towpath
(*Robert A. Mullins Collection*)

In addition to the potential revenue, Mayor Sancken advocated the project's added benefit as a flood-control measure.

> The canal poses possible danger of floods in the city and for this reason I'd like to see it eliminated from Lake Olmstead to downtown. With the new generating plant we could clean up the whole canal system and be better off.[5]

Construction of the hydroelectric plant and elimination of the canal would alleviate significant flood concerns. With Sancken's enthusiasm, the FPC awarded a fifty-year license to the city of Augusta and Georgia Power Company the following year for construction of the $2.75 million hydroelectric plant. The fate of the Augusta Canal was all but sealed.

Notwithstanding the issuance of the necessary license, there were still considerable issues to be addressed. If the power plant was built, water flow would stop at Lake Olmstead. What would the canal bed be used for if the water flow was eliminated? Who would own the canal basin? Suggested uses of the canal bed included proposals from train tracks to a roadway. Debate was rampant.

Augusta's next mayor, Millard A. Beckum, declared, "[A]nything that can be done to cover the canal would be good. We desperately need to get rid of this filth and stench . . ."[6] Fortunate for future Augustans, this time period coincided with the beginning of an environmentally conscious era and enactment of the National Environmental Policy Act.

Signed into law on January 1, 1970, the National Environmental Policy Act (NEPA) establishes national environmental policy and goals for the protection, maintenance, and enhancement of the environment. NEPA requires the federal government to use all practicable means to create and maintain conditions under which man and nature can exist in productive harmony, including incorporation of environmental considerations in planning and decision making. Moreover, the act requires all federal agencies to prepare detailed environmental impact statements (EISs) assessing the environmental impact of and alternatives to major federal actions significantly affecting the environment.

Public interest and appreciation of the value of the canal and its adjacent lands began to intensify. A requisite component for FPC approval for the power plant was funding for a CSRA Regional Park and a pledge by Augusta to develop recreational areas in the vicinity of the canal. Initial plans for the park incorporated the development of a marina, picnic tables, comfort stations, and a fifteen-acre open area adaptable to multiple recreational uses. In May of 1970, the Augusta City Council formally endorsed plans for the CSRA Regional Park.[7]

Although the canal was not treasured by Mayor Beckum, it found ardent support from Joseph B. Cumming, the grandson of Henry H. Cumming, one of the original fathers of the canal. At the time, Cumming was chairman of the influential Georgia Historical Commission. Largely through Cumming's efforts, initial efforts to preserve the canal were successful when it was placed on the National Register of Historic Places in 1971 and was thereafter designated as a National Historic Landmark by the National Park Service.

Figure 70. The Augusta Canal towpath is a popular site for walking
and bicycle riding (*Robert A. Mullins Collection*)

Canal Park

Momentum was growing for preservation of the canal. As public interest
in the canal and its adjacent lands began to swell, so did the recreational-use
proposals. The idea of further development of the canal and Lake Olmstead area
was part of a master plan adopted by the city of Augusta in June of 1972 for a
regional park that would stretch from Lake Olmstead to Interstate 20 along the
Savannah River.[8] Several months later, plans to include an international tennis
complex integrating twenty-five courts and four covered courts with grandstands
within the park were revealed.[9] With the master plan moving forward, Augusta
purchased an option on the 116-acre tract of land between Lake Olmstead and
the Savannah River with anticipation of developing a multiple-use area, including
the tennis center, facilities for Olympic-type sports, an international village and
marina, as well as a shopping center and housing sites.

The Georgia Department of Natural Resources, city of Augusta, and
Richmond County commissioned Eric Hill Associates Inc., an urban planning
consultant, to prepare a conceptual plan for the revitalization of the Augusta
Canal.[10] The plan integrated a proposed state park to portray the historic

significance of the canal in the early growth and development of Augusta. Pursuant to the plan, the state would build and maintain the park facilities, including nature trails, golf courses, and other recreational aspects. The only caveat was that the city would have to donate the land.

Subsequently, former president, then Georgia governor Jimmy Carter created the Georgia Heritage Trust, which was tasked to preserve Georgia's recreational, historical, natural, and cultural resources. The Commission recommended the purchase of 230 acres along the canal's first level for the proposed state park. Governor Carter concurred with the recommendation and spent over a million dollars to acquire the necessary property.[11]

Elected in 1973, Augusta Mayor Lewis A. "Pop" Newman was a staunch advocate for the state park. After taking office, Mayor Newman began efforts to clean up the canal. He ensured that when the canal was drained for several months in early 1974 for installation of storm sewers and utilities, it also received a much-needed cleaning. Pop was quoted as saying, "We're in the process of dredging now and this will let us do some more cleaning up of the canal."[12]

Acknowledging the significant recreational and historic aspects of the canal, negotiations evolved into a proposal to develop an eight-mile-long Augusta Canal State Park. The park would stretch from Oglethorpe Park in downtown Augusta to the beginning of the canal in Columbia County.[13] At the canal headgates in Columbia County, canoe rentals and tours, picnic areas, and hiking were designed. To the south toward Augusta, a primitive camping area would be set aside accessible only by hiking or biking. Commenting on the proposed camping area, Jake Ingram of the Georgia Department of Natural Resources observed, "Although you're only a mile or two from downtown Augusta, when you're on the water's edge, you are in the wilderness."[14]

The Augusta Canal State Park plan, however, faded away with the demise of the state Heritage Trust Commission. As a result, the state exchanged its land along the canal with the city for land it needed to extend Bobby Jones Expressway.

Fortunately, in the late 1980s, community leaders united in an endeavor to conserve the important natural and historical canal resources. Subsequent lobbying efforts led the Georgia legislature to create the Augusta Canal Authority in 1989 to "promote the revitalization and development of the City of Augusta through the creation of parks, recreation areas, and . . . develop and promote the public good and general welfare, trade, tourism, commerce, industry, and employment opportunities . . ."[15] Led by the Augusta Canal Authority and other leaders, preservation of the canal would become a reality.

XX

Augusta Canal—A National Heritage Area

P erhaps, most significant for Lake Olmstead's future is its eastern boundary with the Augusta Canal. Today, the Augusta Canal, Lake Olmstead's mother, is protected as one of forty-nine designated National Heritage Areas nationwide. To receive designation as a National Heritage Area by the United States Congress, an area's natural, cultural, historic, and recreational resources must combine to form a cohesive, nationally distinctive landscape arising from patterns of human activity shaped by geography. The designation, received in 1996, is an acknowledgment of the outstanding significance of the canal to Augusta.

The Augusta Canal Discovery Center at Enterprise Mill offers visitors an opportunity to encounter the people behind the canal's development and learn about its history through historical exhibits, film, and interactive demonstrations. Visitors can enjoy the Augusta Canal on foot, by bicycle, by canoe, by kayak, or even on one of the Petersburg Boat replicas, which travels up and down the canal on a daily basis.

Figure 71. Petersburg Boat on the Augusta Canal (*Credit: Rebecca Rogers, Augusta Canal NHA*)

Departing from the Discovery Center, boat tours along the canal are a highlight for many tourists. In 1999, Rusty Fleetwood was hired to design a replication of the historic Petersburg Boat for tours along the canal. The tour boat was modeled after the cigar-shaped Petersburg boats that once shipped cotton and freight on the Savannah River and Canal. Fleetwood's design called for a sixty-five-foot, twenty-two-thousand-pound tour vessel with a seating capacity for forty-eight adults and a two-person crew.[1]

The first Petersburg tour boat was built and arrived in Augusta in October 2004. The boat was appropriately named after Henry Cumming, the Augustan who first proposed building the canal in the 1840s. The second tour boat to arrive was named after the young canal engineer, William Phillips, who in 1845, helped convince skeptics that a canal could bring growth and prosperity to Augusta. Over 165,000 visitors have enjoyed boat tours over the last 10 years.

Access to the canal and its eight miles of navigable water and seven miles of towpath is provided via a footbridge or by nonmotorized boat. Several noteworthy sites can be experienced along the canal, many of which can be accessed by the numerous hiking and bicycle trails. The majority of the sites are located on the canal's first level between the headgates in Columbia County and Thirteenth Street in downtown Augusta. Along the first level of the canal still stands one of several cotton mills built along the canal, King Mill, named after John Pendleton King, one of the canal's founding fathers. The mill continues to generate operating power from the canal, as do several other mills.

The site that stands higher than any other site is the confederate powder works chimney. The chimney is the only remnant of the powder works that occupied two miles along the canal during the Civil War. The chimney was preserved as a memorial to Augusta's Confederate dead.

Figure 72. Archibald Butt (ca. 1910)

The Butt Bridge crosses the canal at Fifteenth Street in downtown Augusta. The ornate stone bridge, complimented by guardian lions on both sides, is a historical reminder of Major Archibald Willingham Butt, an Augustan who died valiantly on the *Titanic* in 1912. Major Butt was a military adviser to presidents Theodore Roosevelt and William Howard Taft. Returning home from a European mission for President Taft, he was aboard the *Titanic* when it struck an iceberg off the coast of Newfoundland and sank. Butt was credited with ceaselessly helping women and children into lifeboats until the ship went down. Ms. Marie Young, staff correspondent for the *Washington Star*, praised Major Butt's efforts.

> His brave face smiling at me from the deck was the last I could distinguish as the boat I was in pulled away from the steamer's side. Archie himself put me in the boat, wrapped blankets around me and tucked me in carefully, as though we were merely starting for a motor ride.[2]

In April 1914, President Taft dedicated the bridge to his former aid. "He died," declared President Taft, "like a soldier and a gentleman."[3]

Figure 73. Butt Memorial Bridge (*Historic American Engineering Record*)

Another site of interest is the aqueduct near Lake Olmstead. Before the creation of Lake Olmstead, the aqueduct carried the canal across Rae's Creek. The aqueduct fascinates visitors because of its ancient stone arches and rushing waterfalls.

Savannah Rapids Park, owned and operated by Columbia County, is located at the headgates of the Augusta Canal. Developed during the 1990s, the prominent feature of the park is the Savannah Rapids Pavilion, a multipurpose community conference center erected atop an eighty-foot bluff overlooking the canal and Savannah River. Within the park, numerous historical features have been restored, such as an old wooden dance pavilion and the old lockkeeper's cottage, which recently was transformed into a visitors' center. The park also has bicycle trails, playgrounds, picnic shelters, and barbecue pits and is often frequented by bicyclists, runners, and walkers who enjoy the scenic beauty as they traverse up and down the old canal towpath.

The canal, although man-made, is a vital urban wildlife habitat. Much of the seven mile area along the first level of the canal is undeveloped and heavily wooded. Ash, elm, red maple, and sweet gum trees forest the wetland area in between the canal and the Savannah River, providing invaluable habitat for waterfowl and other wildlife. Over time, a wetland area has been formed on the undeveloped land between the canal and the Savannah River, creating an urban wildlife sanctuary that is home to varied flora and fauna, including several rare and endangered species. Typical wildlife one might encounter include beavers, muskrats, otters, several breeds of fish and turtles, bald eagles, wood storks, wild turkeys, blue herons, loons, geese, ducks, a variety of snakes, and even an occasional alligator.

Unique flora and fauna include the endangered Rocky Shoals spider lily (*Hymenocallis coronaria*, listed on the federal species of concern), a flowering aquatic plant native to large streams and rivers; the federally endangered confederate trillium (*Trillium reliquum*); and the bog spicebush (*Lindera subcoriacea*, a candidate for federal protection), a rare shrub common to sandhill bogs that produces a small yellowish flower. Other rare species include the Georgia aster (*Aster georgianus*), a perennial, colonial herb that produces white flowers with dark-purple rays in early October through mid-November; the sweet pitcher plant (*Sarracenia rubra*), a carnivorous plant that produces small red flowers in the spring; and the Pickering's morning-glory (*Stylisma pickeringii var. pickeringii*), a spreading, herbaceous, perennial vine characteristic in the sandhills that produces small white morning glory—like flowers in the summer months.[4]

Figure 74. Lake Olmstead (*Robert A. Mullins Collection*)

XXI

Lake Olmstead Today

The social clubs of the early nineteen hundreds have long since vanished. Private residences border the north side of the lake, while the Augusta Canal creates the eastern border and Julian Smith Park encompasses the south side of the lake. Adjacent to the park stands Lake Olmstead Stadium, where Augusta's minor league baseball team plays; the old city stockade, which now houses the CSRA Humane Society; a National Guard armory; an American Legion Post; and public housing.

After consolidation of Augusta and Richmond County governments in 1996, a plan for a $2.8-million improvement project was advanced to transform Julian Smith Park into a first-class attraction.[1] In his site analysis, Augusta architect Roger W. Davis declared that Lake Olmstead "has the potential to become a major water recreation destination point." The project's primary goal was to renovate Julian Smith Casino by adding palladium windows overlooking Lake Olmstead to its main hall. Now, the main hall offers amazing vistas of the lake's glistening waters. Entrances to the park were rebuilt to ease parking and traffic problems and the fishing pier and gazebo bandstand were refurbished. Unfortunately, other goals of the project, such as adding rental boats, installation of reflecting pools, and lighted fountains and creation of a satellite canal visitors' center, were scrapped.[2]

Today, Julian Smith Park encompasses approximately twenty-eight acres on the shores of Lake Olmstead. The casino and barbecue pit overlook the lake and feature heart-of-pine hardwood floors. The recently renovated gazebo is a popular location for an occasional wedding. All three facilities are available for rent. The park has a softball field, picnic tables, barbecue grills, paved walkways, and a fishing-boat pier. It also boasts one of the area's most popular disc golf courses and a convenient walking track.

Lake Olmstead has been host to numerous events, such as Augusta Technical College's annual paper-boat races. These races required that the only supplies allowed in constructing the boats be glue, tape, paint, nails, staples, and of course, paper. The race's organizer and Augusta Technical Institutes Teacher of the Year (1999-2000), Tim Lewis, said the strategy is simple: "Build the boat any way you want and with whatever you want—so long as it's paper."[3] The lake was the site of the Annual Great Augusta Bicycle Race during the early 1970s. Held on a 1.5-mile course around Lake Olmstead, the race was sanctioned by the ABLA (Amateur Bicycle League of America). It was also home for the Lake Olmstead Road Race, a four-and-a-half-mile race, sponsored by the Augusta Athletic Association; the Lake Olmstead Invitational Sailboat Race (1980); and the 1994 Rowing Regatta, boasting more than one thousand rowers, ages 27-80.

Lake Olmstead is still polluted and full of trash. Yearly efforts are made to remove trash from Lake Olmstead. Science teacher Carl Hammond-Beyer, a teacher at Davidson Fine Arts Magnet School, takes his class to Lake Olmstead yearly to study the environment around the Lake and participate in the cleanup.[4] One volunteer collecting trash from Lake Olmstead commented. "[W]e haven't even left the dock—it's been five minutes and we already almost have an entire trash bag filled."[5] During a 2002 cleanup effort by Sierra Club, members and volunteers picked up paper, bottles, cans, a box of clothes, fishing corks, bait cups, balls, tires—so much trash it took a Dumpster to hold it all.[6]

Figure 75. Trash litters the water's edge at Lake Olmstead (*Robert A. Mullins Collection*)

Today, environmentalists assert the need for intervention and protection of Rae's Creek based on the evidence of significant contamination issues. In addition to typical urban runoff, the previous historical use of the creek by grist mills, lumber mills, a foundry, and a possible gold mine might have caused the creek to have elevated levels of heavy metals. In 2008, for example, research led by Augusta

State University biology professor Donna Wear found elevated levels of mercury, arsenic, and other toxic materials in fish and sediment samples taken from Lake Olmstead.[7] Other concerns included low oxygen, siltation, and erosion.

Figure 76. Lake Olmstead Stadium (*Robert A. Mullins Collection*)

Lake Olmstead Stadium—Baseball Returns

On the same grounds that horses and motorcycles raced now stands Lake Olmstead Stadium. In 1988, thanks to the persistence of Bill Heaton, minor league baseball returned to Augusta after a twenty-five-year absence. Heaton's love for the sport led him to build Heaton Stadium, located where Lake Olmstead Stadium now stands, with his own money and efforts. The first team that called Heaton Stadium home was the Augusta Pirates of the South Atlantic League. On the cold, rainy night of April 12, 1988, over 2,500 people witnessed baseball's return on opening day at Heaton Stadium.[8]

Most recently, Lake Olmstead spawned the name for Augusta's newest minor league baseball stadium, Lake Olmstead Stadium. The park was built in 1994 and seats 4,322 for baseball. The GreenJackets, a low Class A affiliate of the San Francisco Giants, have played in Lake Olmstead Stadium since 1995. Since the opening of Lake Olmstead Stadium in 1995, the GreenJackets have ranked in the top 7 in the South Atlantic League in attendance, averaging more than 2,600 fans a game.[9]

A partial list of players that played at Heaton Stadium and/or Lake Olmstead Stadium include such Major League baseball greats as Tim Wakefield and Kevin Youkilis, Moisés Alou, Emmanuel Burriss, Carlos García, John Grabow, Brian Horwitz, Jason Kendall, Orlando Merced, Hanley Ramírez, Pablo Sandoval, Eugenio Vélez, Brian Wilson, David Justice, John Smoltz, and Tony Womack.

More than baseball has been played at the stadium. Numerous noteworthy concerts and events have been held in Lake Olmstead Stadium. A series of annual concerts, dubbed the Hot Southern Nights held at Lake Olmstead Stadium to benefit the local Red Cross, have hosted such musical performers as Charlie Daniels, the Marshall Tucker Band, Travis Tritt, Charlie Robison, Mark Wills, Blake Shelton, Rebecca Lynn Howard, Orleans, Poco, Firefall, the Little River Band, Atlanta Rhythm Section, and Blackfoot. Other concerts at the stadium have featured Bob Dylan, Jimmie Vaughan, Junior Brown, Elana James, and John Michael Montgomery.

Figure 77. Cormorants on Lake Olmstead (*Robert A. Mullins Collection*)

Wildlife

Today, the lake's waters are polluted. Swimming has not been permitted for over sixty years. Irrespective of the pollution, Lake Olmstead, located within minutes of downtown Augusta, is still a site of scenic beauty and an important wildlife habitat. Fishing is permitted, and the Georgia Department of Natural

Resources has not listed any restrictions on consumption. Lake Olmstead is also a virtual inner-city wildlife refuge for waterfowl. Ducks commonly seen on its waters include mallards, wood ducks, blue-winged teals, ring-necked ducks, and canvasbacks. American coots and egrets are also common, as are cormorants. Canadian geese also make yearly migratory appearances.

The Savannah River and its shoals and rapids create a typical Fall Line environment and essential habitat for fish and other river life.[10] The American shad and endangered shortnose sturgeon, one of the planet's oldest living fish species, have been found in the Savannah River. Typical fish species in the Lake Olmstead area include largemouth bass, striped bass, bluegill, redear sunfish, white catfish, smallmouth bass, shellcracker, spotted sucker, gar, and freshwater perch.

XXII

Stories and Trivia

Although numerous stories are intertwined through this book, several noteworthy events stand out through short stories. Beginning with the Great Escape of 1924 and the image of shackled prisoners attempting to escape their confines and ending with the story of a brave young lifesaver, these stories convey the reader back in time while providing insight, humor, social pride and hope.

The Great Escape of 1924

While Augusta's real estate boom was taking place, something else was in the works right up the road—the great escape of 1924. On the morning of August 4, 1924, Lonnie Clark, a Richmond County prison guard, went to work at the convict camp located off Washington Road near Lake Olmstead like any other morning. Little did he know that he would soon experience the eruption of a coup d'état. Clark was in the process of shackling his prisoners on the morning of August 4, 1924, when eleven convicts made a break for freedom.[1]

Dewey Abrams, serving a sentence for burglarizing several local gas stations, led the escape. After somehow acquiring a gun the previous afternoon, Abrams waited for just the right moment to make his escape. As Clark began shackling the prisoners, Abrams pulled the pistol from his jacket and ordered Clark to "throw them up." Clark, however, chose not to put his hands up, instead going for his gun. Abrams fired, shooting Clark in the abdomen.

Fortunately, Clark was able to fight through his injury and managed to run out of the room to seek help. As Clark ran for help, Abrams turned the gun on the large chain and lock that held him and ten other prisoners captive. It was no easy task to shoot through the chain and lock. As Abrams was shooting the lock, bullets struck two of his fellow prisoners. Frank Green was shot in the leg and Charley Glenn over the left eye. Finally, the lock gave, and Abrams, with seven other like-minded prisoners, dashed out of the room in their shackles, dragging the remaining three prisoners behind them. Although the three prisoners in the rear attempted to thwart the escape, they were powerless to stop the others. "With the big chain, which is 30 feet long, dangling from their shackles they were dragged through the room and out into the prison yard."[2] Eventually, the three protestors ceased their struggle and followed along. The shackled convicts made their way to the yard overturning chairs, tables, and a stove in the process.

Figure 78. Photo of a Richmond County Convict Camp

After reaching the yard, "the entire eleven in column formation with their shackles on proceeded at a dog trot up the road and disappeared into thick woods that surrounded Lake Olmstead."[3] Word of the escape quickly spread, leaving nearby residents in fright. Doors were bolted shut, and the women huddled with their children while the men, grasping their guns, watched from behind closed doors and windows for the emancipated and armed convicts that had "killed a guard."

When city and county police arrived, they combed the hillside above the camp for the escaped convicts. Motorists stopped, afraid to pass through the stretch of woods where the convicts had escaped. "With the woods throwing out mysterious shadows and rumors flying thick and fast, the terror stricken occupants of the automobiles on the road near the big stretch of woods knew not what to do or which way to move. The road was being traversed by men with guns on their shoulders who peered with anxious eyes into the woods looking for some sign of the escaped convicts."[4]

Although bloodhounds were commandeered, before they could arrive, the convicts had been discovered in the woods about a mile and a half from the convict camp, lying flat on the ground. Their two hours of freedom had come to an end. The ringleader, Abrams, was charged with assault with intent to murder.

Plunge to Death

On the same day a tornado struck Lincolnton, Georgia killing three people, a young soldier from Camp Lee, Virginia, and his bride of nine months also met with tragedy. The couple met a dreadful death in Lake Olmstead on the morning of December 2, 1942, when their automobile left the highway leaping forty feet before plunging from Broad Street into the icy waters of Lake Olmstead.[5] The soldier was Pvt. James Bussey, twenty-five, formerly of Kathwood, South Carolina, and his wife was the former Ms. Wilma Beckum, twenty-four, of Augusta. Apparently, Bussey's vehicle plunged into Lake Olmstead after he lost control of it coming down the hill before the Broad Street Bridge.

A brave but futile effort was made to rescue the trapped couple by James Hooper, eighteen, who jumped from his car, pulled his shoes off, and plunged into the icy waters of the lake. He made several dives in an effort to unlock the doors of Bussey's vehicle, but they were locked from the inside. Although almost exhausted and numb from cold, Hooper eventually managed to break the windshield, but being exhausted and numb from cold, he had to be pulled into a boat and carried to a nearby home where he was wrapped in blankets; an ambulance could arrive and carry him to the hospital. Mr. Hooper told a *Chronicle* reporter that "what I regret is that I could not do anything for the people in the car."[6]

The "Murder" of Barbara Ann West

A most interesting murder case made it to the court in 1944. The criminal case of Isaac West, a fifty-eight-year-old textile worker, accused of drowning his seven-year-old daughter in 1944, was closely followed by Augustans with countless spectators packing the courtroom throughout the trial.[7] Officers alleged that West shoved his daughter, Barbara Ann West, into Lake Olmstead on the night of November 19 to recover payouts from several life insurance policies he had purchased on her life.

The bitterly contested case began with a motion for mistrial by defense counsel, court-appointed attorneys Nathan Jolles and Starkey S. Flythe, when Solicitor General George Hains, in his opening statement, improperly introduced evidence of an alleged confession by West. After hearing the arguments, the honorable judge, A. L. Franklin, struck the evidence of West's confession.[8]

Issac West explained that he and his daughter had walked to the lake to go fishing. When they reached the lake, they stopped and talked with a man who was fishing from a boat. They also stopped to get persimmons from a persimmon tree before casting into the lake with hopes of catching a fish.

> When we had walked around, we went back to the hook and she [Barbara Ann] was holding my fingers. She made a dash and fell down the incline and I went after her and fell and my knee struck her in the back and knocked her in the water. I tried to get to her and couldn't. I hollered as loud as I could.[9]

In his testimony, West explained to the jury that he "did just like any father would have done. I didn't throwed my young'un in the water. I was tore up so bad, I didn't know what I was doing."[10]

After Barbara Ann fell in the water, West said he went to the city stockade for help.

> I had to kick down the door to get the woman at the stockade to come, and when the police came I didn't see no lights. I hollered as loud as I could the whole time. That man [pointing to Assistant Solicitor Charles Britt and others] went up to the lake and dug out the bank to make it look like she couldn't have got into the water.[11]

West's testimony made it seem like he had been framed. Mrs. Jesse Clemmer, matron at the stockade, testified that West came to the door and asked her if she had a phone. West then proceeded to tell her his daughter had fallen in the lake and he needed an ambulance. According to Mrs. Clemmer, at no time did she hear him holler for help or request further assistance.

Officer C. D. Jones, who answered the call to the city stockade, said that after arriving at the scene, he spent twenty minutes looking for West before West came running up to him and told him that his "girl had fell in the lake." Officer Jones noted that only the bottom of West's trouser legs was wet. He testified that West told him Barbara Ann broke away from him and ran down the embankment. West heard her hit the water and then pulled off his clothes and waded as far as he could into the water by holding on to the bank. When Officer Jones found Barbara Ann's body, it was floating facedown about eight feet from the bank.

Special Detective H. S. Grammar testified that West had purchased over $5,000 in insurance policies on his daughter before the drowning. Grammar said West had ten children: six by his first wife who had died, one by his second wife, and three by his current wife. Grammar took West, West's wife, and his mother-in-law, Mrs. Edna A. Buck, to revisit the scene of the drowning. According to Grammar, West said that when Barbara Ann fell in the water, he took off all his clothes and went in after her, but he couldn't find her, so he put his clothes back on, found his glasses, and walked to the stockade in the dark.

The prosecution presented numerous witnesses regarding seven life insurance policies West had on Barbara Ann. H. C. Fowler, a local insurance agent, was the first witness for the prosecution. Fowler testified that West was the beneficiary on a double indemnity insurance policy insuring his daughter, Barbara Ann, for $800. Fowler also testified that the day after Barbara Ann drowned, West called him to ask when he could pick up his beneficiary check. L. H. Gore, another local insurance agent, testified that West had purchased three policies on Barbara Ann from him, all of which were set to lapse the same week that Barbara Ann died. Two of the policies had a $500 natural death benefit. The third policy had a double indemnity that would have benefits of $924. Upon cross examination, however, Gore testified that West had the same amount of insurance on one of his other daughters, Mary Francis. Another local insurance agent, R. W. Lynch, testified that West was the beneficiary of a policy on Barbara Ann for $800 and had attempted to borrow $40 from him after Barbara Ann's death. On cross examination, Lynch revealed that West had a higher benefit policy for his other daughter. Finally, West also had a $500 policy through G. L. Gordon, another local insurance agent, and a $800 policy through C. H. Thompson, insurance agent, that was set to lapse three days after the death.

Another issue was Barbara Ann's funeral. S. Herbert Elliott, a local mortician, testified that West came to him and wanted to spend $1,200 on Barbara Ann's funeral. Mrs. J. L. Cooey, sister of Barbara Ann's mother, testified that West left Barbara Ann's funeral in Savannah, Georgia before it was over to come back to Augusta.

Although West contended he could not swim, the prosecution presented overwhelming evidence that contrary to his statements, West could swim. G. B. Ewing and Will Galloway of Moultrie, Georgia, testified that they had seen West swim years ago when he was in South Georgia. Mrs. R. C. McCleod, Barbara Ann's grandmother, said she had seen West and Barbara Ann's mother swimming.

After the prosecution rested, the defense proceeded to put forth evidence of West's character. James Huff, who lived with West for about a year, testified that he was always nice to his kids. Ms. Lillian Coxwell, who also lived with West, testified that he was always nice to his children and that they were constantly with him.[12] Robert L. Rabun, a fireman and former worker with West at Sibley Mill, also testified that West was always with his children and had never mentioned his insurance to him. He also testified that West paid back a $10 loan he made to him. Mrs. Edna A. Buck, West's mother-in-law, said he was "always nice to the children" and that she often saw them sitting on his lap.[13]

Thelma Hains, personnel officer at Sibley Mill, testified that West's average weekly wage while working at Sibley Mills was $37.50 and that he had recently obtained a release from her to go to a new job in Savannah.

The prosecution and defense finally finished, and the case was given to the jury for deliberations at 7:10 p.m. In less than two hours, the jury returned with their verdict at 8:45 p.m.[14] Remarkably, West was found not guilty and acquitted on February 14, 1944.

Swept Away

Tragedy almost struck the Wilcox family as well in 1944. The eight-year-old son of Mr. and Mrs. David Wilcox Jr. and another youth were playing along the road near the Wilcox home in the Lakemont subdivision when they were caught in the pouring rainwater following a violent cloudburst.[15] The Wilcox boy was caught in the swift waters and hurled into the storm sewer culvert. Mrs. Wilcox ran to the assistance of her son, reached down into the culvert, and actually grabbed hold of her son's arm. Unfortunately, her grasp failed, and her son fell back into the pipe. Mrs. Wilcox, in shock, screamed for help, but in the meantime, her son was swept toward a larger storm culvert, about twenty inches in diameter, carrying storm water beneath the paved road into Lake Olmstead.

The youth was swept through the pipe's tunnel, but fortunately, he was able to hold his breath until he emerged on a small sandbar in the lake caused by the outflow of the storm sewer. A few feet farther out was deep water. When asked how he got through the tunnel without injury, he said, "I held my breath as I went through the long tunnel."[16]

Twenty-four years later, twelve-year-old Kenny Godfrey would not be so lucky. Kenny was caught in rushing water in a deep ditch on Smith Drive after a cloudburst.[17] He was sucked up against the mouth of an open sewer. Efforts by nearby help tried to pull him loose from the grip of water pressure. Although Kenny was eventually freed, he died a few hours later.

Esther Williams, Bathing Beauty

Years before the popularity of such shows as *American Idol* and *America's Got Talent*, Julian Smith Casino was host of the first round of the Esther Williams Bathing Beauty Contest, which came to Augusta August 14-15, 1946. The event was sponsored by the Miller Theatre, Royal Crown Bottling Company, Radio Station WGAC, and the Augusta Recreation Commission.[18] Ms. Esther Williams (1921-2013) was not only a leading lady in Hollywood but also a champion swimmer who aspired to compete in the 1940 Olympic Games before the games were canceled due to the onset of World War II.[19] Also known as America's Mermaid, she starred in several hit movies, including the 1944 movie *Bathing Beauty* with Red Skelton.

The Esther Williams Bathing Beauty contest included three entry divisions: six through twelve years, thirteen through fifteen years, and sixteen and older. Each of the five city parks, Allen, Chafee, Hickman, May, and Stewart Walker, were allowed to submit five entries in the two divisions.[20] Over eighty bathing beauties entered the contest. The first round of competition took place on a stage erected at Lake Olmstead with music provided by the Richmond Academy Orchestra. An overflowing crowd witnessed the finals at the Miller Theatre between the showings of Ms. William's current movie, *Easy to Wed.*

Eight-year-old Camille Rozier won the "small fry" division and fifteen-year-old Betty Bessinger won the middle division. After a hard fought battle between Athenia Rabun and Agnes Burdie Culpepper, eighteen-year-old Agnes Culpepper was declared the winner of the sixteen and older division. Evidently, Culpepper's physical measurements were almost identical to Esther Williams.

The winners were awarded Metro Goldwyn Mayer trophies in the shape of cups by an MGM representative and talent scout. Pictures of the winners were also sent to Hollywood to be placed on file for further reference by talent scouts.[21]

All-American Music Camp

Julian Smith Park was host to a phenomenal musical event. For the first time, the All-American Music Camp was held in Augusta from June 15 to July 5, 1947.[22] Nearly a thousand young musicians from numerous states converged upon Augusta for the three-week event featuring musical instruction, entertainment, and recreation in a camp-like atmosphere. Students could receive training in a variety of musical groups, including concert symphonic band, marching band, sight-reading band, green concert band, chorus work, girls' choir with mixed-group sight reading, boys' glee club with mixed-group sight reading, junior choir, elementary choir, master piano ensemble, piano ensemble, all-girls dance orchestra, and boys dance bank, with minor courses in harmony, public school music, ear training, theory, arranging, composition, baton twirling, cane twirling, student conducting, and a number of other instructive sessions.

The purpose of the camp, as described by George T. Bennett, camp director and director of music education at the Junior College of Augusta, was to assemble together the best young music talent in the nation in one setting. The young musicians worked hard during the day mastering their various lessons. In the evening, they relaxed and enjoyed social activities, receptions, dances, picture shows, and excursions, including a boat trip to Savannah and another to Charleston for an ocean cruise.

The first person to arrive in Augusta for the All-American Music Camp was eighteen-year-old Richard Parmeter of Hansen, Idaho, just twenty miles south of the Canadian border.[23] It took Richard five days to travel over 2,500 miles to attend the South's first music camp. The first thing he did upon his arrival in Augusta was to inspect the campsite at Julian Smith Park and take a swim in Lake Olmstead.[24]

Approximately 350 students representing twenty-one states came by bus, airplane, and train from all parts of the country. Numerous state governors designated official representatives for the opening reception. State flags and state colors were hung in the auditorium, and the songs of the various states were sung during the evenings. The first concert was attended by over 1,500 Augustans who braved threatening weather to enjoy the All-American Music Camp's Symphonic Band concert held on the Watergate stage overlooking Lake Olmstead.[25]

The camp finale was a combination of all the young musicians under the direction of Glenn Cliffe Vainum of Northwestern University.[26] The event was staged to coincide with Augusta's Fourth of July celebration at Lake Olmstead.[27] C. K. Fields put on a display of motorboat racing, followed by an evening concert by the music camp student at the lakeside bandstand. Simultaneously, boats began a procession on the lake lighted by Chinese lanterns. After the concert, boats formed a semicircle in the lake flanking a large raft from which a fireworks display was launched. Concluding the display and commemorating the conclusion of the music camp was the setting off of fireworks in the shape of a gigantic American flag.

The combined event was so large that all Augusta stores, city and county offices, the Chamber of Commerce and Merchants Association Office, banks, the Richmond County Health Department, and Board of Education Offices were closed all day. Even the county sheriff's office was closed, with business conducted from the jail.[28]

Maid of Cotton Contest

Augusta's storied history as a large inland cotton market was celebrated during the finals of the Augusta area Maid of Cotton contest held under the shade trees on the shores of Lake Olmstead at Julian Smith Park in 1954.[29] The affair was sponsored by the Georgia Unit of the National Cotton Council, the Augusta Cotton Exchange, the city of Augusta, Chamber of Commerce, Merchants Association, and the Maid of Cotton merchants group. Following a parade, the Cotton Maids went to Julian Smith Park, where each two contestants were assigned a box containing burlap string, wrapping for baling cotton, and access to full bins of cotton. Within a set period of time, each couple had to fill the box with cotton, pound it firmly, and bale it securely and neatly.

Explosive Lake

An explosive situation occurred on Monday, August 30, 1965, following an arrest of three young males by Augusta police after the young males went on a racially motivated bombing spree, throwing a gas bomb at a group of African-Americans and bombing two autos with hand grenades. After arresting three boys, the police learned that one of the suspects, Jack Bailie III, had dumped an activated rifle shell containing thirty pounds of TNT explosives into Lake

Olmstead.[30] Baile told the police that he had eased the recoilless rifle shell used to destroy tanks during wartime into Lake Olmstead eight months earlier. Bailie, a seventeen-year-old former Eagle Scout and church worker, admitted stealing the "dud" rifle shell from a Fort Gordon range and then dumping it in the lake.

The police immediately sealed off the lake and cautiously warned that the shell could be triggered by any movement of the water. The police, Fort Gordon demolition men, and divers from the Neptune Scuba Club began the search for the projectile. Hampered by the murky lake water, explosive charges were set off in the area where the shell was supposedly dumped. A section of the lake was subsequently drained after several days without success.

A cache of explosives was found inside a crate buried in the backyard of one boy's home. Investigators found twelve training-type hand grenades with caps, eleven packages of high-explosive powder, enough to charge 275 grenades, nineteen grenade fuses, eighteen canister-type smoke bombs, a grenade without cap, and a fused homemade bomb.[31]

A Young Lifesaver

Jamie Yarbrough, a sixteen-year-old high school student at Southgate Baptist Church, became an Augusta hero on June 18, 1972, after saving a man and boy who almost drowned in Lake Olmstead. Jamie was sitting near the boat dock during the early evening when he saw two people struggling in the water about thirty yards away. When Jamie saw Arthur Scott, thirteen, go under, he quickly took off his shirt and shoes and dove into the water. After pulling Scott to shore, Jamie looked back to discover he had assistance in his attempts to save the older boater. He saw an unidentified boater jump in the water and began searching for Willie James Hallman, thirty-seven, who had also gone underwater. The boater pushed Hallman to the surface after finding him lying on the bottom of the lake. Yarbrough credited the boater, as well as a woman who jumped into the water with a life preserver, with helping save Hallman's life.[32]

Trivia

The Country Club of Augusta had a large frontage on Lake Olmstead. The *Augusta Chronicle* urged the board of directors of the Country Club to consider development of a boat club.[33]

*   *   *

Figure 79. Sikorsky amphibian plane

Colonel Robert R. McCormick, publisher of the *Chicago Tribune* and one of the nation's foremost businessmen, would land his Sikorsky amphibian plane on the Savannah River and Lake Olmstead.[34]

*   *   *

Lake Olmstead froze over in 1899.

*   *   *

In 1904, a pony was seen swimming in Lake Olmstead and rescued.[35]

*   *   *

In 1929, malaria eradication was an issue of great concern. Richmond County lakes, streams, and ditches were sprayed with Paris green as a method of malaria eradication in an effort to kill the larvae of the anopheles mosquito. The mixture used is one part Paris green to ten parts of hydrated lime, which is sprayed or dusted over the entire surface of the streams and lakes.[36]

*   *   *

In 1940, Augusta had the coldest weather it had had in a dozen years since January 2, 1928, ten degrees expected.[37] For the first time since 1899, the lake froze over.

*   *   *

A huge forty-foot candle was set up on Lake Olmstead as a public demonstration and the Light-a-Candle campaign to focus attention on the dangers of cancer.[38]

*   *   *

In 1958, a four-foot alligator was found in Lake Olmstead.[39]

*   *   *

In 1959, W. L. Crisler, nine, while fishing at Lake Olmstead, caught what was tentatively identified as a freshwater jellyfish.[40] The glob measured one and a half feet across and weighed five pounds.

*   *   *

A tense silence settled over Augusta on the night of May 12, 1970, as state troopers, National Guardsmen, and police, armed with loaded weapons and a dusk-to-dawn curfew, brought order after the violence and chaos of previous day's racial riot left six dead.[41] More than one thousand guardsmen pitched tents on the banks of Lake Olmstead. James Brown volunteered to help.

*   *   *

Authorities got a scare in January 2002 when a fisherman thought he saw a baby floating in the water of Lake Olmstead. Deputies—along with rescue divers, firefighters, and Richmond County Emergency Management Agency—spent several minutes on a bridge near Milledge Road and Lakeshore Loop trying to pull the object from the water.[42] They recovered a rubber *E. T.* doll.

Figure 80. Dawn of Lake Olmstead (*Robert A. Mullins Collection*)

ENDNOTES

Chapter I

1   *Augusta Chronicle*, May 6, 1904.

2   *Augusta Chronicle*, Sep. 26, 1914.

3   *Augusta Chronicle*, Apr. 6, 1933.

4   *Augusta Chronicle*, Sep. 15, 1985 (emphasis added).

5   Ibid.

6   Charles C. Jones Jr., *Memorial History of Augusta, Georgia; from Its Settlement in 1735 to the Close of the Eighteenth Century*; Salem Dutcher, *From the Close of the Eighteenth Century to the Present Time* (Syracuse, NY: D. Mason & Co., 1890), 25.

7   The Central Savannah River Area (CSRA) includes thirteen counties in Georgia and five counties in South Carolina. As of the 2010 American Community Survey from the US Census Bureau, the CSRA had a total population of 709,433, and the six-county Augusta-Richmond County Metropolitan Statistical Area had a population of 543,738.

Chapter II

1   *Workers of the Writers' Program of the WPA of GA, the Story of Washington-Wilkes* (Athens: University of Georgia Press, 1941), 38.

2   "Charleston-Hamburg Railroad," American Society of Civil Engineers, last accessed January 21, 2014, http://www.asce.org/People-and-Projects/Projects/Landmarks/Charleston–Hamburg-Railroad/.

3   "Georgia's Railroad History and Heritage," RailGa.com, last accessed January 21, 2014, http://railga.com/georgia.html. The Georgia Railroad & Banking Company was originally chartered in 1833 as the Georgia Railroad Company, with one of its first tasks being to build a railroad from Augusta to Athens, Georgia. Within two years, its charter was amended to provide for banking services and its name changed to Georgia Railroad and Banking Company. The bank was instrumental in financing for the Augusta to Atlanta railroad and the Augusta Canal.

4   "Seeds of Industry," National Park Service, last accessed January 21, 2014, http://www.nps.gov/lowe/photosmultimedia/prologue.htm.

[5]   Lowell National Historical Park Handbook, National Park Service, last accessed January 21, 2014, http://www.nps.gov/lowe/photosmultimedia/canal_system.htm.

[6]   Edward J. Cashin, *The Brightest Arm of the Savannah: The Augusta Canal 1845-2000* (Augusta: Augusta Canal Authority, 2002), 67.

[7]   Robert F. O'Neill, "The Accomplishments of a Railroad Leader Are Brought to Light a Sign at Baltimore Pike and Thomson Road Honors J. Edgar Thomson. He Made the Pennsylvania Railroad an Industry Giant," *Inquirer*, Nov. 15, 1992, http://articles.philly.com/1992-11-15/news/26006990_1_marker-railroad-man-civil-engineer.

[8]   Junior Achievement, last accessed Jun. 1, 2013, http://www.ja.org/hof/viewLaureate.asp?id=174&alpha=T

[9]   "Thomson History," Thomson-McDuffie County Convention and Visitors Bureau, last accessed January 21, 2014, http://www.exploremcduffiecounty.com/heritage/ThomsonHistory.php. In 1975, Thomson was honored as an original inductee into the Junior Achievement and Fortune Magazine's Business Hall of Fame. http://www.ja.org/hof/viewLaureate.asp?id=174&alpha=T.

[10] George White, S*tatistics of the State of Georgia: Including an Account of Its Natural, Civil, and Ecclesiastical History; Together with a Particular Description of Each County, Notices of the Manners and Customs of Its Aboriginal Tribes, and a Correct Map of the State* (Savannah: W. Thorne Williams, 1849), 503.

[11] Michael C. White, *Down Rae's Creek: A Famous Stream at Augusta, Georgia's Fall Line Hill* (Aiken, SC: Howell Printing Company, 1996). Reportedly, Rae was responsible for 75 percent of the Indian trade in the South during the eighteenth century, *Irish Times*, Apr. 5, 1995.

[12] Edward J. Cashin, *The Brightest Arm of the Savannah: The Augusta Canal 1845-2000* (Augusta: Augusta Canal Authority, 2002), 77.

[13] *Augusta Chronicle*, Oct. 6, 1890.

[14] *Workers of the Writers' Program of the WPA of GA, the Story of Washington-Wilkes* (Athens, University of Georgia Press, 1941), 38.

[15] *Augusta Chronicle*, Mar. 22, 1898.

[16] Peggy Robbins, "The Confederacy's Bomb Brothers," *Journal of Mine Action*, vol. 6, issue 1 (Apr. 2002), available at http://maic.jmu.edu/journal/6.1/notes/robbins/robbins.htm.

[17] *Augusta Chronicle*, Mar. 22, 1898.

[18] *Augusta Chronicle*, May 8, 1877.

[19] *Augusta Chronicle*, Mar. 22, 1898.

[20] *Augusta Chronicle*, Apr. 3, 1877.

[21] *Augusta Chronicle*, Feb. 20, 1883.

[22] Ibid.

[23] "History of the Chinese and CCBA in Augusta," Chinese Consolidated Benevolent Ass., last accessed January 21, 2014, http://www.ccbaaugusta.com/history.htm

[24] *Augusta Chronicle*, Aug. 17, 1872.

[25] *Augusta Chronicle*, Mar. 7, 1873.

[26] *Augusta Chronicle*, Apr. 3, 1877.

Chapter III

[1] Edward J. Cashin, *The Brightest Arm of the Savannah: The Augusta Canal 1845-2000* (Augusta Canal Authority, 2002), 92.

[2] *Augusta Chronicle*, Aug. 17, 1872.

[3] Although it is hard to pinpoint the date, a November 30, 1872, advertisement for property along Rae's Creek references that the property will be located at the head of the new lake made by the stoppage of waters of Rae's Creek. *Daily Chronicle & Sentinel*, Nov. 30, 1872.

[4] *Augusta Chronicle*, Apr. 4, 1872.

[5] *Augusta Chronicle*, May 6, 1881.

[6] *Augusta Chronicle*, July 13, 1873.

[7] *Augusta Chronicle*, Aug. 4, 1877.

[8] "Lake created in canal project," *Augusta Chronicle*, Jan. 13, 1999.

[9] *Augusta Chronicle*, Jul. 2, 1899.

[10] *Augusta Chronicle*, Aug. 3, 1873.

Chapter IV

[1] *Augusta Chronicle*, Jul. 24, 1898.

[2] Drew Goins, "History of Augusta's Waterworks," Augusta Utilities Department, available at *gawaterhistory.com/AugustasWaterworksHistory.pdf*.

[3] *Augusta Chronicle*, Aug. 4, 1877.

[4] *Augusta Chronicle*, Jun. 25, 1881.

[5] *Augusta Chronicle*, Jun. 11, 1882.

[6] *Augusta Chronicle*, Sep. 11, 1888. Hawks Gully, located on the western edge of downtown Augusta, was utilized as a return outlet for water from the canal to return to the Savannah River.

[7] *Augusta Chronicle*, Sep. 15, 1888.

Chapter V

[1] *Augusta Chronicle*, July 13, 1873.

[2] *Augusta Chronicle*, May 7, 1873; *Augusta Chronicle*, Jun. 20, 1873; *Augusta Chronicle*, Jul. 27, 1873; *Augusta Chronicle*, Sep. 21, 1873 (the *Home Made* was outfitted for either sailing or rowing).

[3] *Augusta Chronicle*, Nov. 6, 1873.

[4] The Clinch Riffles were an elite militia named in honor of General Duncan Clinch who served in the War of 1812. It was considered an honor and a privilege to be voted

into membership. The Clinch Riffles formed Company A of the Fifth Georgia Infantry Regiment and were known by their distinctive green uniforms.

[5]   Saint Paul's Church was established on the grounds of Fort Augusta in 1750 by the Church of England. http://www.saintpauls.org/history/.

[6]   "Manuscript Collections of the Nantucket Historical Association Research Library," Nantucket Historical Association, available at http://www.nha.org/library/ms/ms6.htm.

[7]   *Augusta Chronicle,* Jun. 8, 1873.

[8]   *Augusta Chronicle,* Jul. 16, 1873.

[9]   *Augusta Chronicle,* Apr. 2, 1873.

[10] Ibid.

[11] Ibid.

[12] *Augusta Chronicle,* Jun. 14, 1874.

[13] *Augusta Chronicle,* Jun. 4, 1875.

[14] *Augusta Chronicle,* Aug. 6, 1875.

[15] *Augusta Chronicle,* Jul. 17, 1879.

[16] *Augusta Chronicle,* Jul. 24, 1879.

[17] Charles C. Jones Jr., *Memorial History of Augusta, Georgia; from Its Settlement in 1735 to the Close of the Eighteenth Century;* Salem Dutcher, *From the Close of the Eighteenth Century to the Present Time* (Syracuse, NY; D. Mason and Co., 1890), 146.

[18] Ibid, 476.

[19] *Augusta Chronicle,* Jul. 24, 1877.

[20] Ibid.

[21] *Augusta Chronicle,* Feb. 4, 1887. The AGCH Club sought to ensure high society amusements. Although the club presented several elaborate balls including, but not limited to, the Domino Ball at the Augusta Hotel.

[22] *Augusta Chronicle,* Jun. 8, 1889.

[23] *Augusta Chronicle,* Mar. 23, 1898.

[24] *Augusta Chronicle,* Jul. 3, 1904.

[25] *Augusta Chronicle,* May 8, 1899.

[26] *Augusta Chronicle,* Nov. 25, 1902.

[27] *Augusta Chronicle,* May 6, 1904.

[28] *Augusta Chronicle,* May 3, 1907.

[29] *Augusta Chronicle,* May 23, 1883.

Chapter VI

[1]   http://www.usclimatedata.com/map.php?location=USGA0032.

[2]   "Augusta Arsenal [1826]," Augusta State University, last accessed January 21, 2014, http://www.aug.edu/public_relations/history/arsenal.html.

[3]   *Augusta Chronicle,* Nov. 13, 1949.

4   American State Papers, House of Representatives, 19th Congress, 1st Session Military Affairs: vol. 3, p. 242, no. 312

5   Breana Walton, *Walker Family History on Augusta State's Campus*, available at http://www. rajarmstrong.com/projects/summerville/walker/. The property was purchased in a deed dated November 9, 1826.

6   The city of Augusta subsequently annexed Summerville in 1912.

7   Edward J. Cashin, *The Brightest Arm of the Savannah: The Augusta Canal 1845-2000* (Augusta: Augusta Canal Authority, 2002), 136.

8   *Augusta Chronicle*, Mar. 7, 1999.

9   *Augusta Chronicle*, Apr. 3, 1890.

10   *Augusta Chronicle*, Dec. 1, 1889.

11   *Augusta Chronicle*, May 29, 1887.

12   "Bon Air a comfortable retreat for wealthy," *Augusta Chronicle*, Mar. 7, 1999.

13   David Ogilvie also designed the Augusta Municipal golf course, now known as the Patch, in 1928.

14   *Augusta Chronicle*, Aug. 9, 1933.

15   *Augusta Chronicle*, Aug. 9, 1933.

16   *Augusta Chronicle*, Nov. 14, 1942. The Lake course was sold to F. A. Calhoun, George C. Blanchard, local realtors; P. S. Knox Jr., building contractor of Thomson, G. A.; E. C. Harvey, Holley Hill, S. C., and Jeff Curry, an Augusta attorney.

17   *Augusta Chronicle*, Aug. 30, 2007.

18   *Augusta Chronicle*, Jan. 21, 1922.

19   *Augusta Chronicle*, Dec. 3, 1922.

20   The Bon Air Hotel was one of four hotels the Vanderbilts established so they could cover every season of the year with their grand hotels.

21   *Augusta Chronicle*, Dec. 29, 1945.

22   "The Partridge Inn," National Park Service, available at http://www.nps.gov/nr/travel/augusta/partridgeinn.html.

23   "The Partridge Inn Self Guided Tour," Partridge Inn, last accessed January 21, 2014, www.partridgeinn.com/d/.../Self20Guided20Tour20Bookleteb1ca5.

24   Lee Ann Caldwell, "Open for the Season," *Augusta Magazine* (Oct. 2010).

25   Ibid.

26   *Augusta Chronicle*, Apr. 7, 1923.

27   Lucian Knight, *A Standard History of Georgia and Georgians*, vol. 6 (Lewis Publishing Co., 1917), 3094.

28   Ibid.

29   Ibid.

30   http://cityofdust.blogspot.com/2005/05/hollywood-south-carolina.html.

31   Ibid.

32   "History of North Augusta," Lookaway Inn, last accessed January 21, 2014, http://www.lookawayinn.com/local-information/history-of-north-augusta.

33   *Augusta Chronicle*, Jan. 1, 1917.

[34] Ibid.

[35] *Augusta Chronicle*, Aug. 22, 1915; Aug. 29, 1915. In 1915, special rates were secured from the railroads for out-of-town visitors to come to Augusta's Labor Day celebration.

[36] *Augusta Chronicle*, Feb. 16, 1908.

[37] *Augusta Chronicle*, Apr. 9, 1908.

[38] *Augusta Chronicle*, Oct. 23, 1906.

[39] *Augusta Chronicle*, Oct. 29, 1911.

[40] *Augusta Chronicle*, Oct. 4, 1925.

[41] *Augusta Chronicle*, Nov. 22, 1925.

[42] *Augusta Chronicle*, Sep. 28, 1936.

[43] *Augusta Chronicle*, Aug. 8, 1941.

Chapter VII

[1] *Augusta Chronicle*, Jun. 2, 1935.

[2] *Augusta Chronicle*, Oct. 28, 1900. Augusta was renowned for its abundance of social, athletic, literary, and musical clubs. One reason given for this phenomenon was that one could obtain amusement and pleasure for a limited or low cost, and in many instances, club members who would not be able to entertain otherwise were enabled to do so.

[3] These lanterns, similar to luminaries, are typically made of colored paper, which surrounds a candle or light projecting vibrant colors and images.

[4] *Augusta Chronicle*, May 5, 1881.

[5] *Augusta Chronicle*, Apr 5, 1881.

[6] *Augusta Chronicle*, May 13, 1881.

[7] *Augusta Chronicle*, Dec. 24, 1972; see also *Augusta Chronicle*, Apr. 26, 1973; *Augusta Chronicle*, Dec. 19, 1972.

[8] *Augusta Chronicle*, Jul. 31, 1873.

[9] Edward J. Cashin, *The Brightest Arm of the Savannah: The Augusta Canal 1845-2000* (Augusta: Augusta Canal Authority, 2002), 143.

[10] *Augusta Chronicle*, Mar. 25, 1887.

[11] Mathewson was a general commission merchant and agent for Hazard & Dupont Powder Cos., Georgia and North Carolina Cotton Mills, North Carolina and Virginia Tobacco Manufacturers, and the Pacific Guano Company.

[12] *Augusta Chronicle*, Apr. 3, 1890.

[13] Judge Boarman (1839-1916), a former mayor of Shreveport, Louisiana, and lieutenant of the Caddo Rifles of the Confederate Army during the civil war, was nominated by President James Garfield on May 18, 1881. He was confirmed by the Senate and received commission that same day. He served until his death in 1916. http://bioguide.congress.gov/scripts/biodisplay.pl?index=B000579.

[14] *Troy Daily Times*, Feb. 19, 1902, p. 6.

[15] Ibid.

16 Ibid.

17 *Augusta Chronicle,* Jun. 23, 1911.

18 *Augusta Chronicle,* Dec. 23, 1912.

19 *Augusta Chronicle,* Feb. 13, 1890.

20 *Augusta Chronicle,* Dec. 23, 1912.

21 Ibid.

22 The camp was initially located in the Turpin Hill area in the south part of Augusta but was later moved to the Murray Hill area in west Augusta in late August.

23 *Augusta Chronicle,* Dec. 23, 1912.

24 *Augusta Chronicle,* Jul. 27, 1902.

25 *Augusta Chronicle,* Oct. 28, 1906.

26 Ibid.

27 *Augusta Chronicle,* Oct. 20, 1906. At the request of Dyer and Mayor William M. Dunbar, City Engineer Nisbet Wingfield located and staked out a portion of the proposed boulevard along the canal and around Lake Olmstead. In 1906, a steel bridge was built across Rae's Creek at Lake Olmstead by the Roanoke Bridge Company for $1,385.

28 *Augusta Chronicle,* Jul. 20, 1902.

29 *Enclyclopaedia Britannica,* s. v. "Kinetoscope," accessed on January 21, 2014, http://www.britannica.com/EBchecked/topic/318211/Kinetoscope.

30 *Augusta Chronicle,* Jun. 14, 1899.

31 *Enclyclopaedia Britannica,* s. v. "Vitascope," accessed on January 21, 2014, http://www.britannica.com/EBchecked/topic/631191/Vitascope.

32 *Augusta Chronicle,* Jul. 2, 1899.

33 *Augusta Chronicle,* Jul. 23, 1899.

34 *Augusta Chronicle,* Jun. 10, 1898.

35 *Augusta Chronicle,* Sep. 21, 1898.

36 *Augusta Chronicle,* Mar. 12, 1900; Oct. 21, 1900; Apr. 23, 1904. The turkey rabbits were donated by Mrs. R. W. Burnham of Harlem, Georgia.

37 *Augusta Chronicle,* May 1, 1912.

38 *Augusta Chronicle,* Dec. 23, 1898.

39 *Augusta Chronicle,* Aug. 17, 1901.

40 *Augusta Chronicle,* Aug. 10, 1902.

41 "Prairie Dog," *National Geographic,* accessed on January 21, 2014, http://animals.nationalgeographic.com/animals/mammals/prairie-dog/.

42 *Augusta Chronicle,* May 25, 1904.

43 *Augusta Chronicle,* May 30, 1904. Due to their pest-like nature, approximately 98 percent of the prairie dog population in the United States was exterminated during the twentieth century.

44 *Augusta Chronicle,* Oct. 14, 1901.

45 *Augusta Chronicle,* May 1, 1912.

46 "1916 fire destroyed more than 740 Augusta buildings," *Augusta Chronicle,* Mar. 15, 1999.

47 "1916 Fire devastating to Augusta," *Augusta Chronicle,* Aug. 30, 1999.

[48]   *Augusta Chronicle*, Apr. 2, 1904; May 6, 1907.

[49]   *Augusta Chronicle*, Apr. 11, 1942.

[50]   *Augusta Chronicle*, Nov. 12, 1911. Colonel Dyer and Cody formed the Cody-Dyer Arizona Mining and Milling Co. with hopes of finding gold.

[51]   *Augusta Chronicle*, Dec. 23, 1912.

[52]   *Augusta Chronicle*, Jul. 29, 1899.

[53]   *Augusta Chronicle*, Oct. 28, 1906.

[54]   *Augusta Chronicle*, Jun. 1, 1925

[55]   *Augusta Chronicle*, Jul. 9, 1922.

[56]   *Augusta Chronicle*, Mar. 17, 1907.

[57]   *Augusta Chronicle*, Mar. 17, 1907.

[58]   *Augusta Chronicle*, Apr. 19, 1908.

[59]   *The New York Dramatic Mirror*, Nov. 18, 1893.

[60]   *Augusta Chronicle*, Mar. 15, 1908.

[61]   "History," *Seven Venues*, accessed on Jan. 21, 2014, http://www.sevenvenues.com/about/history/wells.

[62]   *Augusta Chronicle*, Jun. 11, 1911.

[63]   *Augusta Chronicle*, Jul. 13, 1908.

[64]   *Augusta Chronicle*, May 17, 1908; Jul. 13, 1908.

[65]   *Augusta Chronicle*, Apr. 19, 1908.

[66]   *Augusta Chronicle*, Apr. 13, 1908.

[67]   "Mullins Boats," *Salem Ohio History*, accessed on Jan. 5, 2014, http://www.salemohiohistory.com/HistoryMakers/Mullins-Boats.aspx.

[68]   *Augusta Chronicle*, Feb. 28, 1909.

[69]   *Augusta Chronicle*, May 2, 1909.

[70]   *The Pittsburg Press*, Aug. 3, 1916.

[71]   *Augusta Chronicle*, Sep. 4, 1909.

[72]   *Augusta Chronicle*, Jun. 23, 1911.

[73]   Ibid.

[74]   *Augusta Chronicle*, Jul. 20, 1912.

[75]   *Augusta Land Co. v. Augusta Ry. & Electric Co.*, 140 Ga. 519, 79 S. E. 139 (1913).

[76]   *Augusta Chronicle*, Jul. 27, 1912.

[77]   *Augusta Chronicle*, May 23, 1915.

[78]   *Augusta Chronicle*, May 2, 1915.

[79]   *Augusta Chronicle*, May 4, 1915.

[80]   *Augusta Chronicle*, Sep. 26, 1914.

[81]   *Augusta Chronicle*, May 4, 1915.

[82]   *Augusta Chronicle*, May 2, 1915.

[83]   *Augusta Chronicle*, Apr. 14, 1952. Dr. Murphey was a descendant of Nicholas Murphey, who came to Georgia with Governor Oglethorpe on his second journey, as a member of His Majesty's Troop of Rangers, stationed at Fort Augusta as a unit of the garrison at the time of the founding of Augusta.

[84] "Old Government House," National Park Service, accessed on Jan. 21, 2014, http://www.nps.gov/nr/travel/augusta/oldgovernment.html. The Old Government House was the seat of local government until 1821, when it was sold to former Mayor Samuel Hale, who made it his residence. The Murphey family bought the property in 1877. Dr. Murphey's estate sold the property to the Augusta Junior League in the 1950s. The Junior League gave the property to Historic Augusta, which in turn sold it to a development firm in the late 1970s. The City of Augusta purchased it in 1987 and is the current owner of the property.

[85] *Augusta Chronicle*, May 5, 1915.

[86] *Augusta Chronicle*, May 23, 1916.

[87] *Augusta Chronicle*, May 2, 1915.

[88] *Augusta Chronicle*, Jun. 27, 1915; Jun. 29, 1915.

[89] *Augusta Chronicle*, Jun. 17, 1915.

[90] *Augusta Chronicle*, Jun. 27, 1915.

[91] *Augusta Chronicle*, Jun. 14, 1915.

[92] *Augusta Chronicle*, Jun. 6, 1916; Jun. 8, 1916; Jun. 11, 1916.

[93] *The Evening Independent*, Apr. 9, 1915.

[94] *Augusta Chronicle*, Jun. 22, 1918

[95] *Augusta Chronicle*, May 31, 1890.

[96] Unfortunately, Alexander was the subject of national news in 1906, when he disappeared and discrepancies of $145,000 were discovered in the accounting of Alexander & Alexander. *New York Daily Tribune*, Jul. 13, 1906.

[97] *Augusta Chronicle*, Jun 1, 1890.

[98] "Fleming, Lamar, Jr.," *Texas State Historical Association*, accessed on Jan. 21, 2014, http://www.tshaonline.org/handbook/online/articles/ffl09.

[99] *Augusta Chronicle*, Dec. 6, 1907.

[100] *Augusta Chronicle*, Aug. 13, 1909.

[101] *Augusta Chronicle*, Apr. 25, 1909.

[102] *Augusta Chronicle*, Sep. 20, 1905.

[103] *Augusta Chronicle*, March 15, 1891; *The Princetonian*, Mar. 11, 1891.

[104] *Augusta Chronicle*, March 19, 1890.

[105] *Augusta Chronicle*, Mar. 12, 1891.

[106] *Augusta Chronicle*, Mar. 17, 1891.

[107] *Augusta Chronicle*, Mar. 6, 1891.

[108] *Augusta Chronicle*, May 27, 1890; May 31, 1890.

[109] Patrick Robertson, *Robertson's Book of Firsts: Who Did What for the First Time* (Bloomsbury Publishing USA, Nov. 11, 2011).

[110] *Augusta Chronicle*, Aug. 22, 1909.

[111] *Augusta Chronicle*, Oct. 28, 1900.

[112] *Augusta Chronicle*, May 24, 1898.

[113] Ibid.

[114] *Augusta Chronicle*, Oct. 28, 1900. By 1900, the members of the Lakeside Club represented a list of prominent Augustans. The members included: Thomas W. Alexander, J. B. Alexander, Irvin Alexander, W. M. Alexander, J. A. Anderson, W. E. Andrews, Hugh Alexander, William H. Barrett Jr., Prosper J. A. Berkmans, Charles S. Bohler, F. C. Barnes, J. T. Bothwell Jr., E. C. Burwell, H. C. Brown, William E. Bush, Walker Beeson, R. C. Berkmans, Louis A. Berkmans, W. C. Bewley, J. D. Bansley, Everard Blackshear, F. C. Bush. Charles Biggars, Charles Bush, N. B. Baxley, A. S. Bayles, W. G. Basinger, James Brotherton, J. C. C. Black Jr., W. H. Bishop, L. A. Burkmeyer, R. M. Bissel, Irvine Branch, H. W. Buxton Jr., Geo. P. Butler, H. Gould Barrett, C. H. Cohen, Bryan Cumming, Jack Cranston, Bryson Crane, J. W. Chaffee, H. W. Clark, G. R. Coffin, Campbell Chaffee, W. C. Cleckley, J. Treut Cleckley, William J. Cranston, Chas. Crane, C. R. Clark Jr., J. J. Cohen Jr., L. H. Charbonnier Jr., J. M. Clark, C. D. Cohen, Harry Chaffee, J. B. Caswell, Harry Carr, Geo. Crane, Wylie Crowley, Harry Cashin, Antoine Carr, Louis Cole, Geo. A. Cunningham Jr., M. B. Dunbar, E. W. Deveney, F. X. Dorr, V. J. Dorr, A. O. Dawson, L. A. Dorr, W. E. Berry, C. E. Dunbar, E. R. Derry, E. S. Dunbar, W. T. Davidson, B. S. Dunbar, W. A. Doyle, F. M. Dunbar, S. C. Durban, John W. Dickey, A. H. Davidson Jr., H. H. D'Antignac Jr., J. P. Doughty Jr., Arthur Deveney, L. B. Evans, H. J. Eve, J. C. Fargo, F. P. Farrow, T. R. Ford, Dan Fogerty, Claude Fleming, W. H. Gage, Thos. Goldsby, H. B. Garrett, George N. Garvin Jr., Thomas Hopkins, T. I. Hickman, John Hook, E. B. Hook, L. C. Hayne, J. S. Hall, James Henderson Jr., C. C. Howard, George Hardwick, Judge Henry C. Hammond, Roy Heart, C. H. Howard, Geo. Howard, H. M. Houston, W. R. Houston, William Irvin, William E. Jackson Jr., George T. Jackson, E. S. Johnson, Marion Jones, Chas. E. Jones, T. C. Jowett Jr., G. Jowett, H. B. King, Charles Key, Harold Lamb, Abe Levy, Clinton Lee, E. R. Laney, B. C. Lester, Lloyd Lyon, J. B. Lockheart, Frank Lowe, W. P. Lamar, P. R. Lamar, P. D. Langdon, George S. Lombard, George R. Lombard, William Law, Dr. Eugene E. Murphey, William Martin, William Lyon Martin, J. Moore, T. T. Miller, C. P. Mulherin, C. E. Marks, Samuel Martin, Arthur Martin, John Manly, W. W. May, C. J. Montgomery, F. H. Miller Jr., E. B. Merry, W. B. Merry, N. M. Moore, R. B. McLaws, C. B. McAuliffe, E. W. Miller, C. M. Miller, Frank Moore, F. C. Meyer, Adrienne Miller, Ernest Morris, W. M. Nixon, E. M. North, F. M. North, F. E. Obenauf, T. E. Oertel, George C. Oates Jr, L. F. Platt, W. L. Platt Jr., D. M. Potter, Roscoe Perkins, Dr. C. D. Perkins, Raliegh Perkins, H. C. Parker, Henry Plunket, T. C. Plunket, Bowdre Phinizy, Jacob Phinizy, Montgomery Ridgely, Marion Ridgely, W. R. Rood, Hy. Raworth, C. A. Robbe Jr., J. Righton Robertson, Theo. Richards, Eugene Roseborough, Charles Ridgely, Marshall Shewmake, Henry Saxon, H. P. Shewmake, J. R. Stokes, W. H. P Shepard, W. P. Smith, M. A. Stovall, T. H. Stafford Jr., Julian Stevens, Colden Stokes, William Schwiegert, H. Claude Smith, Terence Sheron, P. A. Steiner, John Sylvester, A. A. Thomas, James Tobin, Robert Tannahill, L. A. Thomas, J. W. Turnet, John D. Twiggs Jr., P. B. Tobin, R. R. Vaughn, W. C. Wardlaw, Walker Wallace, T. C. White, Clarence White, Fielding Wallace, A. T. White, Howard Wilcox, M. P. Walsh, C. Stanley Weisiger, B. W. Wall, Warren Walker, Jos. D. Weed, Rutherford Walton, George W. Whitney, A. S. Wilson, J. B. Walker, J. W. Wallace, and George Wilcox.

[115] *Augusta Chronicle*, May 24, 1899.

[116] *Augusta Chronicle*, Nov. 1, 1908.

[117] *Augusta Chronicle*, May 23, 1901.

[118] *Augusta Chronicle*, May 20, 1902.

[119] *Augusta Chronicle*, May 19, 1908.

[120] *Augusta Chronicle*, May 23, 1908; Aug. 3, 1908.

[121] *Augusta Chronicle*, May 23, 1908; *Augusta Chronicle*, Jul. 13, 1908.

[122] *Augusta Chronicle*, Aug. 13, 1911.

[123] *Augusta Chronicle*, May 20, 1911.

[124] *Augusta Chronicle*, May 7, 1909; *Augusta Chronicle*, Jun. 25, 1909; *Augusta Chronicle*, May 14, 1922. The annual city tennis tournament began in 1907.

[125] *Augusta Chronicle*, Apr. 6, 1909.

[126] *Augusta Chronicle*, Jun. 9, 1919.

[127] *Augusta Chronicle*, Aug. 30, 1912.

[128] Ibid.

[129] *Augusta Chronicle*, Jul. 27, 1961.

[130] *Augusta Chronicle*, Mar. 6, 1960.

[131] *Augusta Chronicle*, Mar. 6, 1960.

[132] *Augusta Chronicle*, Apr. 17, 1918.

[133] *Augusta Chronicle*, Jun. 3, 1913.

[134] *Augusta Chronicle*, Jul. 18, 1915.

[135] *Augusta Chronicle*, Aug. 10, 1915.

[136] Ibid.

[137] *Augusta Chronicle*, Jun. 8, 1913.

[138] *Augusta Chronicle*, Apr. 2, 1914.

[139] *Augusta Chronicle*, Jun. 17, 1914.

[140] *Augusta Chronicle*, Jul. 25, 1915.

[141] *Augusta Chronicle*, Apr. 30, 1915.

[142] *Augusta Chronicle*, Feb. 9, 1906.

[143] *Augusta Chronicle*, Jul. 25, 1915.

[144] *Augusta Chronicle*, May 24, 1898.

[145] *Augusta Chronicle*, Apr. 30, 1915.

[146] *Augusta Chronicle*, Aug. 7, 1918.

[147] *Augusta Chronicle*, Jul. 22, 1928.

[148] *Augusta Chronicle*, Sep. 8, 1918.

[149] *Augusta Chronicle*, May 15, 1921.

[150] Although the *Augusta Chronicle* reported that Sam Baron sold the Lakeside Club to Dave and Shier Levkoff for $5,500, the real estate records do not support the reported sale. See *Augusta Chronicle*, Jun. 24, 1921.

Chapter VIII

1   In 1870, the US Congress made July 4 an unpaid federal holiday. It was not until 1941 that July 4 became a paid holiday for federal employees. http://www.history.com/topics/july-4th.
2   *Augusta Chronicle*, Jun. 27, 1898.
3   *Augusta Chronicle*, Sep. 3, 1899.
4   *Augusta Chronicle*, Jul. 4, 1911.
5   *Augusta Chronicle*, Sep. 25, 1919.
6   *Augusta Chronicle*, Jul. 9, 1920.
7   Ibid.
8   *Augusta Chronicle*, Jun. 3, 1922.
9   *Augusta Chronicle*, May 25, 1923.
10 *Augusta Chronicle*, Jul. 6, 1924.
11 *Augusta Chronicle*, Apr. 2, 1926.
12 *Augusta Chronicle*, Jul. 9, 1920.
13 *Augusta Chronicle*, Jul. 1, 1979.
14 *Augusta Chronicle*, Jul. 4, 1958.
15 *Augusta Chronicle*, Jul. 1, 1979.
16 *Augusta Chronicle*, Jul. 6, 1937.
17 *Augusta Chronicle*, Jul. 5, 1939.

Chapter IX

1   The American Football League (AFL) would later become the National Football League (NFL).
2   *Augusta Chronicle*, Jun. 24, 1921.
3   *Augusta Chronicle*, Mar. 22, 1923.
4   "The Forrest Hills-Ricker Hotel," *The Hill-Top Magazine*, vol. 31, no. 8, Aug. 21, 1926; available at http://www.baharris.org/historicpolandspring/ForrestHillsRicker/ForrestHillsRicker.htm.
5   *Augusta Chronicle*, Dec. 27, 1925.
6   *Augusta Chronicle*, Oct. 16, 1925.
7   *Augusta Chronicle*, Sep. 7, 1937.
8   *Augusta Chronicle*, Mar. 22, 1923.
9   In those days, the team names were a little different than today. The Boston Red Sox were then known as the Boston Americans. The Atlanta Braves were then known as the Boston Doves, Boston Rustlers, and Boston Braves. The Minnesota Twins were then known as the Washington Nationals. The Los Angeles Dodgers were then known as the Brooklyn Dodgers, and the San Francisco Giants were then known as the New York Giants.

10 *Augusta Chronicle*, Nov. 22, 1906; Jun. 23, 1921.

11 *Augusta Chronicle*, Mar. 21, 1922.

12 *Augusta Chronicle*, Apr. 8, 1923.

13 *Augusta Chronicle*, Apr. 14, 1929.

14 *Augusta Chronicle*, Mar. 14, 1924.

15 Ibid.

16 *Augusta Chronicle*, Dec. 27, 1925.

17 *Augusta Chronicle*, Jan. 18, 1925.

18 Rossignol's father, Charles F. Rossignol Sr., had engaged in the musical instrument business for years and later the automobile accessory business, during which time he invented the first visible gasoline pump.

Beginning on Tuesday night, February 2, 1926, Rossignol began a weekly lecture at the Bon Air Vanderbilt Hotel, preceding the evening motion picture performances. "Know the City You Are Visiting" was the subject of the lectures. Rossignol, who is splendidly versed on Augusta, devoted his lecture time to acquainting visitors as to the historical points of interest and the city's great commercial, industrial, and resort advantages. *Augusta Chronicle*, Jan. 26, 1926.

19 *Augusta Chronicle*, Sep. 9, 1925.

20 *Augusta Chronicle*, Oct. 15, 1925.

21 *Augusta Chronicle*, Jun. 11, 1926.

22 *Augusta Chronicle*, Oct. 9, 1925.

23 *Augusta Chronicle*, Feb. 5, 1926.

24 *Augusta Chronicle*, Jan. 31, 1985. The Washington Heights Development Company had control of the Berckmans' tract when Stoltz came to Augusta. Stoltz had the option to buy, provided he built the hotel.

25 "Memorial Web Page for the 1926 Great Miami Hurricane," National Weather Service, accessed on Jan. 21, 2014, http://www.srh.noaa.gov/mfl/?n=miamihurricane1926.

26 *Augusta Chronicle*, Oct. 28, 1946. While serving as mayor, Mr. Smith was a staunch advocate for development of the Savannah River. He was instrumental in obtaining rights for the city to operate a commercial steamboat, the *Altamaha*, on the Savannah River.

27 *Augusta Chronicle*, Jun. 24, 1921.

28 *Augusta Chronicle*, Jan. 31, 1924.

29 *Augusta Chronicle*, Nov. 13, 1924.

30 *Augusta Chronicle*, Dec. 4, 1923; Jan. 12, 1924.

31 *Augusta Chronicle*, Jul. 11, 1931.

32 *Augusta Chronicle*, Nov. 13, 1924.

33 *Augusta Chronicle*, Nov. 11, 1924; Nov. 13, 1924.

34 *Augusta Chronicle*, Mar. 8, 1925; Nov. 6, 1924.

35 *Augusta Chronicle*, Mar. 22, 1925.

[36] *Augusta Chronicle,* Sept. 24, 1925.

[37] *Augusta Chronicle,* Nov. 19, 1924.

[38] *Augusta Chronicle,* Nov. 19, 1924. The property was subsequently sold to Alexander and Garrett, managers of the real estate department of the Southern Finance Corporation.

[39] *Augusta Chronicle,* Jan. 13, 1925.

[40] Ibid.

[41] *Augusta Chronicle,* Dec. 14, 1924.

Chapter X

[1] Rob Pavey, "Depression Hit Augusta Early," *Augusta Chronicle,* Mar. 1, 2009.

[2] *Augusta Chronicle,* Oct. 11, 1927.

[3] *Augusta Chronicle,* Mar. 29, 1928.

[4] *Augusta Chronicle,* Apr. 4, 1928.

[5] *Augusta Chronicle,* Jul. 29, 1928.

[6] Ibid.

Chapter XI

[1] *Augusta Chronicle,* Jul. 15, 1931.

[2] Ibid.

[3] Michael Reynolds, "A History of Fruitland Nurseries, Augusta, Georgia, and the Berckmans Family in America," *Magnolia* (Bulletin of the Southern Garden History Society, winter 2002-2003), 3.

[4] Ibid.

[5] David Owen, *The Making of the Masters: Clifford Roberts, Augusta National, and Golf's Most Prestigious Tournament* (Simon and Schuster, Mar. 25, 2003).

[6] *Augusta Chronicle,* Jul. 15, 1931 (emphasis added).

[7] *Augusta Chronicle,* Oct. 29, 1931.

[8] *Augusta Chronicle,* Jul. 15, 1931; Oct. 29, 1931.

[9] *Augusta Chronicle,* Nov. 15, 1954. Fielding Wallace was president and treasurer of the Southern Press Club Manufacturing Company, former owner and operator of the People's Oil Co., and a director of the First Railroad and Banking Co. and Georgia Railroad Bank and Trust Company. Wallace served as secretary of the Augusta National from its inception until his death.

[10] *Augusta Chronicle,* Mar. 2, 1956. Alfred Severin Bourne provided land for Augusta's first golf course. His winter home in Augusta was known for its beautiful gardens. Alfred's father, Frederick Gilbert Bourne, was president of the Singer Sewing Machine Company. Bourne served as vice president for the Augusta National from its inception until his death.

[11] *Augusta Chronicle*, Jul. 15, 1931.

[12] *Augusta Chronicle*, Oct. 29, 1931.

[13] *Augusta Chronicle*, Dec. 2, 1931.

[14] *Augusta Chronicle*, May 20, 1932.

[15] *Augusta Chronicle*, Jun. 12, 1934.

[16] *Augusta Chronicle*, Nov. 18, 1944. At the time of Crowell's death, Quaker Oats had grown into a $250-million business. When he died in 1944, he left an estate of $3,100,000. Crowell was noted for his philanthropy and, in later years, devoted a majority of the profits from his business enterprises to churches and educational institutions, including the Moody Bible Institute in Chicago. Crowell also created the Crowell Trust in 1927 to advance and support the doctrines of evangelical Christianity through approved grants to qualified organizations. http://www.crowelltrust.org/.

[17] "Leadership," Harvard Business School, accessed on Jan. 21, 2014, http://www.hbs.edu/leadership/database/leaders/henry_p_crowell.html.

[18] *Augusta Chronicle*, Apr. 20, 1932.

[19] *Augusta Chronicle*, Oct. 28, 1931.

[20] Originally, there were sixty-one magnolia trees, but a thunderstorm in 2011 severely damaged one of the trees.

[21] Steve DiMeglio, "Augusta's living landmarks have seen, heard all the history," *USA Today*, Apr. 9, 2009, available at http://usatoday30.usatoday.com/sports/golf/masters/2009-04-08-course-landmarks_N.htm.

[22] *Augusta Chronicle*, Jan. 13, 1933.

[23] *Augusta Chronicle*, Jan. 4, 1933.

[24] *Augusta Chronicle*, Dec. 2, 1931.

[25] Ibid.

[26] *Augusta Chronicle*, Jan. 14, 1933.

[27] *Augusta Chronicle*, Jan. 13, 1933.

[28] *Augusta Chronicle*, Aug. 9, 1933.

[29] http://www.masters.com/en_US/discover/timeline.html?decade=1930.

[30] "Augusta National Golf Club members list," *USA Today*, Aug. 4, 2004, accessed on January 23, 2014.

Chapter XII

[1] *Augusta Chronicle*, Jul. 11, 1931.

[2] *Augusta Chronicle*, July 12, 1931; Aug. 1, 1931.

[3] *Augusta Chronicle*, Jul. 11, 1931.

[4] *Augusta Chronicle*, Aug. 1, 1931.

[5] Maurice Steinberg (1914-2000), an Augusta native, would go on to attend the University of Georgia, School of Law, before returning to Augusta to practice law and engage in a

real estate career. Extremely active in the Jewish community, Steinberg would also serve as president of the Augusta Jewish Federation.

6   *Augusta Chronicle*, Oct. 23, 1931. The former Lakeside Club property was acquired from Sam Baron for $1,001 and an agreement to satisfy outstanding state and county taxes.

7   *Augusta Chronicle*, Mar. 26, 1933.

8   *Augusta Chronicle*, May 15, 1950. E. Lynn Drummond had outstanding success as an architect in the Augusta area. He was responsible for the architectural work for numerous beautiful Augusta residences, Sue Reynolds School, Wilkinson Garden School, Allen Park swimming pool, etc.

9   *Augusta Chronicle*, Sep. 25, 1933. Red was a wrestling promoter for the New Coliseum, which opened at 704 Ellis Street in 1933. The New Coliseum had seating for 1,500 and a balcony with one hundred reserved box seats.

10 *Augusta Chronicle*, May 1, 1936; Jun. 28, 1936.

11 *Augusta Chronicle*, May 1, 1936.

12 *Augusta Chronicle*, Dec. 8, 1935.

13 *Augusta Chronicle*, Jan. 31, 1936.

14 *Augusta Chronicle*, Jun. 2, 1935.

15 *Augusta Chronicle*, Jun. 26, 1938. Under Councilman Joe Allen's administration, the Trees and Parks Committee repaired the boardwalk, floats, and diving facilities.

16 *Augusta Chronicle*, Apr. 8, 1938.

17 *Augusta Chronicle*, Sep. 4, 1938.

18 William "Bill" Goll, Marathon Pioneer and Hall of Famer, *Daily News of Open Water Swimming* (Nov. 18, 2010), accessed on Jan. 21, 2014, http://dailynews.openwater swimming.com/2010/11/william-bill-goll-marathoning-pioneer.html.

Chapter XIII

1   *Augusta Chronicle*, Apr. 29, 1949.

2   *Augusta Chronicle*, Jun. 2, 1949.

3   *Augusta Chronicle*, May 8, 1949. Dr. Abe J. Davis was also known as quite the cook, and his book *Reckless Recipes by Dr. Abe* included recipes such as barbecue pork and Brunswick stew.

4   *Augusta Chronicle*, May 18, 1949.

5   Evidently, the name Aumond resulted from a contest and combines *Augusta* with *Richmond County*. http://www.augusta.com/node/118.

6   *Augusta Chronicle*, May 18, 1949.

7   *Augusta Chronicle*, May 18, 1949.

Edwin Fulcher and his brother, William M. Fulcher, subsequently founded the Augusta law firm, now known as Fulcher Hagler LLP, employing over twenty attorneys.

8   *Augusta Chronicle*, Jun. 10, 1949.

9   *Augusta Chronicle*, Jun. 19, 1949.

10 *Augusta Chronicle*, Jun. 22, 1949.

11 *Augusta Chronicle*, Jul. 8, 1949.

12 *Augusta Chronicle*, Nov. 13, 1949.

13 *Augusta Chronicle*, Jul. 31, 1955.

14 *Augusta Chronicle*, Nov. 14, 1954.

15 *Augusta Chronicle*, Jul. 29, 1956.

Chapter XIV

1   *Augusta Chronicle*, Jan. 24, 1974.

2   *Augusta Chronicle*, Aug. 11, 1956

3   *Augusta Chronicle*, Aug. 15, 1956.

4   *Augusta Chronicle*, Aug. 17, 1961.

5   *Augusta Chronicle*, Aug. 17, 1960.

6   *Augusta Chronicle*, Jul. 11, 1961.

7   *Augusta Chronicle*, Sep. 24, 1961.

8   *Augusta Chronicle*, Oct. 17, 1961.

9   *Augusta Chronicle*, Nov. 21, 1961.

10 *Augusta Chronicle*, Nov. 23, 1967. In 1967, Dick Ransom was appointed the American Institute of Chemical Engineers' representative to the Augusta Citizen's Committee for Clean Air.

11 *Augusta Chronicle*, Jul. 4, 1965.

12 Ibid.

13 *Augusta Chronicle*, Jul. 18, 1966.

14 *Augusta Chronicle*, Apr. 24, 1967.

15 *Augusta Chronicle*, Aug. 5, 1970.

Chapter XV

1   *Augusta Chronicle*, Jun. 18, 1911.

2   "A Moving Tribute," *Boating*, accessed on Jan. 21, 2014, http://www.boatingmag.com/moving-tribute.

3   *Augusta Chronicle*, Sep. 28, 1919. Louis Edelblut was also the drummer in the local Adonegui Orchestra.

4   *Augusta Chronicle*, Oct. 10, 1927.

5   The American Outboard Motor Association was a national organization pledged to promoting interest in water motoring. The Augusta Outboard Motor Club became a member on August 27, 1928. *Augusta Chronicle*, Aug. 26, 1962.

[6]   *Augusta Chronicle*, Aug. 22, 1928.

[7]   *Augusta Chronicle*, Jun. 24, 1934.

[8]   *Augusta Chronicle*, Feb. 20, 1949; Apr. 23, 1949.

[9]   *Augusta Chronicle*, Apr. 13, 1952.

[10] *Augusta Chronicle*, Mar. 1, 1922. Dales won the standing broad jump with a jump of 9'3" and the fence vault at 6'½".

[11] *Augusta Chronicle*, Dec. 31, 1954.

[12] Armchair Golf Blog, accessed on Jan. 21, 2014, http://armchairgolfblog.blogspot.com/2009/04/q-walker-inman-jr-first-augusta-native.html.

[13] *Augusta Chronicle*, Aug. 17, 1999.

[14] *Augusta Chronicle*, Jul. 29, 1928; Aug. 18, 1928.

[15] *Augusta Chronicle*, Jul. 29, 1928; Aug. 13, 1928.

[16] *Augusta Chronicle*, Aug. 16, 1928; Aug. 18, 1928.

[17] *Augusta Chronicle*, Aug. 16, 1928.

[18] *Augusta Chronicle*, Feb. 6, 1972.

[19] Ibid.

[20] *Augusta Chronicle*, Aug. 16, 1928.

[21] *Augusta Chronicle*, Sep. 3, 1928.

[22] *Augusta Chronicle*, Jul. 5, 1933.

[23] *Augusta Chronicle*, Jun. 29, 1933.

[24] *Augusta Chronicle*, Aug. 7, 1933.

[25] *Augusta Chronicle*, Aug. 28, 1933.

[26] *Augusta Chronicle*, Sep. 5, 1933.

[27] *Augusta Chronicle*, Feb. 12, 1935; Aug. 6, 1944. Charles Johnston Goodwin was a well-known businessman and active in the Augusta Rotary Club and the Junior Chamber of Commerce.

[28] Barnwell purchased its first motorized fire apparatus in 1933. This apparatus was manufactured by the American La France Company and was capable of pumping five hundred gallons per minute, in addition to carrying fire hose, ladders, and equipment. The apparatus was built on a Chevrolet truck chassis and had an open cab. Mr. Clyde Vickery and Mr. Lloyd Plexico were the two engineers assigned to operate the new fire truck. http://www.cityofbarnwell.com/departments/fire/History.aspx.

[29] *Augusta Chronicle*, Sep. 1, 1933.

[30] *Augusta Chronicle*, Jun. 28, 1934.

[31] *Augusta Chronicle*, Jul. 5, 1934.

[32] Ibid.

[33] *Augusta Chronicle*, Aug. 26, 1962.

[34] *Augusta Chronicle*, Jul. 5, 1936.

[35] *Augusta Chronicle*, Apr. 26, 1937.

[36] *Augusta Chronicle*, Jul. 6, 1937.

[37] Claude Smith of Atlanta, Georgia, took first place, followed by Carl Flock of Jackson, Georgia; Ralph Cutter of Atlanta, Georgia; and veteran skipper George Guy from Greenville, South Carolina.

[38] *Augusta Chronicle*, Sep. 7, 1937. In the Free-for-All race, Carl Flock took first place, with Claud Smith coming in second, trailed by Tom O'Fiechi of Atlanta.

[39] *Augusta Chronicle*, Jul. 5, 1939.

[40] *Augusta Chronicle*, Apr. 18, 1939.

[41] *Augusta Chronicle*, Jul. 5, 1941. Bum Holliday, Wyman Tyler, and Morris Rock monopolized top honors, emerging with the lion's share of the more-than-$100 prize money.

[42] *Augusta Chronicle*, Apr. 11, 1947.

[43] *Augusta Chronicle*, Jul. 12, 1948.

[44] *Augusta Chronicle*, Apr. 24, 2011. Three of Casella's uncles—Victor, Vincent, and Louie Casella—operated businesses close by. Victor owned an optometry practice, Vincent operated Snappy Hamburgers, and Louie was the owner of a sandwich shop on Eighth Street.

[45] *Augusta Chronicle*, Apr. 13, 1952; Apr. 14, 1952.

[46] J. M. Propes of Greenville, South Carolina, won first place in the Class D Runabouts. In the Class D Hydroplanes event, it was Joe Elder of Lenoir, North Carolina, that emerged victorious.

[47] Danner was followed by Lee Leary and Tommy Sly.

[48] Walter Sweet came in second. John Danner finished in third place.

[49] H. G. Rosier finished first; Alfred Gormley, second; and Jim King, third.

[50] *Augusta Chronicle*, Jul. 21, 1952. Sligh was followed by W. Bateman and Bob Bernard in the Class B Hydroplane race and Dale Locke and Bob Bernard in the Free-for-All Dash.

[51] *Augusta Chronicle*, Jun. 7, 1953.

[52] *Augusta Chronicle*, May 11, 1985.

Chapter XVI

[1] *Augusta Chronicle*, May 22, 1949.

[2] *The Billboard*, Jun. 11, 1949, p. 55.

[3] Buster's father, George Bohler Sr., a chemist for Augusta, had traveled all over the world with the Barnum and Bailey Circus, where he played the cornet and flute as a member of the circus band. *Augusta Chronicle*, Mar. 12, 1955.

[4] *Augusta Chronicle*, Aug. 20, 1950.

[5] *Augusta Chronicle*, Aug. 13, 1950. Constance Tabb's mother and sister had died in a car crash in 1947, coming back from a trip to Tybee Island. *Augusta Chronicle*, May 26, 1947. Her father, Howard Oliver Tabb, who owned and operated the Tabb Finance Company, died six years later. Connie would marry Thomas Hugh Herndon.

[6] *Augusta Chronicle*, May 23, 1948.

[7] *Augusta Chronicle*, Aug. 20, 1950.

[8] *Augusta Chronicle*, May 9, 1958. The Water Thrill Show took place on May 10, 1958.

[9] *Augusta Chronicle*, Jul. 5, 1962.

[10] Louie was an avid sailor, hunter, and fisherman. Professionally he was a realtor employed by Meybohm Realtors and served several years on the Augusta Richmond Co. Tax Assessors Board. *Augusta Chronicle*, Mar. 22, 2009.

[11] *Augusta Chronicle*, Jun. 27, 1965.

[12] *Augusta Chronicle*, Jul. 4, 1965.

[13] *Augusta Chronicle*, Jun. 27, 1965.

[14] *Augusta Chronicle*, Sep. 15, 1971.

[15] *Augusta Chronicle*, Jul. 1, 1984.

[16] *Augusta Chronicle*, Jun. 30, 1985.

[17] *Augusta Chronicle*, Jul. 1, 1984.

[18] *Augusta Chronicle*, Sep. 4, 1983.

[19] *Augusta Chronicle*, Apr. 3, 1960.

[20] *Augusta Chronicle*, Aug. 18, 1958.

[21] *Augusta Chronicle*, Jul. 5, 1959.

[22] *Augusta Chronicle*, Aug. 24, 1959.

[23] *Augusta Chronicle*, Oct. 31, 1965.

[24] *Augusta Chronicle*, Aug. 1, 1998.

[25] *Augusta Chronicle*, Jul. 21, 2005.

[26] *Augusta Chronicle*, Jun. 25, 1990.

[27] *Augusta Chronicle*, Jan. 26, 1999.

[28] *Augusta Chronicle*, Mar. 28, 1972.

[29] *Augusta Chronicle*, Jul. 19, 1998.

[30] *Augusta Chronicle*, Aug. 10, 1997.

[31] *Augusta Chronicle*, Jul. 24, 1960; Jul. 25, 1960.

[32] *Augusta Chronicle*, Aug. 9, 1960.

[33] *Augusta Chronicle*, Aug. 29, 1960.

[34] *Augusta Chronicle*, Aug. 22, 1977.

[35] *Augusta Chronicle*, Jul. 31, 1977.

[36] *Augusta Chronicle*, Jun. 29, 1980.

[37] Ibid.

[38] *Augusta Chronicle*, Aug. 10, 1981.

[39] *Augusta Chronicle*, Jun. 29, 1981.

[40] *Augusta Chronicle*, Jun. 2, 1985.

[41] *Augusta Chronicle*, May 15, 1988.

[42] *Augusta Chronicle*, Jul. 1, 1984.

[43] *Augusta Chronicle*, Jun. 2, 1985.

[44] *Augusta Chronicle*, Aug. 10, 1981.

[45] *Augusta Chronicle*, Apr. 22, 1985.

[46] *Augusta Chronicle*, May 4, 1986.

[47] *Augusta Chronicle*, Mar. 9, 1986.

Chapter XVII

[1]   *Augusta Chronicle*, Mar. 28, 1874.

[2]   *Augusta Chronicle*, May 31, 1885.

[3]   *Augusta Chronicle*, Nov. 12, 1936.

[4]   *Augusta Chronicle*, Nov. 13, 1935.

[5]   *Augusta Chronicle*, Nov. 12, 1936.

[6]   *Augusta Chronicle*, Mar. 11, 1949.

[7]   Ibid.

[8]   *Augusta Chronicle*, Aug. 2, 1957.

[9]   *Augusta Chronicle*, Sep. 28, 1964.

[10] *Augusta Chronicle*, Aug. 2, 1957.

[11] *Augusta Chronicle*, Aug. 1, 1963.

[12] *Augusta Chronicle*, Apr. 30, 1939.

[13] *Augusta Chronicle*, Sep. 12, 1976.

[14] *Augusta Chronicle*, Jul. 7, 1976.

[15] *Augusta Chronicle*, May 4, 1986.

[16] Bill Baab, "'Larger' fish await anglers in Lake Olmstead," *Augusta Chronicle*, Aug. 22, 2013.

Chapter XVIII

[1]   *Augusta Chronicle*, Apr. 7, 1999.

[2]   *Augusta Chronicle*, Oct. 26, 1969.

[3]   *Augusta Chronicle*, Jan. 5, 1956.

Chapter XIX

[1]   *Augusta Chronicle*, May 21, 1929.

[2]   *Augusta Chronicle*, Sep. 5, 2005. Mr. Sancken worked in leadership roles with the First of Georgia Insurance Company and First of Georgia Credit Life Company, as well as Sherman and Hemstreet Inc., a local real estate company, until he retired in 1983. Mr. Sancken served on the city council from 1957 to 1963 and was elected for two terms as mayor from 1964 to 1970. He was reelected to the city council in 1974 and served in that capacity until 1983. Mr. Sancken held many directorships, including the First Union National Bank of Georgia, the First Union Bank of Augusta, and the Atlanta Gas Light Company, as well as serving as president of Westover Memorial Park, president of the Tuttle Newton Home, director of the American Cancer Society, trustee and president of Augusta Preparatory School, and a trustee of Pendleton King Park. He was a member of the Augusta Aviation Commission, the Augusta National Golf Club, the Augusta Assembly, and the Augusta Golf Association, in addition to being a member of the

Robert A. Mullins

Augusta Country Club, the Beech Island Agricultural Club, the Veterans of Foreign Wars, and the Military Order of the Cootie Pup Tent.

3   *Augusta Chronicle,* Jan. 7, 1964.

4   *Augusta Chronicle,* Jun. 9, 1967.

5   Ibid.

6   *Augusta Chronicle,* Sep. 20, 1970. Millard Arthur Beckum (1901-1991) was a jeweler by trade. He served three terms as mayor of Augusta from 1958 to 1964 and 1970-1973. He served as the national president of the Exchange Club in 1956 and national treasurer for twenty-three years. *Augusta Chronicle,* Oct. 1, 1991.

7   *Augusta Chronicle,* May 19, 1970.

8   *Augusta Chronicle,* Aug. 6, 1973.

9   *Augusta Chronicle,* Dec. 24, 1972.

10   *Augusta Chronicle,* Aug. 26, 1974.

11   Edward J. Cashin, *The Brightest Arm of the Savannah: The Augusta Canal 1845-2000* (Augusta: Augusta Canal Authority, 2002), 247-48.

12   *Augusta Chronicle,* Dec. 5, 1973. A new two-lane bridge was also constructed near the former city stockade.

Augusta Chronicle, Mar. 28, 2002. Lewis A. "Pop" Newman started out in the dry cleaning business, starting during World War II. Lewis A. "Pop" Newman served as an army navigator in England and saw combat during the 1942 invasion of North Africa. After the war, he started White House Cleaners, a business he would operate for over thirty years. Dedicated to public service, Newman served on the Augusta City Council from 1965 to 1971, before being elected to three terms as Augusta's mayor holding office from 1973 to 1981. During Newman's term as mayor, he proclaimed St. Patrick's Day an official day of celebration.

13   Oglethorpe Park was subsequently destroyed when Augusta developed its river walk along the Savannah River Levee.

14   *Augusta Chronicle,* Aug. 24, 1974.

15   *The Augusta Canal National Heritage Area Management Plan,* 3 (Oct. 1999).

Chapter XX

1   *Augusta Chronicle,* Jul. 14, 1999.

2   *Augusta Chronicle,* Jan. 21, 1971.

3   *Augusta Chronicle,* Mar. 18, 1999.

4   Center for Plant Conservation, accessed on Jan. 21, 2014, http://www.centerforplant conservation.org/Collection/CPC_ViewProfile.asp?CPCNum=4157.

Chapter XXI

[1]   *Augusta Chronicle*, Mar. 3, 1997.

[2]   *Augusta Chronicle*, Oct. 14, 2010. Recent discussions for improvements have included a fishery study by the Georgia Department of Natural Resources, as well as additional restoration and expansion of Julian Smith Park and the creation of a high-end, high-rise residential area overlooking Lake Olmstead.

[3]   *Augusta Chronicle*, May 16, 2002.

[4]   *Augusta Chronicle*, Mar. 21, 2005.

[5]   *Augusta Chronicle*, Oct. 23, 2010.

[6]   *Augusta Chronicle*, Aug. 25, 2002.

[7]   *Augusta Chronicle*, Feb. 26, 2010.

[8]   *Augusta Chronicle*, Jun. 27, 2005.

[9]   *Augusta Chronicle*, Nov. 11, 2001.

[10] *Augusta Canal National Heritage Area Management Plan*, 5 (Oct. 1999).

Chapter XXII

[1]   *Augusta Chronicle*, Aug. 5, 1924.

[2]   *Augusta Chronicle*, Aug. 4, 1924.

[3]   Ibid.

[4]   Ibid.

[5]   *Augusta Chronicle*, Dec. 2, 1942.

[6]   Ibid.

[7]   *Augusta Chronicle*, Feb. 15, 1944.

[8]   Ibid.

[9]   Ibid.

[10] Ibid.

[11] Ibid.

[12] Ibid.

[13] Ibid.

[14] Ibid.

[15] *Augusta Chronicle*, Aug. 1, 1944.

[16] Ibid.

[17] *Augusta Chronicle*, Jul. 23, 1968.

[18] *Augusta Chronicle*, Aug. 4, 1946.

[19] *Augusta Chronicle*, Aug. 14, 1946. http://www.biography.com/people/esther-williams-259340.

[20] *Augusta Chronicle*, Aug. 4, 1946.

[21] Ibid.

[22] *Augusta Chronicle*, Mar. 7, 1947.

[23] *Augusta Chronicle,* Jun. 15, 1947.
[24] Ibid.
[25] *Augusta Chronicle,* Jun. 20, 1947.
[26] *Augusta Chronicle,* Jul. 1, 1947.
[27] *Augusta Chronicle,* Jul. 4, 1947.
[28] Ibid.
[29] *Augusta Chronicle,* Aug. 14, 1954.
[30] *Augusta Chronicle,* Aug. 31, 1965.
[31] *Augusta Chronicle,* Sep. 1, 1965.
[32] *Augusta Chronicle,* Jun. 19, 1977.
[33] *Augusta Chronicle,* Mar. 8, 1925.
[34] *Augusta Chronicle,* Mar. 31, 1929.
[35] *Augusta Chronicle,* Mar. 27, 1904.
[36] Ibid.
[37] *Augusta Chronicle,* Jan. 27, 1940.
[38] *Augusta Chronicle,* May 26, 1950.
[39] *Augusta Chronicle,* Sep. 6, 1958.
[40] *Augusta Chronicle,* Aug. 8, 1959.
[41] *Augusta Chronicle,* May 13, 1970.
[42] *Augusta Chronicle,* Jan. 13, 2002.

INDEX

Edwards Brothers Malloy
Thorofare, NJ USA
May 27, 2014